PENGUIN BOOKS

THE FUGITIVE YEARS

Robert Bradshaw was born in Crayford, Kent, in 1934 and after experiencing the worst of the London Blitz emigrated with his parents to South Africa in 1948. Six years later he was excommunicated from the Exclusive Plymouth Brethren and made to leave the family home. Thereafter he worked as a sales representative for stationery companies, developed a gambling compulsion and began a criminal career. This lasted from 1955 to 1982 and Bradshaw has spent over twenty-two years in prison. Whilst in prison he attained a diploma in commerce and, in 1977, began to write. His first, unpublished, novel received a commendation under the Arthur Koestler Award scheme in 1978.

In 1981 he was admitted to a unit in Wormwood Scrubs Prison called the Annexe, which specializes in psychotherapy treating addictions such as gambling. There he wrote *The Fugitive Years*, and it received a Koestler Award in 1983.

Since leaving prison he has collated notes on his time in the Annexe, and these form the basis of a second book, written with Dr Max Glatt, a world authority on addictions.

Robert Bradshaw says of his writing:
'My experiences in prison, often under horrific conditions, are recorded in the hope that someone may read them and realize that however dreadful circumstances may be, there *is* hope. Men *can* and *do* decide to change – and they can *succeed* where previously they had *failed*.'

THE FUGITIVE YEARS

ROBERT BRADSHAW

PENGUIN BOOKS

Penguin Books Ltd, Harmondsworth, Middlesex, England
Viking Penguin Inc., 40 West 23rd Street, New York, New York 10010, U.S.A.
Penguin Books Australia Ltd, Ringwood, Victoria, Australia
Penguin Books Canada Ltd, 2801 John Street, Markham, Ontario, Canada L3R 1B4
Penguin Books (N.Z.) Ltd, 182–190 Wairau Road, Auckland 10, New Zealand

First published by Penguin Books 1986

Made and printed in Great Britain by
Richard Clay (The Chaucer Press) Ltd,
Bungay, Suffolk
Filmset in Monophoto Plantin Light by
Northumberland Press Ltd, Gateshead,
Tyne and Wear

CONTENTS

ACKNOWLEDGEMENTS

This book would not have been written without the help and encouragement of a great many people. I owe a special word of thanks to Patricia Pelly, probation officer, who persevered when I had lost interest in my future. Without her help I might not have taken the steps that opened up a new way of life to me.

The support and guidance I received from Dr David, medical officer, and Dr Shorvan, visiting psychotherapist, led to me being admitted to the Hospital Annexe at Wormwood Scrubs – they did not fail me when I turned to them for help.

The staff and fellow-inmates of the Hospital Annexe played a special role in helping me to come to terms with life. They helped me to recognize and deal with the attitudes and anger of my previous way of life, and they encouraged me to write an honest account of my experiences.

My thanks too are due to Michael Relton, my solicitor; Justin Lewis my barrister, and John Mortimer QC, all of whom have encouraged me and offered help and support.

To Bob and Chris Bell, a special acknowledgement of their friendship and kindness to me.

BOB BRADSHAW
HM PRISON
WORMWOOD SCRUBS
MAY 1983

INTRODUCTION

Between 1955 and 1982, I was sentenced to periods of imprisonment which led to my spending more than twenty years in prison. At the trials that resulted in these sentences I consistently refused to furnish my solicitors with anything they could have used in mitigation. My life remained a secret, and the judges who sentenced me did so without the benefit of medical or probation reports. In the absence of evidence in mitigation, and faced with silence about my past, trial judges have imposed a succession of custodial sentences.

In June of 1981, I was imprisoned at Wormwood Scrubs, facing a very large number of charges in respect of offences committed whilst I had been on parole. I had come to accept my role as a criminal, and I believed that my behaviour was a natural consequence of my criminality. Prison was accepted as an unavoidable hazard. My reaction to the charges I faced was one of apathy. I wanted to get to court, plead guilty, get sentenced, and get it all over with.

It was a probation officer at the prison who made me realize that to adopt this attitude was no different to the flight from reality, and the refusal to face up to life, that had been a feature of my past. My solicitor was brutally frank. He told me that if I did not change my way of life I would die in prison.

I began to make notes to furnish my solicitor with material on which to base a plea in mitigation, and as I did so I became interested in the way my life had developed. I was curious and wanted to try to understand how I had built up the record of criminal convictions the police would submit to the trial court.

After my admission to Wormwood Scrubs, discussion with my probation officer made me admit that I was a compulsive gambler. I was encouraged to seek medical help – and under the care of the prison doctors I began to be interested in the attitudes that had given rise to my gambling and criminal behaviour. My notes became copious, covering every aspect of my life, and eventually gave rise to this book.

I have called my story *The Fugitive Years*. It is the story of my life and, from the time I was asked to leave home at the age of sixteen, I have been a fugitive. For most of my life I have been a fugitive from law-enforcement agencies or I have been in prison – but throughout the whole of my adult life I have been a fugitive from reality. I have refused to stop and face the fact that I elected to be a gambler and a criminal – and that I remained one by choice. I am confident that my fugitive years are now over. With the help of prison staff and fellow-prisoners in the Hospital Annexe at Wormwood Scrubs, I have been able to face the past honestly and, in doing so, I have found the confidence to face the future.

I hope that this story may help someone who, like me, has refused to face reality – who may feel that he cannot change. I believe that for every man in prison there is an alternative to criminality; that seemingly insuperable difficulties can be overcome; that many-time losers can win. We *can* choose the way we lead our lives – we *can* elect to reject attitudes, influences and compulsions that controlled us in the past.

I have changed many names to protect those who have paid their debt to society – but everything I have written is based on personal experience. I hope it may be instrumental in improving the very bad conditions in British prisons.

Prologue

I looked around the reception office and recognized no one; they were all strangers. So much had changed in the twelve years since my admission to Pretoria Central Prison. I had been a celebrity then, described by the media as one of South Africa's most wanted men. Now it was 1972, and the years had swallowed up my reputation.

'Teken hier,' a guard said as he pushed a property and private-cash record towards me for signature. 'Het jy alles?'

'Yes, I've got everything.'

It was 7.30 a.m., but already the heat of the high veld sun had found its way into the office, and I realized with surprise that I felt tired. I had waited so long for this moment, never really daring to hope that it would come. Now I was a little afraid.

The faces I had known over the years had disappeared and I was being processed by strangers. I was a little resentful that they did not recognize who I was. They were too impersonal. Over my years in this prison I had become used to abuse and insults, and now the politeness seemed strange. The discharge procedure was strange too; it was so long since I had experienced it. I was about to leave a prison environment I had grown used to, and I was apprehensive – afraid of the world I was about to be returned to.

From the prison I would be escorted to the airport and put aboard a South African Airway's Boeing 747. I would be accompanied by two members of BOSS, South Africa's Bureau of State Security. Their duty was to see that I did not leave the plane en route to London.

It was all unreal; the sort of thing you read about in books. I found it hard to accept that it was happening to me. The reception guard handed me over to my escorts, and they signed a receipt for me. A few minutes later I stood outside the gates of the prison. I climbed into the back of the unmarked car that had been provided and my escorts squeezed in on either side of me. As we pulled away I looked back and saw the sun shining on the weathered red brick and grey stone of the prison walls. The prison gate closed and it all looked just like it had many years earlier when I had first seen it. But it was not the same – this time I was leaving.

I turned around to look ahead, and the car pulled out into the main highway, turned right, heading up the hill leading out of Pretoria. On the left we passed the imposing new buildings of South Africa's Open University. A little farther on, dominating the hill on which it had been erected, stood the Voortrekker Monument. This huge, grey building was not just a memorial to the courage and endeavour of Afrikaner pioneers, it was a symbol of Afrikanerdom itself. With ox-wagons drawn up in laager formation, it was a rallying point for the old and the young of a beleaguered nation. It symbolized the defensive stance of the people, surrounded and outnumbered, their country a white enclave poised at the tip of Africa.

A civilian jet-liner passed overhead, and I realized that it had just taken off from Jan Smuts International Airport, where we were heading. I tried to remember what it had been like to travel by air before I had gone to prison. The planes then had been mainly Skymasters, Constellations and Dakotas; the Vickers Viscount had been quite new. Now I was going to travel by Jumbo-jet.

Suddenly I realized that I was not tired any more.

PART 1

THE FUGITIVE YEARS

I

I was born on 22 March 1934, in Crayford Nursing Home, a cottage hospital tucked into the hill leading down from Bexleyheath to Dartford, in Kent. I was the fourth of five children, with two brothers and one sister older than me, and a younger sister called Rhoda.

My parents belonged to the strict religious sect called the Exclusive Plymouth Brethren. They named me Stephen, after the first Christian martyr, and from as early as I can remember I was reminded how steadfast he had been, choosing death by stoning rather than renounce his faith. Having been born into the faith I knew no other way of life. From childhood I was taught that the beliefs my parents held were to be my heritage. Family life was structured around religious meetings and the obligations of our faith. I learned that my father's business took second place.

I remember my childhood as happy; the large family provided me with a warm, secure home where, as the youngest son, I enjoyed my father's special favour. I did not notice we had no friends or playmates outside the religious group we belonged to, and as a member of a large family I did not feel any sense of loss. We were carefully shielded from the influence of the world outside, and I grew up unaware of life as it really is, unaware that other children had friends and interests outside their immediate family. We had no radio or record-player in our home; they were considered worldly. When my father bought a newspaper we children were not allowed to read it. We lived in a closed environment, singing hymns around the piano, having daily bible-readings and prayers at home, attending religious meetings, cut off from normal social pursuits.

My mother was caring and devoted to us. She provided us with love and attention, but at all times her role was subservient to my father's. She believed that the husband was the head of the household, and I can remember very few occasions when she asserted herself. She was happy in the role of wife and mother, consulting my father in any decisions that were made in the home. She was an excellent cook and took pride in producing dishes of the highest standard. Pastry, pies and pudding took on a special meaning when my mother made them.

Occasionally my father would sing us songs he remembered from his youth. He would take me on his knee as he sang:

'The other night I had a dream
Down underneath the waves,
I dreamt I saw my Nancy
In a coral reef of caves;
She had turned into a mermaid,
She had such a lovely tail;
She was doing double-shuffles
In conjunction with a whale!'

There were other verses that I do not remember, and I had no idea what double-shuffles were, but I welcomed the rollicking tune and the sense of fun it conveyed.

'Sing about the hippopotamus,' I would urge, and my father would oblige:

'My wife's mother is rather stout,
Nineteen stone and a fair knock-out;
She would please the country farmers
If they saw her in pyjamas!

Running up and down our stairs,
Running up and down our stairs:

One dark night she made a bit of fuss,
Snorting like a hippopotamus,
When suddenly a great big nail
Caught poor mother unawares;
She slipped and punctured her india-rubber tyre,
Running up and down our stairs.'

In later years I wondered what these songs had got to do with the solemn commitment to godly pursuits my father professed, but at the time they provided relief from the strict religious routine we lived by.

We lived at Bexleyheath in a detached house. My father owned some adjoining land, on part of which he had built a small joinery works. The business met all the family's needs and I cannot remember any times of financial difficulty.

Next to the garage on the boundary of our land the previous owner had erected a dovecote, and as a child I watched the fantail pigeons strutting about the roof of their cote; but when the war came they disappeared. My father owned a Morris Twenty saloon and I loved helping him clean and polish it. It was navy-blue, and the gleaming chrome headlights and rich smell of the leather upholstery excited me. When the war came, the car was requisitioned and converted to serve as an ambulance.

My favourite playing-area was a lawn close to the house on which my father had built a summer-house. A good-natured cross-bred labrador-retriever called Floss endured endless attention and harassment from my younger sister and me as we played on the lawn. Floss was our constant companion, and when she died we buried her under the pear tree on the lawn she had shared with us. Other dogs followed, but none took her place.

The first indication I had that we were different to other families came when I began school. The faith we lived by required that I be excused religious instruction and did not attend morning service. I can still recall the embarrassment I felt when made to stand outside the classroom or assembly hall whilst these lessons and services were in progress. The remarks of teachers and pupils hurt and confused me and made me aware that they considered me different, that I did not belong to the world they lived in. My parents' admonition to avoid friendship and contact with 'unbelievers', and my own developing religious awareness and beliefs, strengthened this feeling of being a person apart.

I had no problem coping with schoolwork, but it failed to capture my imagination. My parents regarded schooling as necessary only because it was legally compulsory, and I received no encouragement at home. My life was controlled by religious necessity and was not directed towards developing the skills needed to become a useful member of the community. I was reminded daily that I was *in* the world but not *of* the world. I was a pilgrim, passing through.

It seemed strange to me at that time that the only other pupil who missed religious instruction was the son of an orthodox Jew. As we stood side by side outside the classroom I wondered if he was a pilgrim too, and I had yet to learn that according to our faith Jews could not be pilgrims.

I was too young to understand the beliefs I had been brought up to respect; I simply accepted them and allowed no one to enter or contaminate the private world they created. I viewed all outsiders with apprehension. Sport and physical education, which would have brought me into contact with children who were 'unbelievers', were frowned on by my parents. I was not allowed to take part in team events at school. The effect of these restrictions was to keep me very close to my family, close to the faith, shutting out the rest of the world.

My parents taught me that the accumulation of wealth, preoccupation with business, and academic learning were all 'ungodly' pursuits, and when, in 1945, I was offered a scholarship to Dartford Grammar School, my father advised me to decline it.

'Tell them you want to be a nurseryman,' he said.

I did, and I was not accepted.

Although I was young I was aware of the changes the war made to all our lives: I was five when hostilities commenced and eleven years of age when they ended. Food became scarce and my father built greenhouses on the grass tennis-court at the bottom of our garden. He grew tomatoes, lettuce, cucumbers and radish, and I enjoyed helping him side-shoot the plants, my fingers becoming permanently stained green with the sap of tomato plants.

The joinery works fascinated me as a child. I was never allowed into the works during the day, and the hum of woodworking machinery, the whine of a router, the screech of the circular saw, all combined to stimulate a sense of mystery. When I was allowed into the timber-yard the smell of newly sawn timber and the sight of strange woods from foreign lands conjured up pictures of the ships that brought the timber to us; tall ships heeling under full sail, and fussy little tugboats manoeuvring big ships into the wharf.

Later the factory was requisitioned for the war effort. My father's pacifist beliefs and his refusal to join a trade union led to him being barred from entering his own factory. He now concentrated on cultivating the land, and we kept rabbits, chickens and a few pigs. We opened a greengrocer's stall, and our own produce was augmented by fruit from a rented orchard and purchases from Covent Garden. The preparation and delivery of firewood and kindling provided part-time work for me and my brother Philip.

Bexleyheath was very close to the flight path of German planes heading for London, and during the years of the blitz the unending drone of bombers as they passed over seemed to last from nightfall until dawn. The wail of the air-raid siren was the signal for us to take our bedding down into the cellar, which my father had reinforced with massive timbering. There we were safe from anything except a direct hit: but there was always tension, and our parents would comfort us as we lay trembling with fear, listening to the whine of a falling bomb, wondering where it would land. Even when the crump of its explosion told us that we were safe, the fear and the tension remained.

Strangely I remember an element of adventure too as distant anti-aircraft guns opened fire and air-defence rockets whooshed skywards; but when mobile units of Bofors guns were parked near our home, the sharp bark of their firing shattered windows and seemed somehow more frightening than the threat posed by enemy bombers. We used rubber earplugs and cotton wool to protect our eardrums, but nothing could shut out the sound of war. We only relaxed when the continuous blast of the siren told us that it was 'all clear'.

When the blitz of London was at its height we were evacuated to Hereford. For several weeks we were billeted in a house on the common close to the cider factory. The old man whose home we invaded was a sweetmaker, and he spent hours in his huge kitchen producing the finest acid drops and bulls-eyes I have ever tasted. Not far from the house was a small stream, and I used to take a gauze net and jam-jar when I visited it. My younger sister would come with me and we caught tadpoles, small frogs and newts, and sometimes a stickleback. I remember the small fish glowering at me through the glass wall of the jar. Some were brown and plain, but others glowed with brilliant reds and blues.

Apart from that short stay at Hereford we lived in Bexleyheath throughout the war. The nights of lying listening to the drone of German bombers were followed by the terror of Hitler's V1 buzz-bombs. On several occasions the glass in the greenhouses my father had built was shattered by explosions. One day I was standing beside them when I heard the sound of a buzz-bomb approaching. As it grew louder I turned towards the sound, watching the tall trees that grew behind the greenhouses. Without any warning the rocket engine stopped and almost simultaneously I saw the bomb appear over the treetops, not more than sixty feet from the ground. It glided across our property and over my head, grey, squat and lethal; its short stubby wings and tail whispering in the wind. It crashed and exploded five hundred yards away, killing a young mother and her baby – devastating the houses near them. I was showered by splinters of glass blown out of the greenhouses, but suffered only minor cuts.

As the war progressed the terror of Hitler's flying bombs was added to by the V2 rockets. Late one winter afternoon my brother Philip and I made a firewood delivery and were returning home along Belvedere Road. It was bitterly cold and my hands and feet were frozen. As we began to descend the incline leading into Church Road a shattering explosion occurred directly ahead of us. From where we were the blast seemed to be exactly where our house stood. I remember the fear that gripped me as I saw the blinding flash of the explosion and then watched smoke and debris billow up into the sky. Mini-seconds later the sound of the blast reached us, and we stood frightened and confused as the noise of the rocket's passage through the air lingered on long after the explosion. Neither my brother nor I spoke as we hurried down the road to our home. I can still recall my enormous relief when we found the house undamaged. Later as my mother helped me to bathe my frozen feet in warm water, tears induced by the physical pain mingled with those of relief that our home had been spared.

The rocket had fallen in Oaklands Road, almost a half-mile away, killing several people. It damaged the home of the Bamfords, who belonged to the Exclusive Plymouth Brethren, and later Mrs Bamford told us that she had been in her kitchen when it had fallen. She said she had seen the window-panes shatter and crockery fall to the floor, but at the moment of the explosion she had heard nothing. It was as though she were in a vacuum which excluded sound. When sound did return it was the noise of falling debris and the roar of the rocket's passage that she heard. It had fallen two houses away from where she stood, and in the freak manner of such blasts neither her family nor their house suffered seriously.

A young woman who had been walking past the house where the rocket exploded was stripped of all her clothing by the blast, and blown up into the air to land on top of a tall oak tree. When firemen rescued her she was found to have suffered no serious injury apart from shock. The superficial scratches she sustained were caused by the rough branches of the tree she had landed in.

2

The Exclusive Plymouth Brethren owned a freehold property in Standard Road, Bexleyheath, where a meeting-room had been built. There was a large main hall, a smaller rear room, and cloakroom facilities. A courtyard in front of the main entrance was concreted and surrounded by a wooden fence. It was in this courtyard as a child that I met the families of other members of our faith. Today I cannot remember the name or the face of any child I met there. My memory is completely blank in this respect, and it would seem that the solemnity with which the religious meetings were conducted spilled over into the courtyard, inhibiting normal, playful behaviour and friendships.

On Sunday three meetings were held at the hall: communion in the morning, bible-reading in the afternoon, and a gospel address in the evening. Prayer-meetings and bible-readings were held on some evenings during the week. We attended them all, and on those evenings that were free my father would often travel to a neighbouring town to attend a meeting there.

The war meant that air-raids frequently occurred during a meeting. On one occasion we were seated in the meeting-room during an alert when we heard a V 1 buzz-bomb approaching. As it drew closer and the noise of its engine grew louder we all tensed. Suddenly it stopped. One of the peculiarities of the buzz-bomb was that you could never be sure what it would do. Sometimes it would crash and explode with its engine still going, at other times it would nosedive immediately its engine stopped, and on yet other occasions it would glide for miles after the engine had cut out. We had had several bombs drop quite close to the meeting-room during services, and now we waited in tense silence for the explosion that would tell us the danger had passed. The seconds ticked by, and it was at that moment that a slate, loosened by previous blasts, broke loose and rattled down the steep roof of the hall. At first fear paralysed everyone, and then we instinctively cringed into our seats. I had a front-row view of two eminent brothers shedding all pretence of calm dignity and jostling each other ferociously as they tried to get under a small table that stood at the centre of the circle of chairs we occupied. A few seconds later the bomb exploded some distance away, and the two brothers stopped jostling each other, got up rather sheepishly, dusted their trousers, and took their seats to continue the prayer-meeting, pretending that nothing untoward had happened.

Fellowship meetings were held on Saturday afternoons and the brethren from other areas were invited to them. In the afternoon a bible-reading took place and this was followed by an address in the early evening. In between tea and cakes were served, and these occasions are the only social events I can remember as a child. I looked forward to them as a special treat. Significantly I attached little importance to the meetings themselves, I was more concerned with the breaks in between them – and I called them 'tea-meetings'.

Despite the conscientious objections of the Brethren to the war, there was an air of patriotism during the difficult days of the blitz. But as the Allies gained the upper hand this mood seemed to change. I can remember Mr Bamford praying during the days when thousand-bomber raids were pounding Germany into submission; he prayed for the Brethren in Germany: 'Now that the enemy is, as it were, coming from over this side now'. In later years I could not help thinking that this subtle change in attitude reflected the expediency that underlay much of the Brethren's behaviour.

We lived in Bexleyheath up until 1946, and although I was then twelve years of age I can remember only one occasion on which my father spoke to our neighbours. On the west side of our property our neighbours' house rose three storeys high, the wall that faced us windowless and topped by a brick chimney-stack with clay-red chimney pots. Ivy covered the wall thickly and provided ideal nesting for sparrows, and in the mornings I would be woken by the clip-clop of dairy-cart horses and the noise of the sparrows with their young.

Towards the end of the war a barrage-balloon broke free from its moorings in Dansen Park. Carried by a strong wind it scudded across the roof-tops, demolishing chimneys and damaging slates and tiles. The cable it trailed managed to wrap itself around the chimney-stack of our neighbours' house, and the balloon came to rest there. It was enormous, its silver-grey fuselage shutting out the sky as it hovered over us. Then a stronger gust of wind wrenched it free, demolishing the chimney-stack and scattering the bricks and mortar across our lawn. Fortunately no one was hurt.

When the balloon had first become lodged in their chimney our neighbours had hurried out. I watched from a safe distance as they spoke to my father. Then they disappeared back into their house. That was the only time I saw any of the neighbours speak to any member of our family.

The owner of the house opposite grew roses. He lavished care and attention on them, and armed with a spade and bucket he appeared promptly as soon as the horse-drawn dairy-carts began to appear. He would stand watching, ready to hurry out and collect any droppings they left behind. A little farther along the road another keen gardener kept a similar vigil. Sometimes they would hurry out into the road, spade and bucket in hand, and sprint for the same prize, each pretending he had not noticed the other.

A small public house near our home was often the scene of revelling at weekends. Sometimes the celebrations would spill out on to the pavement. As a child I lay in bed and listened to rowdy farewells and bawdy songs as the drinkers dispersed. I would draw the blankets a little closer and cringe at the sound of broken glass, the cursing and voices raised in anger. The stench of stale beer that hung in the air as I hurried past the pub the next morning convinced me that something bad happened there. Trapdoors giving access to the pub cellar formed part of the pavement, and I carefully avoided them, afraid of the darkness they opened into. My parents' stories of the evils of drink were very real to me and they had no trouble instilling a healthy fear of alcohol in me.

After the war ended we moved to Gorleston in Norfolk, where my father began a speculative building business. I attended Great Yarmouth Grammar School, and the daily trip from our home involved changing buses in the old, cobble-stoned market place. Little stalls offering mouth-watering fish and chips, fresh shrimp, cockles and winkles stood there, and sometimes I was scolded by my mother for indulging and having no appetite for the tea she had prepared when I got home.

One of the highlights of our stay at Gorleston was the annual visit of the Scottish herring-fleet. Trawlers crammed the river Yare, and the quayside smelled of the sea and fresh herring winched ashore in wicker baskets. Occasionally the baskets allowed a herring to drop on to the quayside, and a vigilant policeman would try to prevent the children from picking it up, but he was never very successful. Sometimes I would take a carrier-bag and ask a friendly skipper for a 'fry'. Sixpence bought a dozen or more plump herring, and I would hurry home and wait impatiently with my brothers and sisters whilst my mother gutted them and prepared a late tea.

The flat country around Gorleston encouraged cycling, and as children we spent many happy hours visiting Corton and Oulton Broad to the south, Beccles and picturesque St Olave, with its small marina and swing-bridge, to the west.

At school I achieved only moderate success. I found it hard to become interested, and my family were indifferent to my results. On one occasion the games master persuaded me to disobey the veto my parents had placed on sports. I was tall, and he encouraged me to take part in the high jump. Whilst making my run-up I slipped on wet grass. I fell heavily on my back with the cross-bar under my arm, dislocating my collar bone and completely deflating my lungs. The pain as I struggled to regain my breath was incredible – as I tried to reflate my lungs I was quite sure that God was punishing me for disobeying my father, and the sense of guilt I developed was not assuaged by his stern reproof and lack of sympathy when I got home.

In 1947, we moved to Westcliff in Essex. Our new house stood in more than an acre of ground, a well-kept lawn leading from the rear of the house to a row of tall poplars. The land beyond the trees was overgrown and had become a mini-sanctuary for birds. In the spring after our arrival I found two fledgelings floundering on the ground there. I took them back into the house and nursed and fed them until they had grown to be fully fledged young birds. They were jays, and the soft browns of their plumage glowed against the brilliant blue, white and black of their markings. When I released them they stayed close to the house for some weeks, swooping out of the tall poplars at the end of the lawn and screeching their greeting whenever I appeared. But towards autumn they disappeared.

Belfairs Golf Course was only a short distance from where we lived, and in addition to a splendid eighteen-hole layout it boasted a fine nine-hole miniature course, incorporating all the features and hazards of a real course. My parents allowed me to go and play there with my brothers and sisters, and I spent a lot of my time that summer chipping and putting my way around the course.

I attended Westcliff High School, and a forceful games master put me into the cricket team. He refused to take my religious objections seriously, and I was surprised to find that I was enjoying myself. But when my father came to hear about it he was very angry. He wrote a letter to the headmaster and I did not play cricket after that.

My father's business had begun to falter. He put a part of the land attached to the house under cultivation, and opened a non-dispensing chemist's shop in Leigh-on-Sea. These undertakings were not successful and by the winter of 1947, he had begun to make arrangements to emigrate to South Africa.

At the time that this decision was being made something happened which I believe played a large part in shaping the attitudes I have carried with me ever since. Despite regular attendance at religious meetings I had never made a personal, public commitment to the faith. I accepted my parents' beliefs as right, but felt no strong reason to commit myself to them. I respected them and acted in accordance with them, but the God I prayed to, and the Saviour I sang hymns to, were in reality strangers to me. I believed and hoped that one day that would change; that I would discover the personal relationship with God my father and mother had told me of. I was often reminded that I had been baptized in faith, and that my christening tied me irrevocably to the first Christian martyr. Through the act of baptism my parents had committed me to the Christian community. I found nothing strange in their hopes for me, and I looked forward to the day when I would be accepted as a full member of the brethren.

During the autumn of 1947, I attended a gospel meeting in Southend and heard a Mr Kerr preach. He was a tall young man, and he wore the khaki uniform of the army non-combatant corps. He was attached to a medical unit, and I believe that he had acted as a stretcher-bearer during the final stages of the war. He took as his text the story of the Prodigal Son, and as he spoke of the father's yearning for his son to return and fill the empty place in his house, it seemed that he spoke directly to me. Something moved within me – I was deeply affected. I experienced elation mingled with a sense of relief. These feelings were very strong, and I had no doubts that I was experiencing a solemn conversion. My family shared the joy of that experience with me, and I became publicly committed to the faith my parents had given me.

Six months later I stood on the deck of the liner *Carnaervon Castle.* We were approaching Cape Town and dawn was beginning to lighten the sky as I stood beside my father looking out for our first sight of South Africa. We swayed comfortably with the movement of the ship as a carpet of gold rolled across the horizon, heralding a new day. A new life was about to open up for me – but nothing that had gone before could ever have prepared me for what it was to bring.

3

When I first heard that we were going to emigrate to South Africa I imagined a land full of excitement and untamed beauty. South Africa was all of that – and a great deal more.

The *Carnaervon Castle* was not yet fully restored from her role as a troop-ship during the war when we made the journey in her. The accommodation was cramped, but after a few days of seasickness, and a violent storm in the Bay of Biscay, the voyage was more exciting than I could have imagined.

We stopped briefly at Funchal in Madeira, and then cruised down the west coast of Africa to Cape Town. It was a voyage that introduced me to the heat of the Equator, shoals of flying fish, and schools of gambolling dolphin. Sixteen days after leaving the cold, grey mists of Southampton we docked in Cape Town.

The sun was hot and very bright – the sheer beauty of the scene was intoxicating. Table Mountain always presents an awe-inspiring picture; to a young lad, excited at arriving in a new and dangerous land, the first sight we had of Table Mountain rising out of the sea, capped by its table-cloth of cloud, was quite stunning. It was an unforgettable sight, and I was still overwhelmed by the grandeur of it some hours later when we disembarked.

We were met by members of the Brethren, and they provided transport and gave us advice as we made our way from the docks to the house we were to live in. It was in Mowbray, a suburb of Cape Town, tucked in at the foot of Devil's Peak, quite close to Groote Schuur Hospital, later of heart-transplant fame.

The Plymouth Brethren in Cape Town proved to be far more outgoing than the community we had known in England. The climate and the natural amenities of the Cape created an outdoor way of life, and for the first time I experienced the pleasure of sharing activities with young people outside my immediate family. I found it hard to throw off the reticence I had grown up with, and my father's oft-voiced disapproval of many of my new friends and their pursuits as worldly and improper left me with a lingering sense of guilt. I felt that somehow the pleasure I now experienced was wrong. With the children of other families of the faith I went walking, climbing, camping and swimming. I tried to become part of the happy group they formed, but I always felt a little different – a little guilty. I was never completely at ease.

The meetings of the Brethren, and devotion to bible-reading and prayer, were just as much a feature of life as they had been in England; but the emphasis and some attitudes were different. For the first time I met children whose parents openly expected and encouraged them to do well at school. Interests tended to include material well-being as well as spiritual commitment. This change of emphasis seemed very attractive to me and I wanted to enjoy the relief it offered from the drab life I had led up to then. To my father it represented a worldliness that he was never able to reconcile with the strict orthodoxy he had always lived by, and I found that my desire to be part of this new community often conflicted with my sense of duty towards him.

As I grew older I became aware of hypocrisy in many of the attitudes the Brethren adopted and, later still, I came to see hypocrisy in many areas of my father's behaviour. Despite this awareness I was tied to the community of the Exclusive Plymouth Brethren both by upbringing and belief. I formally entered the fellowship when I was fourteen years of age, at which time I was admitted to the Communion, known as 'the breaking of bread'.

Our family finances had been strained to meet the cost of transporting the family to South Africa, and partly because of this, partly because of my own wishes, I did not renew my schooling in Cape Town. My formal education ended at Westcliff High School in Essex when I was thirteen. In South Africa, I began work with my father, who had started a speculative building business.

Shortly after we arrived in Cape Town, general elections brought a change of government. Jan Christiaan Smuts and his United Party were voted out of office; soldiers returning from the war found that he had failed to keep the promises he had made them, and the voting reflected their anger. The Nationalist Party came to power and since 1948 no other party has come near to ousting them.

The immediate effect of this change of government was a review of the very liberal immigration policies Jan Smuts had believed in. Nationalist Afrikaners were mistrustful of the large numbers of British immigrants encouraged under previous policies. The resultant clamp-down on new immigrants meant a fall-off in the demand for new homes, and this affected the home-building industry.

My father operated his business on a memory-and-trust basis, making any important calculations on the back of an old envelope. He kept no proper books at all. Despite the quality of his workmanship, and possibly because of it, after two years his business failed, and I took work as a junior clerk with a clothing company in Cape Town. During my lunchbreaks I visited a café near the factory and I began to play the fruit-machines and pinball machine there.

At about this time I became very active in evangelical work. Although not yet sixteen I obtained a licence from the Cape Town Municipality to preach in the streets and in the main market-place. Whatever I may have believed my motives were at that time, looking back it seems to me that this activity was part of my effort to identify with my new friends amongst the Brethren – perhaps an effort to appear more worthy in their eyes. On Saturday and Sunday evenings I often met up with other members of the faith and we would venture into District Six, Cape Town's notorious coloured ghetto, or travel to the non-white township of Athlone to preach. We would form a small circle on the pavement, sing hymns, and proclaim the Christian gospel message. I purchased gospel tracts for distribution among bystanders, and on Sunday evenings I patrolled the pavements near the Brethren's meeting-hall, approaching strangers and trying to persuade them to come in and listen to the gospel address.

It was whilst I was engaged in this way that I committed my first criminal act. Playing fruit-machines during my lunch breaks left me short of money, not that I had any real need of money. My parents provided me with a home, but I would have been unable to pay my way among my new friends if I had none. So I stole cash-sale takings from the company I worked for.

When the theft was discovered I was not asked directly if I was responsible, but suspicion fell mainly on me and a young girl who operated the firm's accounting machine. The cloud of suspicion made me feel uncomfortable and the sense of guilt I felt at what I had done made it impossible for me to remain at the company. I left shortly after the theft, working first for a bank, then an assurance company, and finally as a salesman for Caribonum Limited, selling carbon paper and typewriter ribbons.

Soon after joining Caribonum I began to accompany my work colleagues to a snooker club after work, and this was reported to the Brethren. I was confronted by two elders and I admitted the facts to them. A disciplinary meeting was held to consider my behaviour and to decide what to do about it. At that meeting scriptures quoted emphasized the need to avoid 'association with unbelievers', and the mood of the meeting developed into one of hostility towards me. My action in playing snooker with colleagues was clearly 'association with unbelievers', and one older brother, a Mr Stevens, accused me of deceit and pride in concealing my actions until confronted. He was a small, stocky man with greying hair and a goatee beard, and he urged my disfellowship, saying that the Brethren should 'not spare the rod'.

Throughout the meeting I sat at the back of the hall listening to the discussion. I was bewildered when I heard two elders being asked to inform me that the community had 'withdrawn fellowship' from me, and that I was no longer a part of that fellowship.

From that moment I became 'unclean' in the eyes of all those who I had known and grown up with. The worldwide community of the Exclusive Plymouth Brethren rejected me – I would not be allowed to speak to them, eat with them, or do any of the things we had enjoyed together. Parents told their children of the decision and warned them not to breach the barrier my excommunication raised. My own family were required to disown me, and within days I had to leave the family home and live alone in an hotel. I would be allowed to attend meetings, but only if I sat alone at the back of the meeting-hall, pilloried, and spoke to no one.

My whole life had been shattered, and now my sense of guilt made me confess to the theft from the firm I had worked for. This, too, became known to the Brethren, and made me doubly unfit for their fellowship. I still remember my father's anguish at the disgrace I had brought upon the family – then his despair turned to anger. He didn't attack me – I was a big lad – but my younger sister was suspected of holding hands with a young brother, a heinous offence in my father's eyes, and he picked up a thick wooden stick to beat her. He was a powerful man, but as he approached her something snapped inside me. In my fury at his intention I took the rod out of his hands and broke it into pieces. He was stunned, as I was, at my rebellion against his authority. Anything that remained of the relationship we had enjoyed was shattered and was never repaired. The next day I left home, rejected by my family. I was never to return.

The elderly Mr Stevens, who had urged my disfellowship, was to suffer the same fate himself. Six months after the meeting at which he had condemned me for playing snooker he was found in the same hall one afternoon with two little girls, aged nine and eleven. He appeared in court accused of child-molesting, and died shortly afterwards of a coronary thrombosis, a lonely, broken, old man.

After I had left home and had moved into an hotel, I telephoned Mr Osborne, the secretary of the clothing company, to tell him that I had been responsible for the theft. The sense of guilt I felt was heightened by the knowledge that an innocent girl was under suspicion, and I wanted to right that wrong. Mr Osborne told me that he would talk to the directors of the company and he asked me to visit him at his home that evening. When I did so he offered me tea, and whilst his wife busied herself preparing it he told me that the directors had decided not to prosecute me. He thanked me for clearing the girl's name, and he expressed concern when he learned that I had been forced to leave the family home and was now living alone, with no friends of my own age. He suggested that I join the YMCA, or a sports club, but the inhibitions I still harboured made it impossible for me to do this.

I continued to work at Caribonum Limited, and became one of the most successful men at the Cape branch. I was eighteen when I was given a country territory to canvass and, with it, a car. The territory stretched 500 miles from Cape Town to Port Elizabeth in the east; from there it extended almost 200 miles north to Graff Reinet, then west to Beaufort West, and back along the main Cape Town–Johannesburg highway for another 600 miles. It was a huge area and I was expected to cover it once a month. My trips were arranged in such a way that I travelled in the country during the week, but returned to base in Cape Town on most weekends. It was a lonely nomadic life, giving no opportunity to form stable friendships, and I began to seek companionship in pool-rooms, restaurants and late-night cafés. My rejection by the Brethren had shattered me and my life seemed to lose all sense of direction. I changed jobs three times in the next two years, selling stationery and office equipment for Cape distributors.

Most social pastimes had been considered evil or unclean according to the faith I had been brought up in. Drinking, dancing, smoking, cinemas, theatres, snooker, football and numerous everyday pursuits were taboo under the rules of the Exclusive Plymouth Brethren. I experienced a sense of guilt each time I broke one of those rules; I was naive and ill-prepared to live what society regards as a normal life. In later years I believe this sense of guilt may have led to me over-indulging perversely.

After joining Caribonum Limited, I began to gamble. A colleague invited me to spend one Saturday afternoon with him at Kenilworth racecourse in Cape Town. That was in 1951, and I won just over seventy pounds sterling, a small fortune in those days. The excitement of racing, the glamour, and a feeling of comradeship with other racegoers, combined to attract me. I began to realize that there was a world I knew nothing about, and that the summary divine displeasure I had been warned of did not seem to be visited on any of the crowds I saw enjoying themselves. Gambling became a form of escape from loneliness, and looking back I can see how this single pastime was to develop into a compulsion that would leave its mark on my whole life.

At about this time I had my first sexual experience. I met a pretty young girl at an all-night café. She was obviously a prostitute, although at the time I was so naive I didn't really understand what a prostitute was – the word simply was not part of my vocabulary. She invited me to go home with her, and I was grateful to her for not making me feel inadequate, and for allowing me to go to bed with her. I think the experience was a little unusual in that she did not ask me for any money, and seemed genuinely surprised when I pressed a small gold bracelet on her as a gift. I had been carrying it around with me for days waiting for just such an opportunity.

In 1953, my brother Philip left the Plymouth Brethren and went to live in Johannesburg. He wrote to me, giving me his address, and invited me to stay with him should I visit that city. I was becoming increasingly disillusioned at my failure to create a proper life for myself, and soon after I received his letter I decided to take up his offer.

4

I arrived in Johannesburg to discover that my brother had developed homosexual tendencies. His friends were mainly gay and I found their attentions completely alien to me. I attended the parties he went to and tried to join in the jollity, but I found the suggestion that I become one of them repulsive. Their way of life frightened me, I did not understand it, and I began to avoid meeting them.

I started to frequent Turffontein racecourse, joined Tattersalls Club, and visited pool-rooms. I gambled and I lost. At the time I was unemployed and I had already begun to develop the obsession with secrecy that is a feature of every gambler's life. I could not ask my brother for money without explaining why I needed it, and I solved the problem by purchasing goods on his accounts, without his knowledge, and converting them into cash. Within weeks my brother discovered what I had done and he reported me to the police, telling me that he had done so. My actions gave rise to charges of fraud and also to contraventions of the liquor laws designed to prevent sales of liquor to non-whites in South Africa. The police seemed to regard breach of the liquor laws as much more serious than the fraud, and when I heard they were looking for me I ran away.

I set out to hitch-hike to Cape Town, a thousand miles away, and I took my very few possessions with me. I arrived in the Cape short of cash and within a week I had sold my belongings to meet my needs. I was afraid to contact anyone I knew, in the mistaken belief that the police would have told everybody to look out for me. I began to sleep rough, often in the open, on beaches and in promenade shelters. To earn money for food I bought pencils and resold them at a profit. The pencils cost twopence each, and I hawked them to shops and offices for six shillings per dozen. On a good day I earned several pounds; then I would book into an hotel, have a meal, and later visit a pool-room to gamble away whatever money I had left. I learned to keep a dozen pencils at the end of each day so that I would have something to begin with the next morning.

It was whilst I was selling pencils that I met Kai Thorsen, a Norwegian carpenter. He had a small workshop in Canterbury Street, on the fringe of District Six, an area where I had stood on street corners and preached. Cape Town's coloured ghetto was built on the slopes of Table Mountain and had become a teeming slum. Filth and crime soiled its streets, the product of poverty so real that it sapped those who lived there of any hope. The houses were squalid tenements and leaned crumbling against one another; narrow roads and cobbled alleyways were piled high with discarded debris, which rotted and stank as the temperature rose, attracting swarms of flies. In these streets barefoot children roamed and played, and when they tired of their games they sat huddled in narrow doorways, clad in little more than dirty rags, waiting for their parents to return from work in the city below. The unequal opportunities that were enshrined in South Africa's apartheid laws made escape from these slums almost impossible.

Kai Thorsen employed two non-white men in his workshop and he puffed on his pipe as I tried to sell him my pencils. He was about thirty-five, a tall, rangy man with black curly hair. His eyes twinkled as he took the pipe from his mouth and pointed the stem towards me.

'I don't want any fokkin pencils,' he said cheerfully. 'But I could do with a fokkin beer. Why don't you join me?'

The pub was next door to his workshop, and as we talked he asked me about myself.

'Where the fock are you staying?' he asked.

To Kai Thorsen no sentence was complete without his heavily accented expletive. He used the word without any embarrassment or malice, and quite indiscriminately. He told me that he had spent the weekend at a beach party.

'It was fokkin lovely,' he said.

As we finished the third beer I gave up any thought of further work that day. I had told Kai of my position and his response had been typical of him.

'You can come and fokkin stay with me,' he said. 'I have a fokkin big flat that I live in by my fokkin self.'

The flat was half-furnished and reflected Kai's carefree attitudes. I moved in with him and continued to sell my pencils, branching out into other items of stationery as I saved a little capital. Not long after I had moved into the flat, Kai invited me to one of his beach parties.

'You'll have a fokkin good time,' he assured me.

The party began on Friday night and lasted until Sunday evening. Kai had chosen a secluded beach, well away from the popular bathing beaches, and sufficiently inaccessible to make it private.

We took wine in one-gallon jars, cases of beer, yards of a spicy sausage called boerewors, loaves of bread and a bag of mealie meal to make a stiff porridge to go with the sausage. Coffee, milk and sugar were added at the last minute. Kai had a friend who owned an old Ford V8, and somehow we packed a sheet of canvas, the provisions and ourselves into the car – and still managed to find room for three girls whom Kai had mysteriously arranged to meet at his workshop.

It was summer-time and the weather was glorious. We fashioned the canvas into a tent – a blanket each and a few pillows served as furnishing. Kai introduced the girls, and after he and his friend had settled down it was clear that Michelle was to be my partner. She was fair with dark brown eyes and I guessed that she was not older than eighteen. I felt a little self-conscious at first, but she quickly put me at my ease as she helped to carry the jars of wine down to the waterline and secure them to cords so that they rested safely in a cool pool. She kicked off her shoes and caught my hand as we made our way back up the beach. I began to relax and look forward to the party.

As the sun disappeared, Kai fetched his piano-accordion. His enthusiasm more than compensated for any lack of finesse, and we sat around the camp-fire sipping the cooled wine, munching sausages still sizzling from the embers they had been grilled over, and joining in the popular songs and ballads Kai was playing. It was a happy, relaxed party and as we sang I felt safe and unembarrassed in the flickering half-light of the fire. Michelle nestled closer and I put my arm around her. She chuckled and reached up to kiss me, her lips tasting of the spicy sausage she had been eating. I felt myself respond to her and pulled her a little closer.

As the darkness closed in, Kai put his accordion to one side. He pulled out his pipe and began to fill it.

'It's time to have a fokkin smoke,' he announced.

A sharp, sweet scent drifted over the open fire, and after a little while Kai handed the pipe to his girlfriend. I watched it go from hand to hand until it reached Michelle. I realized that it contained dagga, South Africa's indigenous marijuana, and when Michelle offered it to me I demurred.

'Oh, come on,' she urged me. 'You must try it.'

The sharp bite of the smoke made me cough at first, but gradually I felt the drug reach me. I was aware of a heightening of my senses; I felt excited, happy and a little light-headed. Later when Michelle stood up I joined her. I took her hand as we made our way to the tent. I was a little afraid, but anxious to please her, and anxious to enjoy a new experience.

It was very dark in the tent, but I sensed that Michelle had discarded her clothes. I froze briefly as I felt her body against mine; then I held her to me and her hands found the belt to my swimming trunks. She loosened it, and I helped her as she drew the trunks off and put them with her clothes beside the blankets. We lay down, my arm slipped around her waist, my hands surprised at the smoothness of her skin and the soft firmness of her body. For a while we kissed and caressed, and then her hand moved over me, brushing my skin until she held me. She sighed and pulled me on to her, and then she gave herself to me freely and without shame.

I woke to find Michelle asleep, her head nestling against my chest. I had slept well and when Michelle stirred and opened her eyes I leaned down and kissed her. She smiled and nestled closer, her hand moving slowly as she caressed me. She murmured contentedly as she realized that I needed no arousal; then she slowly raised herself until she had mounted me, and we began to make love.

Later we took our towels and raced down to the water's edge. We splashed into the surf, tossing our towels in a bundle above the waterline. An incoming wave caught us and Michelle reached out and took my hand as we leaned against the force of the sea. Breakers broke freely about us and although we were both naked I felt no embarrassment. It seemed quite natural, Michelle appearing quite unaware of her nudity.

The weekend passed much too quickly; very soon we were back in the city. At Kai's workshop we kissed the girls goodbye, and they disappeared as mysteriously as they had appeared.

'When can I see you again?' I had asked Michelle.

'When Kai has another party,' she said, and nothing would make her change her mind.

Kai was no more helpful.

'I don't know where they fokkin live,' he said shortly. 'I met them in the fokkin workshop.'

I knew he wasn't being honest because I had seen Beryl, the girl who had been his partner, at the flat on several occasions. Later I discovered the real reason for the secrecy. The girls were from District Six. Although they appeared to be as 'white' as I was, they had been classified 'coloured' under South Africa's race laws, and associating with 'whites' as they had could have resulted in prison sentences for all of us had we been detected.

Six weeks after I had met him, Kai Thorsen went back to Norway. He closed the flat and the workshop and I moved into an hotel. Before long I was frequenting pool-rooms and gambling again, and within weeks I was destitute. In desperation I contacted my mother. She urged me to go to the police and give myself up, and when I left her I went to Mowbray police station and gave myself up. I waited there while they checked with the police in Johannesburg and confirmed that I was still wanted by them. Then they put me in a cell.

My concern at what was to happen to me was overshadowed by my relief at no longer being a wanted man. I slept more soundly in that cell than I had done for some time. The next day I began the long train journey to Johannesburg in custody. My escort was a kindly, retired policeman and we travelled together with nothing to show that I was under arrest. When we arrived he took me to Marshall Square police station, and there I was put into the filthiest cell I have ever seen. It was the cell they used for vagrants, and the grime and smell were shocking.

At my trial I pleaded guilty and received a suspended sentence. My brother, who regretted his action in reporting me to the police, offered me accommodation until I could get on my feet, and as I walked down the court-house steps I resolved never to get into trouble again.

5

My trial had been conducted almost informally. The police, the prosecution and the magistrate left me with the impression that they had been surprised to find me appearing before them. They were courteous, helpful and understanding. Nothing in the procedure justified any feeling that I had been unfairly treated, and I can remember no feeling of resentment that could have accounted for my behaviour in later years. My brother helped to find me employment with a company marketing Kalamazoo business systems, and I became quite successful.

The work was different from the hard, direct-selling methods used by Caribonum Limited; often a period of weeks or even months would elapse between a preparatory discussion and a successful system-installation. During the course of one of my business calls I met the owner of a stationery company specializing in carbon-paper sales, and when he learned of my training he made me an offer that more than doubled my earnings. I accepted and went to work for him.

Shortly after the trial I had left my brother and moved into an hotel alone, but now, at my new job, I joined a colleague and we moved into a flat near the city centre. It served as a base, for I now did a great deal of travelling. I was given freedom to go anywhere in South Africa and my life developed into a series of stays in small country hotels, with occasional rests back in Johannesburg. I usually travelled alone and my movement from town to town meant that I was seldom anywhere long enough to make friends.

I did make some friends in Durban and they introduced me to an attractive brunette called Gloria. Whenever business took me to that city we would stay together at an hotel on the seafront. She introduced me to the night-life of the city, to the party set, where life was lived at a frenetic pace. It was a promiscuous scene; marijuana was smoked quite freely and we escaped fatigue and depression by taking Benzedrine and other amphetamines. For some reason I always felt that I could not become a part of that way of life and, strangely, I never became addicted to the drugs we took. As my travels continued I found escape from boredom and loneliness in gambling, and gradually gambling began to interfere with my work. I began to earn less, and I needed more.

In 1955, whilst on the road, I began issuing cheques without having the funds to meet them. The cheques were issued in my own name and were drawn on my own current account. I hoped to earn sufficient money in commissions to make a deposit and cover them before they were presented to my bank, but my sales ability seemed to be falling off, and the trip was not very successful. When I returned to Johannesburg I tried desperately to raise the money I needed, but I was unable to do so. Gambling and the deceits it brought with it had exhausted the credit my friends were prepared to extend to me. They were tired of my endless borrowing and the manipulation of post-dated cheques and promissory notes I indulged in. When the cheques I had issued were dishonoured, I was arrested and charged with fraud.

The series of cheques I had issued on that one sales trip resulted in four separate trials; in Johannesburg, Durban and Cape Town in 1955, and in Pretoria in 1957. In Britain the matters would have been centralized, but as I elected to contest all the charges, and because of the cost of bringing witnesses vast distances to any one centre, it was more practical for the authorities to hold separate trials and transfer me to the different cities involved. The trials covered almost a year and resulted in me serving an aggregate of thirty-seven months in prison. I served part of that sentence in each of the prisons in Johannesburg, Durban, Cape Town, Baviaanspoort and Pretoria Local.

I had passed through the Fort, Johannesburg's prison, in 1954, as an awaiting-trial prisoner, but now I was admitted as a convict, sentenced to imprisonment with compulsory labour. The Fort stands on top of Hospital Hill and overlooks the city. It was built in the nineteenth century and as its name suggests it was constructed with ramparts and crenellated walls like a medieval fortress. The grey granite walls were more than twenty feet thick in places, leaning away from the hilltop and reaching high into the sky. They dropped away sharply into what appears at one time to have been a moat; now it is largely filled in, providing car-parking for visitors.

The accommodation reflected the era in which the prison had been built. Passageways ran inside the walls and underground tunnels led into rooms and other parts of the prison. There were dungeons too, and some underground cells were still in use in 1955. As a first-time offender I was allocated to a special wing, and from there I went to work in the reception office as a clerk.

The reception was a huge room and at times catered for up to 600 admissions each day: the work-load often kept us busy until late at night. White admissions seldom totalled more than twelve to fifteen per day, many of them regulars, alcoholics who seemed to have given up hope and had sadly become attached to the security and discipline of the harsh prison regime. The balance of the 600 or more admissions were non-white. Most were guilty of nothing more than being in a white area without a 'pass' allowing them to be there. Very strict laws controlled the movement of non-white South Africans, and these laws were strictly enforced in the 'white areas' of the city.

Apartheid is faithfully followed in prisons in South Africa, and the different ethnic groups were allocated to different wings of the Fort. I never had cause or opportunity to go into the 'non-white' sections of the prison, but from the numbers of prisoners I saw processed daily in the reception room, and from what happened in the admission process, it became clear that stories of overcrowding and cruelty were probably true. The blacks were usually marshalled by guards of their own race – indunas, armed with assegais, a short stabbing spear, and with knobkerries, a seasoned hardwood stave with a bulbous protrusion at one end. The crack of a knobkerrie against a skull, and a cry of pain, were common sounds which came from the holding-room behind the reception where I worked. The indunas did not hesitate to use force to ensure that their orders were obeyed.

The systematic theft of cash and personal belongings from incoming blacks was a regular practice in the reception area where I worked. In common with most prisons, all admissions had to hand over any cash or valuables for safe-keeping. The routine was that a black prisoner with money or a watch or ring would be hustled to the reception desk by two indunas. A white guard then addressed him sharply in Afrikaans, a language he probably didn't understand. The indunas would translate.

'Put your things on the counter.'

The prisoner, frightened by the harsh tones and by the stories he had heard of the way he would be treated, quickly complied. The white guard would count the money and inspect the valuables. If ten pounds and a desirable watch had been put on the counter, he would take eight pounds and the watch and place it on a shelf under the counter, leaving just two pounds on the counter-top.

'How much money has he got?' he would ask the induna.

The question and answer were then translated.

'He say he got ten pounds and a watch, baas.'

The white guard would look up in mock anger.

'How much?' he would shout.

The indunas would pretend to get angry and turn on the frightened prisoner and clout him across the face, shouting and pointing at the two pounds. A few more slaps and shouts and the prisoner would give the answer required of him. If he was stubborn, the indunas would take him away into the holding-room. I don't know what they did in there but the prisoners always gave the answers sought of them when they were brought back. It was a sickening experience, but for me it was short-lived. I was soon to be transferred to Durban to face further charges there.

One incident that illustrates the callous attitude of the indunas and the indifference of the white guards occurred in the confusion that always surrounded the daily transfer of hundreds of prisoners between the prison and the courts. It occurred shortly after I left the Fort. Transport to the courts was in lorries that had been converted to little more than metal boxes on wheels. They were suitable to accommodate fifteen persons at the most and had no seats or hand-holds. They had no windows, and small ventilation ducts cut out at the front and rear were quite inadequate. Up to twenty-five men were crammed into these transports for transfer to the courts.

An urgent request for prisoners to be transferred to the Witwatersrand Supreme Court and the Johannesburg Magistrates' Courts one midday, found the prison with only one lorry available. White guards stood by and watched as black indunas swung their knobkerries and bludgeoned a group of non-white prisoners until thirty-seven men were packed into the lorry and the door pressed in on them and made fast. It was summer-time and the sun was very fierce as it beat down on the metal roof of the lorry. The prisoners cried out in pain and in terror as they felt themselves suffocating. The lorry was caught up in the midday traffic and the police driver took no notice of the cries. When they arrived at the courts and the doors were opened, it was too late. Eleven men had died of suffocation and injuries received from the indunas when crammed into the lorry.

For twenty-four hours the media reported public outrage – then everything was forgotten. After all, it was South Africa, and the dead men were black.

6

In 1955, prisoners in South Africa were transferred between cities by rail. We were dressed in moleskin-type trousers, distinctive khaki-coloured canvas jackets and untanned, ill-fitting shoes. A wide-brimmed sombrero completed the outfit. Standing on a platform waiting for a train we attracted a good deal of attention. My transfer from Johannesburg to Durban was my first experience of this. Our clothing was modelled on a bygone era, and at 5.30 p.m., amid crowds of homeward-bound commuters, we looked like men from another world. We were shackled together in pairs with handcuffs and leg-irons, and were surrounded by uniformed prison guards with rifles and prominent revolver holsters. I did what everyone else did – I pulled down the brim of my hat and hoped that no one would recognize me.

Two compartments had been reserved to accommodate six prisoners and six guards. Once inside the compartments we had some privacy; the windows were closed and the blinds drawn, and they remained that way during the 500-mile journey. The guards put all six of us into one of the compartments and commandeered the other for themselves. In addition to six prisoners, three guards were in our compartment on duty at any one time. So, throughout the journey, nine people were crammed into one compartment whilst three off-duty guards relaxed in the other. The leg-irons and handcuffs were never removed, and we ate, sat and slept in pairs. It wasn't very comfortable; we even had to go to the toilet in pairs. It was degrading and often painful trying to cram into the rail-carriage toilet when shackled to someone else. It was not easy to manoeuvre into the small toilet, unbutton, perform your duty, wipe your backside and button up, all with one hand, whilst at the same time swaying as the train rocked and rolled along the narrow-gauge railway line. It was even less pleasant to manoeuvre so that the man you were shackled to could use the toilet, then to remain still while he performed his needs and rearranged his clothing.

Whilst all this was going on the door of the toilet cubicle was propped open by a nervous gun-toting guard, who kept a close watch on the proceedings. The effort required to negotiate the corridors and the coach-linkages, and the stares of the other passengers, were unpleasant too, and no one used the toilet unless absolutely desperate. During one trip along the corridor my co-prisoner and I fell over luggage someone had left in the passageway. It wasn't funny at the time, but later I could laugh at the confusion we caused. I think our guards were as relieved as we were when we arrived at Durban Prison.

There were two main prisons in Durban. One called Point Prison was near to the harbour, and was used almost exclusively as a prison for non-white convicted prisoners. The prison I was placed in was known as Durban Gaol. It was close to the station, and I believe has since been demolished.

Durban Gaol had a section for white prisoners and several much larger sections for both convicted and unconvicted non-white prisoners. There was a hospital that had separate facilities for whites and non-whites, and whilst I was there it seemed to be run not so much by the doctors or prison guards as by a Swazi prisoner called Samuel. He was highly intelligent and spoke both English and Afrikaans fluently, as well as several African dialects. It was common knowledge within the prison that if you wanted something from the hospital you had to see Samuel. How a black man ever came to have such influence in a South African prison I do not know, but he did, and the guards, black and white alike, took advantage of his obvious skills and let him get on with it. He was pretty ruthless with his fellow blacks and was openly feathering his own nest. Apart from the reciprocal favours he extracted from the guards, he had an insatiable appetite for young boys. The hospital orderlies were all selected by him and they made up his private harem. This may sound incredible, but in the context of Durban Gaol it was fairly normal. Homosexuality amongst blacks was rife and appeared to be countenanced by the guards. It was used as an easy way to control the mass of hardened prisoners.

Upon arrival I was again given a job in the reception office, and so was in daily contact with the non-white prisoners. The majority of them came from nearby rural areas, and they were a good deal less sophisticated than those I had met at the Fort in Johannesburg. Many had not been outside their native village or kraal before finding themselves in prison.

The same systematic theft of cash and belongings occurred here as it had at the Fort, the only difference being that the reception orderlies were black trusties, and not indunas. They were possibly more callous than the indunas had been, and aided the white guards in the pillaging of prisoners' property. Young black youths, some barely in their teens, were hustled into the waiting-room next to the reception, ordered to strip and shower and then physically assaulted before being allocated to a cell where they became the plaything of their seniors. Black prison guards stood by and watched whilst this was going on.

My trial in Durban took several days, but was spread over a period of months, and when I was not at court I worked in the reception. I was allocated a cell in the white prisoners' section, and the guard in charge was a pig of a man called Walkenhorst. He terrorized the men unfortunate enough to be in his care. As a clerk in the reception I enjoyed the protection of the administrative staff, and they stopped Walkenhorst from charging me with offences under the prison regulations on more than one occasion. Once he forced open my cell locker and found two thousand cigarettes, excess toiletries and two bottles of whisky. I was called to the Chief Guard's office and confronted with the goods, and I told him that I had never seen them before.

'There must be some mistake,' I said a little lamely.

The Chief picked up the cigarettes and the whisky and put them in a cupboard in the office. He locked it and put the key in his pocket.

'If you've never seen them, you won't miss them,' he said. 'Now take your toiletries away and get out of here.'

Walkenhorst was furious but the Chief would not let him charge me. After that incident I kept my contraband goods in a locker in the reception office, out of Walkenhorst's territory.

One of the functions of the reception office was to accept payment of fines. A sliding window opened directly on to the street outside the prison, and relatives and friends of non-white prisoners would queue there all day long to pay fines imposed by the courts and await the release of the prisoners concerned. White prisoners' friends and relatives used the front gate – and there was no queue. The fines window was the conduit for every kind of contraband imaginable both in and out of the prison. Money and drugs were handed in and watches and pillaged jewellery were handed out. The trade went on all day, every day, under the guise of official fines business. Dagga was traded fairly openly, and I got my whisky that way:

Shortly after I left Durban Gaol I heard that the Chief Guard and a white reception guard had been indicted and convicted of marijuana trafficking. Before I left the white guard had shown me a small suitcase full of money.

'I'm going to buy my son a house,' he told me.

The youngest Head Guard in the prison service was in charge of the fines section. He had control of duplicate magistrates' warrants. The system was that when a warrant was lost or incorrectly completed the Head Guard would make out a duplicate warrant and send it to the appropriate court for signature. When it was returned, duly signed, he would destroy the original faulty warrant and file the new one. The black trusties told me that on one occasion five Asian drug dealers arrived at the prison, sentenced to imprisonment without the option of a fine for periods varying from three to six years. They had been detected by Customs officials who had followed their movements from the Far East, and had arrested them when their ship docked at Durban. They were believed to be part of a gang of international drug smugglers.

The Asians had been stunned by the speed of arrest, trial and conviction, and now faced the prospect of spending years in Point Prison. The master of their ship did all he could to help them, but within days he would have to sail and leave them behind. The trusties told me that the Head Guard solved the problem by preparing duplicate warrants, altered to include the option of a fine. They told me that he then forged the judicial officer's signature, pocketed the hastily paid fines and filed the warrants away.

In confirmation of this I heard some time later that Customs officials, arriving to interrogate the five Asians about their Eastern connections, were more than a little surprised to be told that the men had paid their fines, and were probably safely home in Bombay by now. The Head Guard left the prison service shortly after that incident.

When my trial in Durban was completed I was transferred to Cape Town. Again we travelled by train, and the discomforts I experienced on the journey to Durban were repeated, but over a much longer period. The journey to Cape Town, via Johannesburg, covered 1500 miles, and took four days to complete.

In Cape Town I had my first short experience of the infamous Roeland Street Gaol. It was a filthy hell-hole. The cells were cut into the rock-face and opened directly on to a small open-air exercise yard. In this yard we spent the infrequent exercise periods we were allowed. The food was atrocious; parboiled rice, cold and stodgy, frequently with half-dead maggots to be found in it.

We were crammed up to five in a cell originally designed for one. Bedding consisted of two stinking blankets and lice-infested rotting sisal mats. There were no beds, and we laid the mats directly on the rough-hewn rock floor. When it rained, water trickled through the porous rock ceiling and walls, and seeped over the floor. We huddled together, edging towards the one dry patch on the floor, but the water spread inexorably, and soon the whole floor was wet and slimy. A stinking toilet-bucket stood near the door and made conditions even less pleasant.

I didn't stay there long. I changed my plea to guilty and got the case over with.

7

When my trial in Cape Town had ended I was transferred to Baviaanspoort Prison near Pretoria, and en route I was lodged in the 'Big House', Pretoria Central Prison, for a few nights. The air of gloom and despair in the 'Big House' frightened me. It was South Africa's hanging prison, and housed mainly long-term offenders. I was glad when I arrived at Baviaanspoort.

Upon arrival I was allocated to the open section of the prison, which consisted of a camp that had been used to house internees during the Second World War. It was made up of army huts and ablution blocks surrounded by a high barbed-wire fence. My hut contained twenty-odd other prisoners, and I was given a job helping the camp guard in the office.

Near the military-style camp we lived in, a new prison had been built. It was designed to accommodate non-white prisoners, but had a small section for young white offenders who were considered bad security risks. This section was run as a punishment unit.

The open camp I was in ran on military lines, with parades, inspections and roll-calls at every opportunity. Strict rules governed the make-up of beds, cleanliness, clothing, haircuts, and everything else; but the rules were relaxed after 5.00 p.m., and we were free to associate and enjoy the sports and entertainment facilities the camp offered.

Whilst I was there, stories still circulated about the two gold-mining millionaires who had conspired to salt the ore sent for assay from drillings at mines they had holdings in. One had served his sentence in the camp hospital, with a medicinal bottle of whisky in his bedside locker. He was remembered as a thoroughly disagreeable old man. His co-defendant was remembered for the way he helped everyone he could. He provided Christmas parcels for those prisoners who had no money, and added to the inventory of musical and sports equipment in the camp. I remember their case particularly because the assayist who had actually salted the gold-ore samples for them was a man called Campbell-Stephenson, who had been an Exclusive Plymouth Brother. Traces of the gold dust he used to salt the ore were found in his waistcoat pocket, and I recall idly speculating that the same pocket had probably held his offering for the Sunday-morning collection bag at communion service.

Baviaanspoort lay in a valley and seemed exposed to icy winter winds, whilst at the same time it seemed to be shielded from the cool breezes we longed for in summer. It was some 6000 feet above sea level, and the merciless high veld sun in summer was replaced by bitterly cold nights in winter. I experienced both during my stay there.

A few months after my arrival at Baviaanspoort, detectives from Pretoria came to interview me about cheques issued in their city. My prison experiences had hardened me, and I declined to co-operate with them. They arranged for an identification parade, and on the appointed day they brought their witnesses out to the prison by coach. I had been asked who I wanted to stand on the parade with me, and I took advantage of a little-known precedent set in a case involving an army cadet. In that case it had been held that he could have as many people as were available at the parade, as long as they were of similar appearance. He paraded with some three hundred cadets and had not been identified. I asked for all white prisoners of over five feet ten inches to stand on parade with me, and the Head Guard granted my request. We all wore prison clothing and the detectives had to write down the particulars and positions of over sixty men.

The first witness quickly walked along the four rows of prisoners and said that she did not recognize anyone. I then rearranged the parade, requiring the detectives to take fresh particulars and positions before calling their next witness. She was a young lady who clearly wanted no argument with sixty prisoners over a cheque her boss had received some two years earlier – and she too walked past the four rows of prisoners, said she recognized no one, and made her way determinedly back to the coach.

As I began to rearrange the parade yet again, the detectives withdrew and held a short conference. They then informed me that they were abandoning the parade, and would hold the matter over until I was released from the sentence I was serving.

The immediate repercussion of all this was that I was no longer considered suitable for the open prison camp, and I was transferred to the closed penal unit housed in the new prison.

None of the stories I had heard prepared me for the treatment I received in that unit. It consisted of one large cell, thirty feet long and fifteen feet wide. At the time I was there, thirty-four men were accommodated in this one cell. It had no windows. Open slits twelve inches wide and four inches deep had been cut into the unplastered, solid concrete walls. These slits had to provide both light and air and they did little of either. Sited close to the concrete ceiling they admitted very little light to the cell, and they were even less effective in dispersing the heat and stench that accumulated from thirty-four sweating bodies and two open toilet-buckets during the fiery heat of the summer months. In winter they served only to admit the intense cold that seemed to envelop the prison complex once the sun had set. The cell had no lighting, no heating, and no running water. The two open toilet-buckets had to serve the needs of us all, and drinking-water was limited to two four-gallon drums each day. Our bedding consisted of half-inch thick felt mats and two blankets. There were no pillows and no linen. The mats were barely two feet wide, and we laid them directly on to the concrete floor. When all the mats were down there was no room for walking about, and arguments arising from encroachment upon one another's areas happened constantly.

The toilet-buckets stood in one corner of the cell, and throughout the night we were woken by curses and fights when one man stumbled over another in the darkness. Those nearest to the toilet-buckets suffered most, and as in all communities it was the weak and the unprotected who found themselves pushed that way.

All the prisoners were under twenty-five, and some were as young as seventeen. We were subjected to a regime of unremitting brutality, and some did not survive. Nearly all of those who did survive became hardened criminals.

A metal grille stretching from floor to ceiling was set in one corner to protect the door. Roll-call was at 5.30 a.m. – in the summer it was barely light, and in winter it was quite dark. The guards carried hand torches and I stood morning after morning watching as the beam of the torch jerked from one prisoner to another whilst the head-count was being taken in darkness. After roll-call we lined up for breakfast. A pint of thin mealie-meal porridge, a small chunk of rough, dry bread, and a half-pint of the foulest coffee I have ever tasted was served without milk or sugar.

By 6.00 a.m. our bedding was rolled up, the blankets folded to form a block which we called a 'wireless', because it looked rather like one. Two cold-water taps set in the open yard served as washing facilities. They were inadequate in summer and incredibly cold in winter. At 6.30 a.m. we were mustered and counted again. Then the gates of the unit were opened and we were marched out in pairs. Outside the gates we were called to a halt and another roll-call was held; we were counted yet again and then handed over to the guards attached to the work parties.

Throughout all of this the strictest silence was maintained. The work-party guards were joined by others armed with rifles, and then by the dog-handlers and their dogs. When the guards were satisfied they gave the order for us to proceed. It often happened that all of this took place whilst it was pouring with rain, and on those occasions the guards would pull their weatherproofed clothing more tightly about them, whilst the prisoners stood without protection and simply got soaked. During the summer months it mattered very little, but in winter the cold made it unbearable. I saw men punished for stamping their feet and rubbing their frozen hands together whilst 'on parade'.

We worked in a clay quarry that was sited more than a mile from the unit. En route we stopped at the tool-yard, where each man was issued with a pick, a spade and an iron-wheeled barrow. The handles of the barrows were of plain metal, and they were unbearably hot in summer and so cold in winter that the skin of my fingers seemed to stick to the frozen metal as I held it. Having collected the tools we were marshalled into a double line, re-counted, and the order was given to march. We proceeded to trundle the barrows along the track to the quarry. The noise was deafening. Pick-axes and spades rattled as the barrows creaked and bounced over the ruts in the track. Many of the tools were badly in need of repair, and it was difficult to keep a place in the double line we were expected to maintain when the wheel of your barrow was out of alignment or bent.

The quarry was really just a huge open pit. A small mountain of heavy, wet clay stood at one end, and our work was to move it to the other end some 300 yards away. During my time, that huge heap of clay was moved first one way and then the other three times. It was the hardest labour I have ever known. In later years I was to work uprooting trees and in stone-yards, but nothing compared with the sheer back-breaking work in that pit.

Our barrows were numbered, and when we arrived at the quarry the number of the barrow each man had been issued was noted. The guards positioned themselves on the high slopes around the pit and leaned on their rifles, while the dog-handlers took up positions next to the small shelters that had been erected to provide protection for the dogs. The prisoners were then ordered to start work.

A record was kept of how many loads each man collected and wrestled across the soggy ground to the new dumping area. Failure to achieve the undisclosed number of loads required resulted in punishment. The punishment was usually the loss of one or more meals in any one day but, for persistent failure to meet the quota, solitary confinement and up to twenty-one days on rice-water were standard punishments. These sentences could be increased and insolence or more provocative behaviour could result in a man being sentenced to whipping with the heavy cane.

It was a vicious circle. The rations we were given were inadequate for young men engaged in such stamina-sapping labour; and when the men were unable to maintain the tempo required of them they panicked and used up still more precious energy trying to do more than they were physically capable of. So they failed to meet the quota and as a result lost the rations they had found insufficient in the first place.

At lunch-times we were marched back to the prison unit. The procedure on returning was exactly the same as on the way out – but in reverse. We left our tools at the tool-yard, were counted and marshalled and inspected several times. Back at the prison the gates to the unit were opened and we were marched in, counted, issued with a bowl of thin stew and a chunk of bread and locked in the cell. We ate our meal in the cell, amid the stench of the open toilet-buckets.

Within the hour we were marshalled, marched back to the quarry and ordered to carry on with the work. We finished at 5.00 p.m. in winter, and at 6.00 p.m. in summer. There were no rest periods and any drop in the tempo was met with shouts, curses and threats from the guards – and, if persisted in, led to punishment.

Under the fierce heat of the summer sun I saw some young men collapse and others simply give up. Occasionally someone would run amok, his sanity snapping suddenly under the unremitting physical pressure. The guards would look on impassively, and they only took action when the man tried to break through the cordon they formed. Sometimes they would let him break through and then loose the dogs to chase him. They laughed and cheered as the dogs pounced and dragged the man down; and then two guards would make their way to where he lay and, calling the dogs off, they would take it in turns to beat the prisoner unconscious with their batons.

I saw a young man, his reason broken by the pressures, gather 'malpitte', a type of poisonous berry with hallucinogenic properties, and chew on them until he dropped to the ground foaming at the mouth. That young man's life was saved, but the poison had so damaged his nervous system that he remained an uncoordinated, helplessly crazed being, committed to an asylum for the remainder of his life.

Those who survived, hardened and changed. The young and the weak gravitated towards those able to protect them, and often the strong took advantage of the weak. We were allowed no tobacco, no reading material, no music, no radio, no recreations at all. The sheer brutality of the life induced animalism. Liaisons were formed and flourished. The joyless, unending pressures made excursions into homosexuality one of the few reliefs open to the prisoners. Jealousy and hate accompanied uncontrolled emotion and led to brutal fights and bitter disputes breaking out in the cell. The fighting was more frequent in the summer months when the heat and stench of the cell became unbearable.

Men did survive – I survived. In desperation we found strengths we had never imagined we possessed. But I believe that the legacy we took with us when we left Baviaanspoort, and which would affect our lives most, was the legacy of hate. Men subjected to the inhumanity of that place emerged embittered and hardened, dangerous products of a system that was a blot on the face of a professedly civilized community.

When I had completed my sentence at Baviaanspoort I was transferred to Pretoria Local Prison to await trial on the fraud charges which had led to the aborted identification parade. The prison stands at the foot of Vulture's Hill, just below the 'Big House', which I was later to know so well. It was in fact the same prison which Sir Winston Churchill had written of so revealingly as the State Model School. He had escaped from there during the Boer War, and his experiences had deeply affected him. Many years later he would write:

'[The] . . . hours crawl like paralytic centipedes. Nothing amuses you.

Reading is difficult: writing impossible. Life is one long boredom from dawn till slumber. The whole atmosphere of prison, even the most easy and best-regulated prison, is odious. Companions in this kind of misfortune quarrel about trifles and get the least possible pleasure from each other's society. I certainly hated every minute of my captivity more than I have ever hated any other period in my whole life. Looking back on those days, I have always felt the keenest pity for prisoners and captives. What it must mean for any man, especially an educated man, to be confined for years in a modern convict prison strains my imagination. Each day exactly like the day before, with the barren ashes of wasted life behind, and all the long years of bondage stretching out ahead.' (Churchill, *My Early Life*, pp. 256–7)

During my short stay in that prison I felt that not much had changed since Churchill's day. Time still crawled past, companions still quarrelled over trifles, and the boredom and sameness of each day became increasingly depressing. I would walk into the exercise yard and look up at the place on the wall where Churchill had climbed over in making his escape. The wall was eighteen feet high and a jacaranda tree peeped over from the outside, its vivid lilac petals a splash of colour against the grey stone. It seemed so peaceful now, and it was difficult to imagine the desperation that had driven Churchill to defy his armed guards and break out of the enemy stronghold. In later years I came to understand that desperation and how it drove men to act beyond normal human boundaries. Churchill belonged to a rare breed of men, but even so, looking up at the wall, I recall thinking that he must have been a little lucky to have got away with it. I suspect that in later years he would have agreed with me.

My trial in Pretoria lasted only one day. I pleaded guilty, and my former employer offered to re-employ me. In view of the sentence I had just completed I was given a suspended sentence – five years' imprisonment suspended for three years.

It was late December 1957, and the jacaranda trees that line Pretoria's streets were shedding their petals, covering the pavements with a carpet of pale lilac and filling the air with their scent. The sun was hot as I left the court-house to be met by my brother Philip, my solicitor and my former employer. Together we travelled back to Johannesburg.

8

I began working on the same day that I was released, and from the outset I was successful. I worked mainly outside Johannesburg, travelling from town to town. Occasionally another salesman would join me and we would canvass an area together.

Early in 1958, I accompanied my employer to Cape Town. We arranged the trip so that it included a long weekend, combining business with relaxation. We worked quite hard during the week and on the Friday I decided to dine out. That evening I made my way along St Georges Street to the Café Royal; I ordered a dry sherry whilst waiting for my table. A very pretty girl stood waiting at the head of the stairs leading to the dining area, and it was clear that she was waiting for someone to join her. As she waited it seemed that her date had let her down, and I persuaded her to join me. She told me that her name was Ruth, and after dining we agreed to go out to the Clifton Hotel, perched on the rock-face overhanging Clifton beach. There we sipped sparkling wine and watched the moon play on Atlantic rollers as they crashed against the rocks below us. We danced a little, shuffled really, because I have never learned to dance, and, reluctant to end the mood we had found, we decided to spend the rest of the weekend together. After telephoning hotel reservations and collecting overnight bags we set out for Hermanus, a picturesque resort eighty miles east of Cape Town.

When we arrived it was quite late and we were shown directly to our room by the night porter. We unpacked, and Ruth sat at the dressing-table combing her thick black hair. It reached down to her waist and I lay on the bed watching as she brushed and combed it. We had undressed, and now she reached behind her and unfastened her brassière. She stood up to come to bed and as she turned towards me her hair tumbled down almost hiding her breasts. Then she tossed it over her shoulders and smiled as I took her hand and drew her to me.

The next day I rented a speedboat and we explored the lake near Hermanus. The boat bounced over little waves that a light breeze had set up, and as I opened the throttle the bow rose and we began to plane. Ruth stood with her hair streaming out behind her, her eyes hidden behind huge sunglasses. She wore an impudent bikini – wisps of pale blue which only emphasized what they tried to cover. A shower of spray burst over the bows and she laughed as it struck us, stinging momentarily and cooling us before it dried under the hot sun. Her skin was a rich brown and she glowed with well-being. I sensed her watching me behind the glasses and I laughed with her as she moved closer until she was pressed against me.

Towards midday we headed back to the jetty, drinking in the sound and smell of the water. As we drew closer I throttled back and the boat wallowed slightly. Slowly we nosed our way in to the jetty.

We spent three days at Hermanus, relaxed and free from care, lazing in the sun, boating on the lake, and retreating to our room as soon as night fell. It was an experience I needed – I had spent more than three years in prison, and as we relaxed and found satisfaction in one another I began to cast off some of the shadows that had followed me since my release. I began to regain a little of the confidence and self-respect that prison had taken away.

When I returned to Johannesburg I rented a flat in a tower-block overlooking the city. From there I could look out and see the outline of tall city buildings, and at night they would merge and light up, multicoloured neon signs flashing on top of them. Gradually a social life began to emerge. I joined a sports club and was elected to captain the snooker team. I was invited to parties and I entertained at my flat. For a short while I had a passionate affair with an air hostess, but my constant travelling and her varying work schedule made us drift apart. As I became more confident, my earnings increased, and I spent quite freely.

Towards the middle of 1958, I met Georgina. She was twenty-one, just three years younger than I was, and as a young girl she had won beauty competitions and trained as a model. She had long golden-blonde hair, and the beauty she had shown promise of as a child had blossomed so that, now, men turned their heads to watch when she passed by. We met at a party given by friends who lived in the same apartment block as I did, and from that first meeting we were irresistibly attracted to each other. I courted her assiduously, forgoing and cutting short sales trips in order to be near her. She responded and we became inseparable.

Georgina's parents were solid Afrikaners and they were wary of me. I was an Englishman, and they were suspicious of the way I appeared to have captivated their daughter. Whilst I had told Georgina about my past, we had agreed not to share this with her parents, and it may be that they sensed we were hiding something from them. In August of 1958, I asked Georgina to marry me, and she accepted my proposal.

Her parents were unhappy; they did not believe that I could provide Georgina with the security they wanted her to have. My employer objected; he suspected that he would be losing a free-roaming salesman. But none of these objections altered our resolve to go ahead with the marriage. Two weeks after I had proposed we were wed by special licence. We had kept the arrangements a secret, and after a short celebration with a few friends we left to honeymoon in Durban.

The first few days and nights of our marriage introduced me to a new world. We had made love prior to our marriage, but the happiness and sense of fulfilment I now experienced were quite new to me. I began to learn what it was to love and to be loved freely, without any sense of wrongdoing. I began to learn to satisfy and to be satisfied, to care and to be cared for.

We made trips seeking out the secluded beaches near Durban – to Isipingo and Amamzimtoti in the south, and travelling as far as St Lucia Bay to the north. We would find an isolated stretch of sand and lie listening to the warm rollers of the Indian Ocean as they broke on the golden beach. The murmur of small wavelets and the crunch and hiss of the breakers combined until they became a rhythmic background sound, reassuring in its constancy, cutting us off from the real world. We would lie late into the afternoon, waiting to watch as the sun set. The clear blue of day would falter until the sky seemed to come alive. It was never still – blues, greens, yellows and reds intermingled in a riot of colour. As the short, sub-tropical evening darkened, the colours faded and were replaced by the deep blue of the night sky. Stars appeared, hesitantly at first, and then more boldly until they covered the sky. Then the moon appeared and as it rose the stars faded. At first it appeared as a pale silvery yellow, edged with blues and greens. The edges seemed liquid, and blue drops of colour fell back into the sea as it rose. Gradually it became darker until it had taken on an orange hue; it was incredibly large and seemed to fill the horizon. The orange deepened into reds and purples, the colours changing endlessly until it stood full and free above the horizon. It grew a little smaller as it rose, but still seemed to be so near that you could reach out and touch it. Gradually the reds disappeared and the orange slipped away as it settled into a warm yellow circle set in a sky of deepest blue. The beach was bathed in its soft light and the stars began to reappear, twinkling, as though in approval.

The first time we witnessed it we did not speak until the stars had reappeared.

'My God, it's beautiful!' Georgina exclaimed softly.

It was beautiful, one of the most beautiful things I have ever seen.

'What makes it change colour so?'

'I really don't know.'

'I'm glad,' she responded quickly. 'I don't want to know. It would spoil the magic if someone were to explain.'

Those early days of our marriage were amongst the happiest that I have ever known. I still wonder at the memory of them – and then when I reflect and realize how I threw it all away, I feel pain.

From Durban we travelled to Cape Town, taking the coastal route, travelling along the foothills of the Drakensberg Mountains, through the Transkei and Ciskei until we came to East London – and then on to Port Elizabeth. From there we made our way slowly along the scenic Garden Route, through Knysna, George, Swellendam, and over the Hottentot Holland Mountains, dropping down to the flatlands that lead into Cape Town. We had travelled more than 1000 miles, passing through some of the most beautiful scenery anywhere in the world.

Cape Town lies in one of the most dramatic panoramic settings of any city I have visited. Table Mountain dominates the scene, rising 1100 feet above the city and, with Lion's Head, provides a majestic backdrop to the south, shielding the city from the worst of the South Atlantic storms. The rugged contours of Devil's Peak to the east, and the waters of Table Bay to the north, provide natural boundaries to the city. We stayed there for some days, exploring the many wonderful beaches, climbing Table Mountain, and enjoying the good Cape wines.

My employer was becoming anxious – he missed the sales figures I had been turning in, and he telephoned me regularly. It was because of this that I decided to combine business with pleasure and make a trip up into South West Africa. I was particularly interested in visiting the Etosha Pan, and hoped to do business with the American-owned copper mines at Nababiep, Ookiep and Tsumeb. Georgina was enthusiastic about the trip as it would take her to a part of Africa she had never visited.

The Etosha Pan is one of the largest and least developed game reserves in Africa. Today, with neighbouring Ovamboland and other territories, it is the scene of bitter fighting between Swapo supporters and South African security forces. It lies not far from the Kunene river, which forms the border with Angola, and our journey from the Cape was to cover more than 1000 miles of roads that were untarred, compacted, dusty, red earth.

We took the route through Namaqualand to Grunau, some way east of Oranjemund where vast diamonds-from-the-sea operations were carried out. As we travelled north the vast expanse of the Kalahari Desert lay to the east, and far away to the west the unexplored dangers of the notorious Skeleton Coast. We travelled through parts of the Namib Desert, the wheels of the car pounding over corrugations and potholes in the road. The steering wheel chattered and shook and after a while my hands went numb from the vibration. The hiss of sand under hot tyres muffled the sound of the engine, and the occasional crack of a stone thrown up against the car fender sounded discordant and a little frightening. A huge cloud of dust billowed out behind us, completely obscuring the road we had covered. We kept the car windows open, but the wind that blew in was hot and dry and it stirred the fine layer of dust that covered everything. The dust was everywhere; on the seats, on our clothes, in our hair; and it stuck cloyingly to the perspiration that the heat induced, making us feel dirty and uncomfortable. Occasionally we would come to a cattle-gate grille, set in the midst of nowhere, five-strand barbed wire fences stretching away from it to either side until they dropped below the land-line. I would slow down and the wheels of the car beat a brief tattoo as we passed over the grille.

Scrawny scrubland stretched on either side, and outcrops of weathered granite, or a lone cactus, relieved the flatness of the scene. Gaping dongas, huge crevices gouged out of the sand and loose stone, bore witness to the fury of flash-floods when they occurred. Whatever soil the floods had left behind was loose and free, and quickly dried in the fierce heat, breaking up into sandy granules, to be blown away by hot desert storm-winds that periodically swept the landscape. It was a very inhospitable place; nothing seemed to live or move except brightly coloured lizards scuttling between dust-red rocks.

The road followed the natural lie of the land, disappearing into a shimmer of heat on the horizon. A dust-cloud appeared ahead of us and grew larger as a car approached. I slowed down and we closed the windows – then the approaching car was upon us, sweeping by and leaving us enveloped in a cloud of fine dust. We both tensed involuntarily as a stone rang out sharply against the windscreen and then rattled over the bonnet before falling back into the road. For several seconds I drove blindly, following the road as I remembered it before dust made it invisible; then the dust cleared and we were back in fierce sunlight. We relaxed and Georgina resettled herself as we opened the windows. She coughed as the dust found its way into her throat, then she took a cool drink from the iced travelbag, uncapped it and handed it to me.

We arrived in Windhoek, the capital of South West Africa, tired and dirty. We booked into the Grossherzog Hotel, and it was only after a shower, a change of clothing and dinner that life seemed to become real again.

I was anxious to press on and to reach Tsumeb, so we set out early the next morning, taking the road through Otavi. I spent a few days in Tsumeb negotiating with the copper-mining company, and then we travelled on to Namutoni, on the edge of the Etosha Pan itself. Namutoni proved to be an old German fort, built to withstand the attacks of the natives when Germany colonized the territory. It had been converted to accommodate tourists, and we were allocated what appeared to have once been a cell to sleep in. A noisy old generator chuffed and stuttered inefficiently, producing little more than a flicker of light from the dirty bare bulb set in the ceiling. We had been given an oil-lamp to augment the electricity, and we carried it with us as we made our way about the fort after dark. The room was sparsely furnished; a chair, a small table and two trestle-beds with soft rubber mattresses, and as we settled down for the night the generator coughed and spluttered and then gave up altogether, and the light from the bulb in the ceiling dimmed and went out. Life outside the walls of our spartan hotel began to make itself heard. The chorus of a myriad insects was broken by the croak of a bull-frog, the sharp bark of a jackal and the grunts of wild boar as they rooted. In the distance a lion roared, and as the sound rolled majestically across the plain the other animals went quiet. But after a while the sounds began again, and we lay listening trying to guess what they might be. The journey had tired us and eventually we dropped off to sleep, but not before a great many moths had dashed themselves against the glass chimney of our oil-lamp, and I had killed an enormous spider that appeared through a hole in the cornice and threatened to share Georgina's bed.

The next morning we were warned by the game warden that a rogue bull elephant was in the vicinity. A small crumpled car just outside the gates to the fort demonstrated just how dangerous elephant can be. We were distinctly nervous as we set out to follow a single-track dirt road, lined on either side by acacia trees. This was elephant country and we saw plenty of evidence that a herd was nearby. Small trees had been uprooted and stripped of their foliage, and the freshness of the droppings showed that elephant has passed quite recently.

We were headed for Okaukuejo, a game-warden's camp to the west of Namutoni, and we had some ninety miles to cover through the reserve. We travelled slowly, negotiating huge potholes and pockets of sand, following the winding track, never quite sure what each corner hid. Throughout the day we saw huge herds of springbok, wildebeest, zebra and kudu. At times the car would be surrounded by animals so close that they rubbed against the fenders. At other times a herd would stampede and race beside the car. The track was rough and bumpy, but as we left the trees behind us and moved out on to the vast plains we clocked zebra at more than thirty miles per hour; and sometimes they would race beside the car and overtake it, immediately swerving in front of us in a terrifying manner. We saw no elephant, but after inspecting the mess made of the car at Namutoni neither of us was too upset about that. The only other human beings we saw were two young men in a light aircraft. They had landed beside the track on a flat piece of the plain, and they told us that they were collecting snakes.

We arrived at Okaukuejo in the afternoon and were given a native hut outside the main camp to sleep in. It was furnished with the same trestle beds and soft rubber mattresses as the cell in Namutoni and was one of a group of four, our neighbours proving to be the two snake collectors we had met out on the plains earlier. The huts were built as rondavels of split poles, a wicker gate serving as the door, and rough, conical, reed thatching providing the roof. They were sited near to a water-hole frequented by wild animals during the night.

We visited the snake collectors and they told us that they had a contract with a group of laboratories producing snake serum. They were only interested in the dangerously poisonous snakes, and they showed us several writhing sacks containing tree snakes, or boomslange as they called them, and the deadliest snakes of all, green and black mambas. The sacks looked none too secure to me, and Georgina felt the same way as I did about them – rather apprehensive.

After a meal in the main camp we went with the game warden to watch lion feeding. A zebra had been shot and laid down as bait some distance from the camp, and a limited number of visitors were invited to attend what was called 'the lions' tea-party'. We arrived at the place where the bait had been laid and formed a circle with our cars. Two cars switched on their headlights to illuminate the scene and it was some time before our vigil was rewarded. We were warned that lion were close by when the whole area seemed to go very quiet. Suddenly several furry lion cubs tumbled out into the lights of the cars, and they were quickly followed by five sleek lionesses. The adults followed behind the cubs and approached the carcass a little suspiciously, but they became bolder as the scent of fresh blood drew them to it. They licked the carcass and prepared to settle down, but then hesitated and drew back to allow a huge male lion to go ahead of them. Only after the male had selected his position did the others move in again and take part in the feast. There was something primeval and strangely beautiful about the scene as mothers and cubs took care not to encroach on the male, whilst they wrestled to wrench flesh from the carcass and snapped the bones they laid bare.

We didn't sleep very well that night – the memory of what we had seen was too vivid, and we lay talking and speculating about the sounds of the animals outside at the water-hole. Small creatures rustled in the thatch overhead, and when a small lizard dropped through the reeds on to Georgina's bed, she insisted that we make a tent of our blankets and huddle under them together.

We spent three days at Okaukuejo and then it was time to make our way back to Otavi, and begin the long journey back to Johannesburg, and home. The trip had been moderately successful from a business point of view, and we had enjoyed an experience that neither of us would forget. Soon after our return to Johannesburg we moved out of my small bachelor flat into a larger apartment, and we spent many happy hours together selecting new furnishings and planning our new home.

9

Once Georgina's parents had recovered from the shock our impulsive behaviour had given them, they made real efforts to come to terms with it. They invited me into their home and did what they could to make me feel welcome and to bridge the gap that our rash conduct had created. It must have been hard for them to ignore the hurt we had caused them, but they tried to do so, and I admired them for that.

My brother-in-law was the assistant attorney-general for the Transvaal. It must have been especially difficult for him to welcome an ex-prisoner into his home, but he did so. Both he and his wife treated me with courtesy and kindness.

My work required me to travel in the country, but now I took Georgina with me, or made certain that I would not be away for more than one night. Three months after we were married I experienced a new happiness when Georgina told me that she believed she was expecting a baby. I became obsessed with her welfare, and I began to think about the responsibilities of fatherhood.

One month later Georgina told me that her doctor had advised her to go into a private clinic for treatment. At first I did not understand what she was saying, but then I realized that the effect of the treatment would be to abort the child she was carrying. My concern for her welfare was at times overshadowed by my anger that this should have to be, and, later, when I brought her home from the clinic, I sensed that something had gone out of our relationship; she seemed a little remote and cold. She was caring and affectionate, but the magic seemed to have gone. Looking back I can see how ill-prepared I was to help her through that difficult time – my lack of understanding led to subtle changes in my own feelings which made me less careful of her welfare.

Because of the nature of my work, my income fluctuated. My average earnings remained very high, peaking to more than one thousand pounds per week at one time. Despite this I was often short of money. I had begun to gamble again, and looking back I can see how the secretiveness I used to cover up my losses grew into dishonesty. Georgina sensed that all was not well, and my changing attitudes increased the strain on our relationship.

In order to meet the financial commitments I had entered into, and at the same time find the money to cover my gambling losses, I introduced dishonesty into my sales techniques. In mid-1959, I was arrested and bailed to face charges of fraudulent non-disclosure in my sales methods. One condition of my bail was that I report regularly to the police at the Greys, the building which at the time contained the Johannesburg offices of South Africa's Special Branch, later to be renamed BOSS, the Bureau of State Security, and moved to John Vorster Square. The directors and the other salesmen at the company were arrested with me and similarly charged and bailed, having adopted my techniques in their own sales expeditions. The charges brought an abrupt end to my only source of income, and left me with commitments I could not meet.

My arrest came as a crushing blow to Georgina. She had faced the antagonism of her family over our marriage, and we had hoped to prove them wrong in their judgement of me. My arrest left me unmasked and Georgina had the task of coming to terms with my failure. She chose to stand by me and try to help me.

Since our marriage I had made no new friends. The party-goers we knew were at best acquaintances, and at the news of my arrest they quickly disappeared. Our visits to Georgina's parents became strained and gradually I stopped seeing them altogether. Apart from Georgina I had no one to confide in, and my secretiveness, now a well-established feature of my behaviour, made it increasingly difficult for me to share confidences with her. My gambling had become compulsive. The small amounts of money I earned or managed to borrow quickly disappeared on the race-tracks and into pool-rooms or card games. In an effort to salvage the home we had put together Georgina borrowed £1000 from her mother, but I took it from her and, in a single weekend, gambled it all away – and with it our home.

I spent my days looking for money to gamble with, returning to the apartment late at night. Georgina would be waiting, anxious to know how I had managed – it was almost as though for a while she became caught up in my gambling fever, hoping desperately that I would win enough money to solve our problems. But, of course, it never happened, and I lived from day to day, with no thought beyond my immediate need to gamble.

One night when I came home the apartment was empty. It was past midnight and as soon as I stepped into the hallway I sensed that Georgina was not there. As I passed the lounge, with its dining alcove, my eye caught a flicker of light, and I stopped to look in. The dining table had been set with two places. A bottle of wine lay in a wicker basket on the table, and the wine glasses reflected the flames of two candles, spluttering as they burned low. A serving-trolley stood next to the table with unopened dishes on it. At first I was a little puzzled, but when I lifted the covers and saw the meal that Georgina had prepared for us I suddenly went cold. It was the first anniversary of our wedding.

I went through to the bedroom and saw that some of Georgina's belongings and a small suitcase had gone. There was a note on the bedside table. At first I was stunned, and then I remembered the frustrations of the day and, quite irrationally, I became angry.

Two days later Georgina returned. Our finances had reached their lowest ebb and we moved out of the apartment into a small furnished flat. I had reached the stage where I found myself unable to hold down any job at all; I was obsessed with what I believed to be the injustice of what was happening to me. Georgina decided to go back to work to earn the money we needed to live on. While she was at work, I continued to visit race-tracks and pool-rooms, sometimes staying late to take a hand in card games that went on illegally behind closed doors.

For a few months we tried to pretend that everything would work out well. But my gambling became more and more compelling and one day I asked her for her engagement ring, so that I could sell it for money to gamble. She handed it to me without speaking, and I hurried out of the flat to try to win back everything that I had lost. Of course, it was in vain. I lost the money I received for the ring, and I lost whatever self-respect I still retained as well.

The arguments we had about our problems became more heated, and my reactions became less rational. My behaviour became less and less excusable and my anger seemed to grow in proportion. One day, in one of our many arguments, I did something I still do not understand. In an irrational fit of temper I struck out and hit Georgina, blaming her for all my problems.

I remember my remorse and self-pity when she left me. She had stood by me when everyone else had deserted. I remember the pain and the tears in her eyes as she turned to me after I had struck her.

'Why?' she asked. 'Why do you hit me?'

In the days that followed her leaving, I lost all sense of purpose. I had no one to turn to – I was completely on my own. I felt an overwhelming sense of loss, but then, too, I felt betrayed. I continued to act irrationally and two weeks after Georgina left me I issued cheques valued at twenty-one pounds to the sports club I belonged to. The cheques were in my own name and were drawn on my own account, but there were no funds to meet them. The club secretary reported me to the police, and I was arrested.

My bail in the sales-fraud case was withdrawn and I was lodged in the Fort in Johannesburg to await trial. In 1960, I was convicted of issuing cheques to the value of twenty-one pounds, fraudulently. In terms of the Criminal Procedure Act, because of my previous convictions, I was declared an habitual criminal – and I was sentenced to imprisonment with compulsory labour for a period of not less than nine years and not exceeding fifteen years.

10

My conviction and sentence took place on a Saturday morning, and the magistrate who sentenced me was clearly upset that the law required him to pass a nine- to fifteen-year sentence. The offence I had been convicted of was a minor one – the sentence was savage and it shocked him. It bore no relation to the quantum of the offence.

I was taken back to the Fort where I had been held whilst awaiting trial, and I was admitted no longer as a low-risk, short-term prisoner, but as an habitual criminal. My money, watch and ring were taken from me – I was stripped of my private clothing and issued prison garb. There was a finality about the process that seemed unreal. The prospect of spending nine to fifteen years in prison was meaningless – I was unable to relate to it. It seemed inconceivable that such a sentence could be imposed for such an offence; but I knew that it was real and my determination not to give in to it led only one way. I decided that I was not going to serve the sentence. I was going to escape.

I was escorted to the convicted wing of the prison, given a cold shower, a short crew-cut, and handed one of the notorious blue jackets to wear. I had to force myself to put it on. It was worn as a mark of criminality, as the special clothing of an habitual criminal. The stigma of that tag did nothing to lessen my determination to escape, nor did the very strict discipline and security that surrounded me as a long-term prisoner. The way the other prisoners moved to one side to give me preference added to the sense of unreality that cloaked the first few days following my conviction and sentence. I spoke to no one; I followed the routine, and that was the extent of my interest in prison affairs.

The charges relating to dishonest sales technique were soon to be heard, and so I was held at the Fort and not transferred to Pretoria Central Prison as I would otherwise have been. My resolve to escape grew each day, and I believe that it was fired by a growing identification with the criminal culture. I had been publicly declared an habitual criminal, savagely sentenced for a minor offence, and I was reminded each day that my criminality set me apart from most other prisoners. I began to see myself in the role I had been sentenced to, as a long-term prisoner with no realistic hope of rehabilitation – and as my reaction to the sentence hardened my anti-social attitudes, I began to make plans that might allow me to escape.

The Fort was, as I have already described, surrounded by a vast wall – up to twenty-five feet high in places. The ramparts were patrolled by armed guards and at night they were well lit. The open spaces between the cell-blocks and the walls were also patrolled and illuminated at night. Within the cell-block I was locked in a cell-cage. A vast dormitory had been subdivided with fine-mesh steel-wire netting, creating a huge room full of cages. Each cage measured seven feet by six feet and was six feet six inches high. The roofs of the cages were of the same fine-mesh netting and left a space of some four feet between them and the original ceiling of the dormitory. Each cage was fitted with a steel-mesh door, and a secure double-bolting prison lock. A series of steel grilles cut across the room and were placed at intervals along the passageways leading to the cages, and this meant that I had to pass through four sets of steel grilles and gates after leaving my cell-cage in order to reach the forecourt in front of the cell-block. The arrangements appeared to be impregnable, but I continued to search for any weakness in the system.

There were no beds in the cell-cages. The bedding consisted of a felt mat and two blankets. The ubiquitous piss-pot, made of flaking galvanized iron, stood stinking in the corner of each cell-cage. Each time someone defecated the hot stench carried through the room, the wire-mesh of the cages providing no protection.

We were woken at 6.00 a.m. each morning and unlocked. During the following thirty minutes we had to make up our bedding; carry the piss-pots out into a neighbouring exercise yard and empty them down an open man-hole; wash under cold taps in the open yard, and line up for breakfast. Eating utensils consisted of a wooden spoon and a tinned mug. At mealtimes we were issued with a tinned eating-bowl. Breakfast was mealie-meal porridge, black unsweetened coffee, and dry bread. As soon as we had eaten breakfast we were locked up again.

Front view

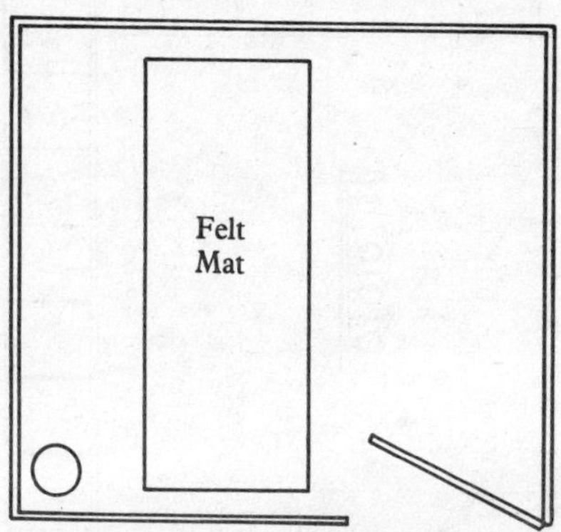

Plan

Figure 1 Sketch of cell-cages in which the author was imprisoned at the Fort, Johannesburg (author's impression).

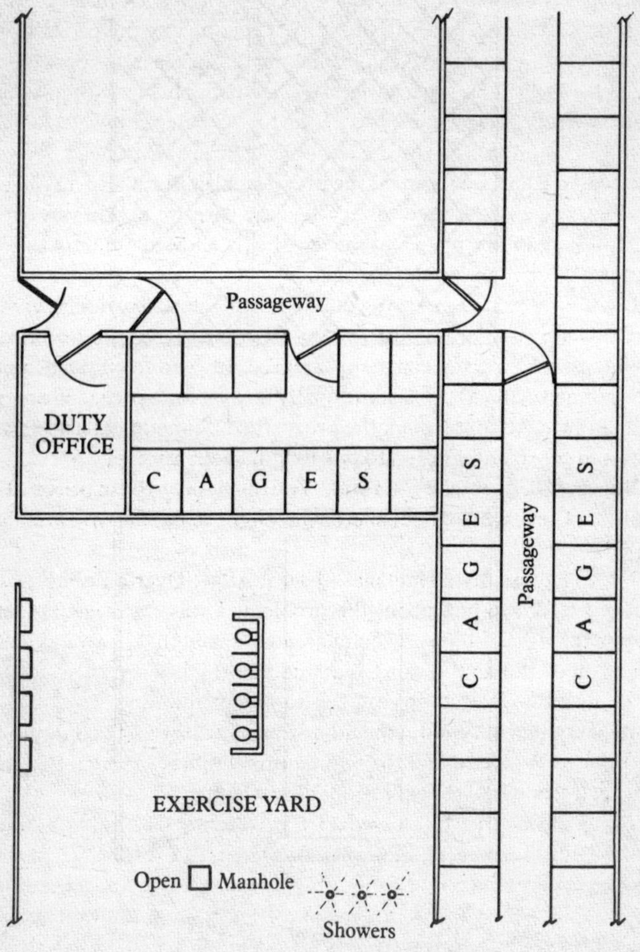

Figure 2 Part of the white-convict section of the Fort, Johannesburg, where the author was kept in a cage (author's impression).

At 10.00 a.m. we were allowed into the exercise yard for thirty minutes. Most of the exercise time was taken up standing to attention during the daily inspection by the head of the prison. We had no music, no reading material, no games or recreation. Contacts with persons outside the prison were limited to one letter and one visit each three months. Smoking was allowed only during exercise periods and tobacco, together with slips of brown paper to roll it in, was issued by the prison guards. No one was allowed to have any smoking requisites in his possession in the cell-block. The tobacco issued was a rough black pipe-tobacco, which we rolled into large 'zolls' in the brown paper provided. The first time I drew on this mixture I felt physically sick. My head swam, my eyes watered and I choked on the biting smoke. But, like everyone else, I persevered and got used to it. When the exercise period was over we were locked up for the rest of the day, being allowed out only to collect meals at midday and in the evening.

I soon realized that breaking out of the cell-block or exercise yard was virtually impossible, and I turned my attention to the opportunities that might arise during my court appearances. I began to cultivate a guard who seemed sympathetic. Occasionally he gave me a packet of cigarettes or a sandwich to supplement the prison food. Sometimes he acted as my escort to court, and I began to talk to him about my case.

'It is a wicked sentence,' he said. 'You ought not to be in prison. There are lots of real bastards out there who ought to be, but you are not the type.'

I didn't press my advantage – I let it grow. Over a period of some weeks I talked to him about the problems I was experiencing getting documents I needed for my defence, and he said that he would help me if he could. But as the weeks became months I began to suffer bouts of depression. Despite my refusal to accept the nine- to fifteen-year sentence, the reality of my position was inescapable. Each day I woke up in my cell-cage to face the same routine, to be reminded that prison was real, that it was actually happening whether I liked it or not.

At about this time I received a letter from my wife's solicitor asking me to agree to a divorce. I knew that our marriage had been irreparably damaged, and I knew that I should agree to Georgina's request, but this realization confused and hurt me and I hung on in the vain hope that something could be salvaged.

Shortly after receiving the solicitor's letter I persuaded the guard to take me to my bank to collect papers I needed for my defence. I had been appearing in the Johannesburg Magistrates' Courts, and he took me out of the court cells and into the street, to take me to the bank. He had removed the handcuffs and he readily agreed when I asked him to wait outside the bank so as not to embarrass me.

'Good luck,' he said, as I went in the front door of the bank.

I left the bank by the side entrance and hurried away from the vicinity. It was not so much a dramatic escape as a careless release, but the media were short of live stories and they made up headlines and wrote pages about the long-term prisoner, a dangerous convict, who had tricked his guards and made a daring escape. It did not occur to them that a prison guard, seeing what an indefensible system of punishment he had been asked to administer, had simply elected to look the other way, allowing me to go free. Unfortunately for the guard he took delivery of a new car a few days later, and he rashly parked it outside the prison. The suspicions of the head of the prison that I had 'bought' the guard seemed pretty conclusively confirmed, and there was nothing that I was ever able to do to change those opinions.

Once I was free I realized that I had made no plans and I had nowhere to go. I had given no thought to what I should do if and when I escaped. At first I hurried to a city park, with the peculiar idea of hiding in the bushes. I was confused and quite unprepared for the situation I had worked so hard to create. I wasted some hours in the park, and then I retraced my steps into the city and made my way to a pool-room where I was well known. When I got there the early editions of the evening paper had already been published. The owner of the club showed me into his office and handed me a copy of the paper. As I read the write-up I realized for the first time what I had done. I was much calmer now – the initial panic was under control, and I began to think about what life would be like as an escaped habitual criminal.

Other club members drifted into the office. An old man came over to me and shook my hand. He took a five-pound note from his pocket and pressed it on me – he said nothing but, as he left the office, other men I had known came in and wished me luck; some gave me money, others just shook my hand.

When it was time to leave the pool-room I had decided what I must do. I contacted a man whom I knew I could trust, and he made arrangements for me to stay in a rondavel in the grounds of a large property near the city centre. I lay up there for the first few days, waiting for the police and the newspapers to find more urgent and current matters to occupy them.

Johannesburg was a city of 500,000 whites and almost double that number of non-whites. The non-whites lived outside the city and away from 'white' residential areas in townships – the one to the south-west, Soweto, being the largest. It was a lively, vibrant city, and the influx of black and white commuters during the day made it fairly safe for me to venture out. Some ten days after my escape I was walking near Ellis Park when I met an ex-prisoner called Andy, and he told me that a man called Don Muniz had escaped and needed help. Don had jumped out of the window of the train taking him to Pretoria Central Prison. He had unfastened his handcuffs and leg-irons, and leapt past the startled guards as the train gathered speed pulling out of a station. He had landed fortunately, slightly spraining his ankle and left wrist and I agreed to help him, taking him back to share the rondavel with me.

The money I had been given at the pool-room was running out, and I decided to call on a man I had met in prison and ask for help. Louis Cabe had been sentenced to four years' imprisonment for running a brothel. His house, at 10 Buxton Street, became a party joke throughout South Africa. I had met him the day after he was sentenced in the exercise yard of the Fort at Johannesburg.

'Come and see me when you get out,' he said. 'I'll fix you up.'

Louis had been released on bail pending his appeal, a fairly normal procedure in South Africa, and I decided to take him up on his offer. The house at 10 Buxton Street had been sold, and now I traced him to his new address outside the city centre. I was greeted by one of his henchmen.

'Louis is busy,' he told me. 'You'd better wait here.'

I looked around the large lounge he had shown me into and helped myself to a cool drink. The door leading to the hallway was open, and I could hear the rhythmic creaking of bedsprings. The man who had shown me in looked at me and grinned.

'Louis is at it again,' he said.

I smiled – I remembered my first meeting with Louis. He had not long changed into prison clothes and he was waiting for his bail application to be processed. He seemed completely unworried about the prison sentence he faced.

'Do you know the addresses of any nice girls?' he had asked me.

That was how Louis' mind worked – in terms of girls and new blood to add to the scores he already had arrangements with. He showed little respect for South Africa's race laws, and he was quite legitimately suspected of recruiting non-white girls to entertain white men. As I sat waiting to see him the noises from the bedroom became more frantic. Then a girl cried out in pleasure – the accent was unmistakably that of a black girl.

'Aah, baas Louis!' she cried. 'You fuck too divinely!'

I burst out laughing – as the man said: Louis was at it again!

Later, when I returned to the rondavel, I arranged to borrow a car. It turned out to be a huge 1937 Lincoln saloon – just like those used by American gangsters in B-movies. I had no clear plans, but I wanted to get away from Johannesburg and so, together with Don Muniz, I set off for Durban. The car began to overheat, and about halfway through the 500-mile journey we pulled into Ladysmith. There was a bookmaker's office next to the garage we got water from, and I went in and proceeded to lay bets. When racing ended for the day the bookmaker gave me almost £300 in cash and a cheque for an additional £460. The win relieved financial pressures and we continued on our way to Durban, arriving safely later that evening.

Next day I visited Durban Tattersalls to cash the bookmaker's cheque, and as I was leaving I ran into a man called Heinz whom I knew. He was on bail on fraud charges, and although I did not know him really well I agreed to meet him again. I spent the rest of the day negotiating the lease of a house at Salt Rock, forty miles north of Durban. The location was ideal as a hideout – the house was on the beach and backed by a golf course. A wide expanse of lawn ran down to the beach, and the property included the sands down to the high-water line. It was isolated, the neighbouring properties being set in quite large grounds and serving as summer retreats for their wealthy owners. They remained vacant whilst I was there. The house I had leased had an enormous picture-window, and after we moved in I used to watch the sunsets that I had found so beautiful on my honeymoon. They were still beautiful, but they were never quite the same as I had remembered them.

Don Muniz moved into the house with me, and a few days later I agreed to accommodate Heinz, his wife and three children, two male friends he had with him and a girl called Dawn. They had no money and nowhere to stay, so I agreed to put them up until they got on their feet. It was a large house and we managed quite well. I had retained the two servants the previous tenant had employed, and whilst a very pretty Zulu girl called Sarah kept house and cooked, James, a Zulu house-boy, acted as butler and valet. I had a very pleasant stay there. The butler had connections who produced large quantities of pot very cheaply, and the habit I had given up after meeting my wife was now revived.

Heinz was becoming restless, and when I asked Don to go into Durban and steal a car, Heinz became very anxious to leave. Dawn had moved into my bedroom as soon as she arrived and she elected to stay with me. Another man, called Charlie, was one of the party Heinz had brought with him – he also wanted to stay on, and I agreed to accommodate him.

Money worries were put off by the efforts of a horse called Left Wing, who won very handsomely, and then went on to win the Durban July Handicap, South Africa's premier race. But even Left Wing could not keep us for ever, and eventually I decided to return to Johannesburg to look for money. Dawn, Don Muniz and Charlie accompanied me, and I took a flat in Berea. It was shortly after I arrived there that Don Muniz introduced me to a man called Peter.

11

Glenton and Mitchell were a company packing and marketing tea and coffee. They had a large depot on Main Street in Johannesburg and they distributed their wares through a fleet of lorries and vans, many of whom sold the products to small retail outlets for cash. Each day this cash was handed into the office, and up to £5,000 was collected and banked at any one time.

Some months prior to my return to Johannesburg from Salt Rock, Peter and two of his friends raided the offices of Glenton and Mitchell and escaped with over £6,000. They were all arrested, and they were on bail awaiting trial on that charge when Don Muniz introduced me to Peter. Peter was diabetic, but active and cheerful. He was an habitual user of dagga, as was Don Muniz, and I became increasingly annoyed at their behaviour which I felt put us all at risk. They were careless where and when they smoked the drug, and the last thing I wanted was for someone to report the smell of 'pot' in the building to the police.

I was becoming tired of providing for so many people. It seemed that as long as I paid the bills no one wanted to make an effort to pay their own way. I smoked dagga, but I did so discreetly, making sure I put neither myself nor others at risk. I made my feelings known, and some days later I overheard Peter and Don planning to commit a robbery. As I listened it became clear that they intended to rob Glenton and Mitchell for a second time. It was a Friday morning and a good deal of alcohol was consumed. Don and Peter were smoking dagga and although I tried to keep out of the way I saw two firearms and asked if they had ammunition for them. Peter laughed and said that both the guns were faulty and incapable of firing a round, but he didn't think that anyone would take a chance on that when they were being threatened. I left them to their discussions and I was glad when towards midday they left, taking Charlie with them.

During the afternoon I went out, leaving Dawn alone at the flat. I tried unsuccessfully to get a stolen cheque book to enable me to raise some cash, and I returned at about 5.00 p.m. Dawn was alone, but a little later Peter, Don and Charlie returned. They seemed jubilant – they carried a Gladstone bag, and Don had a large jar of Koffiehuis coffee, the brand marketed by Glenton and Mitchell. They told me that they had robbed the firm and made good their escape without incident. My reaction was one of relief that no one had been arrested. They had used the car we had stolen in Durban for the robbery, but had abandoned it well away from the flat.

The excitement of success, and the drugs and liquor they had taken prior to the raid, made them pretty rowdy, and I had to remind them that they were not safe yet. Charlie became very quiet; he was beginning to realize for the first time exactly what he had done. Robbery with firearms was a capital offence, and the courts could impose the death penalty if they deemed it proper to do so. I could see that Charlie was beginning to realize that he was in much deeper water than he had bargained for.

Peter and Don tipped open the Gladstone bag and it immediately became clear that the haul was not as big as they had hoped. It totalled £1,200, and later they learned that they had missed a second bag containing over £5,000. They divided the money into five stacks and insisted that I accept one of them. Peter took two shares, Don and Charlie one each.

As soon as darkness fell Peter left the flat to return to his home. Don and Charlie retired to sleep off the effects of the liquor and the excitement of the day. I helped Dawn to clear up the mess, taking special care to get rid of unsmoked reefers. When the place was reasonably tidy we went to bed.

I woke up to find that the reading-lamp beside the bed had been switched on. Dawn stood there and she had been shaking me gently to wake me up. I glanced at my watch and saw that it was almost 3.30 a.m., and I rubbed my eyes and asked her what she was doing. She didn't say anything, but then I saw that she was offering me two bundles of banknotes.

'Take it and get out of here while you are safe,' she said quietly.

I looked up at her and began to realize what she had done. She had taken the money from the room where Don and Charlie slept and had brought it to me.

'You can get right out of the country with this,' she said. 'Take it and go. If you stay you'll only be arrested – these guys will give themselves away and you with them.'

She had taken a very big risk – both the men were capable of violence and would not have hesitated to use it. She had asked for nothing for herself, and suddenly I felt quite small. I took the money and put it on the bed beside me, and she sat down on the edge of the mattress.

'No, Dawn,' I said. 'I can't do that. I can't take their money. I have to manage on my own.'

'But you've spent more than that on them already,' she protested. 'You've got to leave – it's dangerous, I can feel it.'

I lay down and thought over what she had said. She was right – I had to get away before the others drew attention to themselves, and so to me.

'We'll go back to Salt Rock,' I told her. 'You and me. We'll work out something when we get there; but first we must put the money back where you got it from.'

She couldn't remember which money she had taken from which bed, so we counted it and divided it into two equal piles. Then I went with her and watched from the doorway as she replaced it. We pulled the door closed and went back to bed.

The next morning I made arrangements to leave. Don and Charlie were late getting up, and I wondered what their reaction would have been had they known what had happened during the night; but before I had time to do much speculating, Peter arrived. He was in a panic. He had been recognized by staff at Glenton and Mitchell as one of the men who had taken part in the previous robbery, and he had narrowly escaped arrest by police waiting for him at his home. He had spent the night with friends, and now he needed help. We talked about it and I agreed to let him come with me to Salt Rock until things cooled off.

We left Don Muniz and Charlie at the flat and I cautioned them about smoking pot too freely, advising them to get rid of the Gladstone bag, the Koffiehuis coffee jar, and any other evidence of the robbery. We drove out of Johannesburg at 10.00 a.m., in a hired car, and the 500-mile trip south to Salt Rock took just over eight hours. We arrived at the house shortly before sunset. The servants were surprised to see us, but Sarah busied herself preparing a meal for us, and James slipped into his role as butler, pouring the drinks before we all retired to bed.

Two days later the police arrested Don Muniz and Charlie in the flat in Berea. They were acting on a complaint about the smell of dagga in the passageway outside the flat. When the flat was searched, the police found the Gladstone bag and the distinctive Koffiehuis coffee jar still there, and some other evidence of the robbery.

Twelve hours later, five hundred miles away, armed police burst into the house at Salt Rock. Peter, Dawn and I were arrested and taken to a police station in West Street, Durban. After twenty-four hours Dawn was released into her mother's care, whilst Peter and I were transferred back to Johannesburg.

Once again I found myself in the convicted prisoners' wing of the Fort. Once again I was given the blue jacket to wear. But this time I was also put in leg-irons and chains, and placed under special watch. The authorities were taking no chances – they took all the steps possible to make sure that I did not escape again.

12

When we arrived at the Fort I was separated from Peter. He was an unconvicted prisoner and was held in a different section of the prison. Before we were parted I told him that it was my intention to escape again, and he told me he aimed to do so too. A few days later I heard that Peter had been rushed to hospital in a coma. The next day I heard that he had died.

It was some time before I pieced together what had happened. I knew that Peter was a diabetic and took daily insulin injections to control the condition and it emerged that he had administered a large overdose of insulin to himself, in order to induce an insulin coma. The prison staff had rushed him to hospital, and when the reception doctor heard that he was a diabetic he wrongly diagnosed the coma as one induced by lack of insulin. It was only when Peter failed to respond to the insulin the hospital pumped into him that it was realized what had happened. But by then it was too late – Peter died without recovering from the coma. I knew that he had created the situation in order to provide himself with an opportunity of escaping from the hospital – but his plan had gone terribly wrong.

Don Muniz was already at the Fort when I arrived. Like me he was held in chains and leg-irons, locked in one of the cramped cell-cages. Charlie had made a confession and had been released on bail. His confession did nothing to help me, however, as he refused to name anyone in it. Don Muniz also refused to make a statement, but said he would answer questions, depending on the nature of them – and the police had no trouble in getting him to incriminate himself. He, too, refused to name anyone involved in the robbery.

From the outset it became clear that the police had formed the opinion that I was a member of the robbery gang, and they were unimpressed by my denials that I had taken part in it. They believed that I was the fourth man they were looking for, and my refusal to co-operate with them did nothing to reduce their suspicions. They found ample evidence of my stay at the flat where the Gladstone bag and coffee jar had been found, and the fact that Peter had been with me at the time of my arrest at Salt Rock seemed to strengthen their case.

It was whilst I was waiting to appear in court on the robbery charge and other matters that Georgina agreed to meet me in the Fort to discuss her divorce application. I believed that I was still in love with her, and in the confused state of mind my circumstances induced I was reluctant to admit that she really did want to divorce me. I believed that she was being influenced by her family.

The meeting took place in the solicitors' visiting-room at the Fort. I was taken in and seated at a table, with guards on either side of me, and then Georgina was brought in with her solicitor. She was as beautiful as I remembered her, and I had to control an urge to go to her and embrace her. Her eyes searched mine as she approached the table, and for a moment we were the only people in the room. But the moment was broken by her solicitor, an officious little man, who began to make a formal speech about what his client might or might not say at this meeting. I asked him politely to stop talking rubbish, and he seemed so startled that he did so. I then asked Georgina quite simply whether she wanted to divorce me. She looked at me and nodded, and when she spoke it was without any anger.

'Yes,' she said quietly. 'Yes, I do. There is no other way.'

I knew then what had to be done. She had told me what she wanted, and I knew I could not refuse her. Her solicitor was shuffling a sheaf of papers, and I reached over and took them out of his hand. I looked through them and found the consent form he had prepared, crossed out the provision for maintenance that I knew I would never be able to meet, and signed the document before giving it back to him. Georgina had been watching me, and I tried to smile as I looked up at her.

'You've got your divorce,' I said.

There was a little silence and then the guards stood up and motioned to me to do so too. My chains had been hidden under the table up to then, but as I stood up they jangled and I bent down to straighten them. I moved around the table, embarrassed that Georgina should see me shackled, and began to move towards the door. When I reached it, I turned to say goodbye.

Georgina was standing watching me. It was the first time she had seen the chains and they clearly shocked her. She moved towards me, almost involuntarily, and stepped between the guards. I felt her lips touch my cheek, and I drank in the scent I knew so well.

'God bless you,' she whispered.

Then the guards moved in and took me away from her – back to my cell-cage. As I lay on my felt mat on the floor I was not conscious of its hardness. The pain of that meeting welled up inside me. I hid my head under the rough blankets as that pain overwhelmed me, and tears broke through the barriers my mind had created – and I began to weep.

I became determined to escape. The seriousness of the charges I now faced, the pain and the shock of my parting with Georgina, the injustice of the nine- to fifteen-years sentence I was serving, and the squalor and inhumanity of prison conditions combined to fire my resolve. I was certain that it could be done. I had achieved it once, and I could do it again. Of course, it would be much more difficult – I was in chains, locked in a cell-cage, and kept under special observation. Then too, I openly said that I intended to escape. I said it to anyone who would listen. It was sheer bravado, really, defiance of authority, but it satisfied the need I felt to fight back at the adversities that seemed to be heaped upon me.

I could sense that despite their confidence in the security arrangements, the authorities took me seriously. My behaviour was unusual; no prisoner planning an escape goes around openly saying what he is doing. But that is what I did. I had no idea how or when I would achieve it, but, curiously, by simply repeating my intention I came to believe that I would succeed. It became an obsession. I watched every guard, listened to each patrol throughout the night. I tried to analyse the attitudes of the guards individually, probing for any weakness. I carefully examined the cell-cage, the walls and the lighting. Everything that I looked at told me that it was wellnigh impossible; but nothing stopped me from watching and searching for a way through the security imposed upon me.

At this time I was appearing in court on several matters. Preliminary hearings were proceeding in the robbery case. The fraud charges arising from dishonest sales methods still had to come to trial. I was charged with escaping from custody; further fraud charges related to cheques issued whilst I had been a fugitive. There were four different trials, all at different stages, all in different courts, and each requiring my appearance at a different time. I turned my attention once again to the security arrangements surrounding my court appearances.

The security was very tight indeed. I was escorted by an armed guard, in chains and handcuffs. The prison van was often escorted by armed police. Whilst at court I was kept in an underground cell, locked, in chains, and subject to ten-minute checks by guards. I could only be produced in court on the signed authority of a magistrate or judge, and the courts I appeared in were always full of additional police and prison guards, drafted in to maintain security. When a prosecutor or solicitor wanted to interview me I was taken on signed authority under armed guard to their office, in chains and handcuffs. It all seemed impossible – but somehow I believed that I would succeed.

As one court appearance followed the other I found that the guards escorting me were being varied, so that I had no opportunity to get close to any of them, and I could never be sure who my escort would be on any one day. The guard from whom I had escaped before was still in the prison, but he was never allowed to escort me. He remained friendly and, despite the trouble I had caused him, he still smuggled packets of cigarettes to me when he was on duty in the cell block.

The escorts now allocated to me were of a very different breed. They were experienced prison guards who would as soon shoot you as say good morning. I saw then, as I was to see later, how experience of inhuman conditions in prison changes not only the personality of the prisoner, but that of his keeper too. Years of contact with cruel deprivation and treatment that was often brutal had desensitized these men. They had impersonalized the job to the extent that they had created a barrier between themselves and the treatment they administered to the prisoners in their care, and now their normal human attitudes were suppressed and they had lost the capacity to respond to suffering, pain and despair.

Occasionally I had a younger guard as an escort, and it was one of these, a young guard called Ron, whom I decided to try to cultivate. I sensed that he was sympathetic. He had been present at the meeting with Georgina, and sometimes he asked me if I had heard from her. I had no plan in mind, but I felt that Ron would be a part of it when one emerged.

The newspapers had sensationalized my escape from prison, and now they sensationalized my recapture and my court appearances. It was a revelation to me to read the sheer invention that was published and sold to the public as the truth. Other prisoners would smuggle pages of newspapers to me so that I could see what had been printed. The media labelled me as the mastermind in the robbery matter; the evil genius in the fraudulent sales-techniques case, and a dangerous, daring escapist. I was to learn that hyperbole was standard press language, and whenever it improved copy then exaggeration was replaced by sheer fantasy.

Fellow-prisoners approached me and told me that journalists had asked them to make statements about what I said, how I was reacting to imprisonment, and I began to make up stories and then wait to see them published as truth by the media. I began to spread stories that at the time of my arrest I had been forced to abandon a fortune. When the story reached the newsmen it took on shades of reality I would have been hard-pressed to invent. A completely fictitious article appeared in a national newspaper alleging that I had stashed away more than £100,000. To everyone in prison the story that I had started in jest now took on the cloak of truth, and the more I denied it, the more certain everyone was that I had something to hide. I became a wealthy man overnight.

That was how I reached Ron. He was young, he didn't really like the work he was asked to do as a prison guard, and he was in debt. I didn't know that he was in debt, but I guessed it when he responded to my hints that anyone who helped me would be well rewarded. He had seen the new car the other guard had taken delivery of immediately I had escaped and he believed the rubbish the newspapers printed. Surprisingly he was not greedy. He wanted enough money to pay his debts, buy his way out of the prison service, and purchase a new car – about £2,000 in all. I didn't have £2,000; indeed, I didn't have 2,000 pence, but he believed that I did, and we agreed that should he allow me to take advantage of any opportunity that arose he would be rewarded. I knew that he was genuine when he began to take quite serious risks in smuggling cigarettes and tobacco into my cell-cage. It was his way of showing his good faith.

An unforeseen by-product of the 'hidden fortune' story was that my brother, Philip, was attacked and beaten up by a gang of men who tried to get him to tell them where I had hidden the money. As there was no money they had no success, but, incredibly, despite the injuries they had inflicted, they agreed to call back later, giving my brother a chance to obtain the information from me. Philip spent that night in hospital – his jaw was broken and he had it in a steel splint for several weeks. When the gang returned to my brother's flat to get the information they seemed surprised to find a posse of policemen waiting for them. They were subsequently jailed, and I took great delight in letting everyone know what they had done. They did not have a very comfortable time in prison.

Ron continued to be assigned to be my escort quite regularly, and although I believed that in him I had found a guard I could manipulate, the difficulties were still enormous. I spent a great many nights mulling over the problem and I decided to create a diversion to see what would happen. I wanted to see if I could create a situation that would make the security men concentrate on something quite different from what I actually intended to do.

At the time I was appearing in court on the escape charge, and at a preliminary hearing I indicated that my defence would be that conditions in prison were so horrific that my mind had been temporarily unhinged, and that I had acted without malice – or that there was no *mens rea* as the lawyers put it. Alternatively I suggested that even if such a defence was not accepted, prison conditions were relevant to my state of mind at the time of the alleged escape, and would constitute extenuating circumstances which the court ought to take into account in assessing any sentence.

Having set out the direction my defence would take, I logically asked for permission to subpoena witnesses to testify about conditions in prison. As my defence was contentious, and would be strongly attacked by the prosecution, I requested fifteen witnesses. I selected fifteen of the most dangerous hardened white criminals in South Africa. All of them had escape records, some having escaped several times, and I submitted that this made their evidence especially relevant to my defence. All had convictions for violence; all were long-term prisoners who were completely rebellious against any form of authority. Some were in chains.

My request caused a furore. The press were present when I made it, and the magistrate knew that to refuse to issue the subpoenas was wrong in law. He adjourned to take advice, and on his return he overruled the prosecutor's objections and granted my application. I was jubilant. I believed that I had achieved a major tactical advantage. I had given the prison authorities one of the toughest security problems that they had had for some time. The men I had subpoenaed had to be brought from the strict, closed security of Pretoria Central Prison, housed in the Fort, taken to court, made available to me for interviews, and then safely returned to Pretoria. I followed up my success by upsetting everyone I could.

I was decidedly unpopular – but the guards were careful not to step outside the rules in their treatment of me. It is interesting now, some twenty and more years later, to look back and see that the need to escape developed into a vendetta with the system I was subjected to. The inhuman conditions in prisons at that time made it almost inevitable that this should occur.

My witnesses arrived from Pretoria in two batches. They were put into the same cell block and into the same type of cell-cages that I was being held in. Some had already spent some months in segregation, and when I met them they looked at me and just smiled. They were not yet used to conversation – they had been so long on their own under a silent regime. The grey pallor of months in a darkened cell made their skin seem strange, almost deathly, and their eyes squinted in the bright sunlight of the exercise yard. Without exception they thanked me for this break in their isolation. They didn't really care what I wanted them to say in court – they would have said anything. Strangely, the authorities made no attempt to keep us apart. I had made it known from the start that any attempt to intimidate or interfere with my witnesses would be met with an application for a High Court injunction, and we were left alone. When I spoke to the men I told them that I wanted them to tell the truth in court. I made notes of what they told me and, as I listened to them, I realized that the unvarnished truth more than justified the defence posture I had adopted. I spent the days before the hearing reviewing my defence, and trying to think of how best to use this unusual opportunity to stretch security.

Whilst all this was happening I had a visit from my solicitor. He told me that Olga Mann, a senior prosecutor, wanted to interview me about cheque frauds, so that any witnesses I might require could be notified. I suggested that she arrange to see me on the day I went to court to face the escape charge. Later my solicitor told me that this had been arranged.

At night I lay in my cell trying to find a comfortable position on the thin felt mat. My chains clinked as I tossed and turned. Whilst I concentrated largely on how best to present my defence, I never stopped searching for a way through the security cordon that held me in prison. I didn't want to use violence – I never had used violence in any clash with the law – but in the end I saw that the only plan possible was to try to organize a mass escape and break out with the help of my witnesses. I did not like the plan because despite their reputations as some of the hardest men in captivity, I had personal reservations about one or two of them. I was afraid that if I told them too far in advance what my plan was, some of them would inform the authorities. I spent several nights worrying about this and trying to think of a way to ensure that it didn't happen. Then one night I realized that this was perhaps the opportunity I had been waiting for. There would never be a better chance to create a diversion.

I reviewed my plan carefully, and then decided to gamble everything and act on it. The next morning I spoke to all my witnesses and told them that I planned a mass break-out. They all agreed to go along with it. We realized that we could never hope for all of us to be successful, but facing the sentences we did face, and living under the conditions we lived under, we had become men devoid of hope. Even if only one of our number got away we would all derive immense satsifaction from his success.

The air of depression lifted, and the guards noted the change and became wary of us. They could not be sure what was going on, but they knew we looked far too happy to be up to any good. The next day I noticed that the attitude of the guards had changed again. They weren't so suspicious any more. They had a 'we know what you're up to' look about them. Four of my witnesses looked a little subdued - they kept to themselves – and as I saw what was happening I wanted to laugh; it was hard to contain my jubilation. The plan was working; the authorities had got the message; they knew that we planned a mass break-out.

The day before I was to appear in court I put the last part of my plan into operation. When I look back it is incredible that it worked, but my belief in the rightness of what I was doing was so great that I never doubted that I would succeed. I cornered two of the men I suspected of informing and went over the plan with them in detail. They maintained the pretence of solid commitment to it. To each of them, quite separately, I said casually:

'Well tomorrow we'll be free. There's only one thing that can spoil it.'

'What's that?' they asked.

'That bastard guard called Ron,' I said ruefully. 'If I get him as my escort we'll have to call it off. The bastard even holds my hand when I go for a shit!'

They both expressed the hope that we wouldn't get Ron as an escort – and, of course, next morning, we did!

Armed police accompanied the prison van from the Fort to the court. Armed police and armed prison guards stood duty as I was taken with my witnesses to the cells below the courts. There we were separated and I was placed in a cell on my own. There were not enough individual cells for the others, and they were put three or four to a cell. Our mood was incredibly optimistic. I had private reasons for being optimistic, but the others were jubilant too. It was infectious, and when someone began to sing everyone joined in. The guards had strict instructions not to open cell doors, and for a while they rushed from cell to cell, shouting and bashing the doors with their truncheons. Then they gave up and left us alone.

Just by being there we had achieved a small victory over the system. In the harshness of the system we were subject to, any point scored against authority took on a significance out of all proportion to its true value. I had become completely anti-authority, completely anti-law-and-order, and in the context of that attitude the authorities became the enemy – someone I had a duty to take on and defeat if I could. Only those who have suffered the degradation of a harsh prison regime can begin to understand how it breeds rebellion. It distorts values, confuses all sense of right and wrong, and strips a man of his civility. Allegiances become confused and decent attitudes are overwhelmed by the need to survive. The mind creates barriers to shut out pain, and those same barriers shut out the memory of a previous way of life – what were previously regarded as normal values have no meaning any more.

Whilst the singing was going on my cell door was suddenly opened. I looked up from my papers and saw Ron standing there.

'Olga Mann wants to see you,' he said.

I nodded and picked up my case papers. I had a raincoat over my arm and the desk-sergeant checked my handcuffs and chains before Ron led me away. I had tied my chains to a piece of string around my waist and wore my trousers over them. Although they were not visible, they clinked as I walked with Ron up the stairs to Olga Mann's office. I asked Ron how he had come to be on the escort, and he told me that he didn't know. The head of the prison had assigned the duty only an hour before we left the Fort.

My interview with Olga Mann was short. She was pleasant and inquired how I was getting on. She seemed genuinely interested, and I recall that she advised me to write a book about my experiences. She gave me a writing-tablet and wished me luck.

When we had left her office, I asked Ron to take me to the toilet. I told him that he could collect his money from my solicitor as soon as I was free. We went into the toilet and he unfastened the handcuffs. I used my shoelaces to tie the chains tightly to my trouser pocket linings – that way they remained fairly taut, and if I moved carefully they didn't clink and jangle.

'This is it,' I said to Ron a little unoriginally.

'I can only give you a few minutes' start,' he said.

I walked out of the door and down to the main concourse of the court buildings. I had put on my raincoat and I had my hands in my pockets, holding the chains as tightly as I could. The handcuffs were in my coat pocket, and they rubbed coldly against my hands. I held my case papers tightly under my arm. I did not experience any sense of doubt or feel any need for hesitation. I knew that I was about to be free.

As I crossed the concourse and headed for the rear doors of the court building, I developed the feeling that everyone was watching me. But I looked straight ahead and carried on, pausing in the sunshine as I reached the doorway. A police patrol-car was making its way slowly round the corner of the block the building occupied. The driver and his partner were carefully scanning the pavements as they encircled the block. I waited until they had passed and then I moved down the steps on to the pavement and joined the stream of pedestrians as they moved towards the city centre. A second patrol-car came around the corner and proceeded slowly towards me. I felt a twinge of panic, but then I controlled it and, judging my position so that two pedestrians were between me and the patrol-car, I walked on. As the car came level with me I turned my head and began a conversation with the startled pedestrian next to me. I quickly apologized.

'I thought you were someone I knew,' I said lamely.

The moment of danger had passed and I kept on walking, not having any plan. I knew that I had to get well away from the area – it would not be long before Ron would have to raise the alarm. Incredibly I had given no thought to what I would do were I to succeed in escaping. I had planned to act instinctively. I had a ten-shilling note hidden in my clothes – that was all I had. I had seized the opportunity that had come my way – now I had to make the most of it.

My first concern was with the chains. The authorities had inserted metal rivets in them to prevent me opening them. As I made my way towards the city I passed a hardware shop and I stopped and went in to buy two hacksaw blades. I didn't have enough cash for the frame to take the blades. There was a moment of near-panic when I realized that I would have to let go of the chains in order to take out my ten-shilling note and pay for the goods. I held my breath and slowly let go with one hand, trying to take up the slack with the other. I heard a clink as I did so, but no one else seemed to notice, and the moment passed.

After I left the hardware store I continued across the city towards the park. I intended to use the public toilets as a place to saw off the chains. An hotel stood on the corner of the street leading to the park and, instinctively, I turned into it. I had decided to use the hotel toilets instead. I walked across the hotel lounge and I heard a gasp come from a table behind me. I turned around and could not believe my eyes. Dawn sat at the table with a girl-friend. She whispered something to her friend and took a latch-key from her. Then she snatched up her bag and almost ran towards me.

'Jesus Christ!' she said, grabbing my arm. 'Let's get out of here!'

By blind chance I had walked into the lounge of an hotel in a city of one and a half million souls and had found one of only three people I felt I could really trust. It was incredible – it was just one of a chain of completely fortuitous events that came together to make the escape possible.

Dawn took me to a flat close to the hotel, and together we struggled and sweated and cursed as we cut through the rivets that held my chains in place. It took us over two hours, and my hands were bruised and bleeding when we had finished. Dawn had said little – she had grimly held the chains taut as I cut at them. She had fetched rags to wrap around the blades to form makeshift handles. Both blades had snapped under my initial furious assault on the chains, and I finished the job with half-blades, sore hands and bleeding shins.

Dawn had asked me nothing about the escape – only when the chains were lying in a heap on the kitchen floor and she had helped me to put Band-aids on my cuts, did we talk about what had happened. The small radio in the flat had carried the news. I was described as dangerous –

not to be approached – and my solicitor and my brother had both been detained. The guard was said to be helping police with their inquiries, and it was clear that the authorities were taking the matter very seriously indeed.

Dawn explained that I would have to leave the flat as soon as it was dark. The owner would be returning later that night. As soon as she felt it was safe for us to do so she took me across the city and booked a double room in the Grosvenor Hotel. She paid in advance for two nights and she kept the desk busy whilst I made my way up the fire escape into the room. No one had seen me arrive.

Two days later I had arranged transport, and I left Johannesburg. I took the back roads leading out into the country. I passed through Kimberley, famous for its diamonds and Big Hole, said to be the biggest man-made hole in the world, and headed north-west. I crossed the southern edge of the Kalahari Desert, through Posmasburg and Grunau, heading for South West Africa. I skirted the Namib desert, passed Rehoboth, the Bastard settlement, and came to Windhoek. Here I hoped that I would be able to live openly. I had travelled well over 1500 miles in two days, and I had arrived in a territory administered under mandate, with a separate police force and administration.

I booked into the Kaiserhof Hotel and slept for twelve hours.

13

The next day, after an early lunch, I walked down Kaiser Street, the main thoroughfare, window-shopping, drinking in the fresh air and recovering from the long journey. I looked at the people around me as they went about their business and wondered what they would do if they knew who I was. My attention was drawn to a man coming along the pavement towards me, and I smiled as I thought I recognized him. Then I went cold. It was very clear that he recognized me, and suddenly I remembered who he was. His name was Jock, and he had often attended the parties I gave before my marriage to Georgina. As he advanced along the pavement towards me there was no way I could escape him, and I felt a sense of relief as he held out his hand and greeted me quite warmly. He suggested we have a cup of coffee, and we went into a nearby café. Over refreshments he asked about Georgina, and then he said how surprised he was to see me.

'You needn't worry,' he said. 'I shan't give you away.'

He asked how he could help me, and later took me to see a friend of his who immediately gave me a job as a freelance furniture salesman.

For the next two months I travelled all over South West Africa. I was quite successful, selling household appliances and furniture to the scattered farming community. I played golf at Okahandja, where the greens were made of sand and an essential part of the golfer's equipment was a stout stick with which to kill the snakes that basked on the fairways. I enjoyed fresh kudu steaks at the homes of farmers I visited, and got used to chewing savoury springbok biltong on the long drives between towns. Driving at night I wondered at the rock formations of the arid scrubland – in the silvery light of a full moon the landscape seemed unreal, and it would have been easy to imagine that you were on another planet.

I quickly adapted to what was a very pleasant way of life – but it was soon to be disrupted. Jock came to me in a state of some agitation and told me that he had overheard police members at a local rugby club discussing my case. He said that they had been given special instructions to look for me – they suspected that I might be in the territory.

There was nothing to do but to leave. The population was small and scattered over a vast area, and the white population was even smaller. Once a proper instruction was issued it would only be a matter of time before I was arrested. I hastily settled my affairs and flew out of Windhoek by regular air-schedule – heading back to Johannesburg. The plane was an old Dakota. It had seen much better days, and it bumped and bounced its way over the hot air pockets of the semi-desert we were crossing. It would drop a hundred feet one minute, and bounce back up the next. I was very glad indeed when we made a short stop at Upington – the whisky I hurriedly ordered and consumed restored my courage and helped me on the final leg of the journey to Johannesburg. Later I learned that a detective had actually travelled on the same plane with me, but had failed to recognize me.

In Johannesburg I rented a shop and ordered electrical goods from local suppliers. I paid for the goods with dud cheques, and within hours of accepting delivery had sold the goods and decamped.

On the evening I completed this transaction, I met a girl called Suzette. She accepted my invitation to dinner, and as we talked I discovered that she was the daughter of a magistrate and had left home against her parents' wishes. She mentioned the name of a man who I knew was in prison. She spoke of him as a friend and I began to relax a little. She began to ask me about myself, but as I spoke she stopped me and told me that she recognized me. She was clearly friendly, and when she told me that she had arrived in Johannesburg that afternoon, leaving her luggage at the station, intending to look for an hotel, I suggested she let me look after things for her. We collected her luggage and she made no protest when I booked a double room for us in a city hotel. The next morning we both knew that she would stay with me wherever I had to go.

Johannesburg was becoming too dangerous a place for me to stay. My escapade with the electrical goods would have alerted the police to my presence, and in addition I had many former friends and business acquaintances whom I had to beware of. The afternoon after I met Suzette I decided to leave, and I chartered a small plane. We flew out of Germiston airport near to Johannesburg, to Mbabane in Swaziland. The pilot radioed ahead and we were met at the airstrip by a car which took us to stay at the beautiful Swazi Inn. We remained there for a week and then I rented a car and we headed for Lourenço Marques in Portuguese East Africa.

We spent three splendid weeks at the prestigious Polano Hotel, sunbathing by day and spending the evenings roaming between the many taverna the city offered, or listening to the band in the night-club attached to the hotel. Soon the money I had was exhausted and I decided to try to cross back into South Africa. I had no formal documentation and would have been unable to enter Rhodesia or any of the other East African territories. I decided to gamble and try to re-enter South Africa via the main customs post at Komatipoort. Suzette, who was aware of the risk I was taking, behaved impeccably. She was a very attractive girl and she played the part of a doting girlfriend well enough to draw attention away from me during customs procedures. Once through the border-post we both gave a sigh of relief, and then made our way back to the temporary safety of Johannesburg to look for fresh funds.

I leased a flat with Suzette, and for some weeks we lived quietly whilst I tried to set up a business I could exploit. We were getting ready to go to bed one evening when armed police burst into the flat. They were led by Aubrey Marais, a detective I knew well. He was one of the few policemen in South Africa whom I regarded as a friend. He had taken me to his home, and his wife had prepared a meal which we had enjoyed together. My arrest was a considerable feather in his cap, and he told me that it happened quite by chance. He had called at the apartment block to see the caretaker about another matter, and had routinely shown her my photograph. She had immediately recognized me as the quiet Mr Cameron in apartment 502.

After the arrest, Aubrey Marais allowed me to take Suzette out for a meal. Her distress was very real, and it was a very human gesture on his part to allow us that last evening together. He came with us, but never intruded, and later, when he finally handed me over to the guards at the Fort he cautioned them not to mistreat me. It was fairly common for escapees to be given a good beating upon their recapture, but I was treated strictly according to the rules. I was given prison clothes, put in chains and leg-irons, and locked up in one of the now-familiar cell-cages.

I looked in the corner and saw the felt mat and blankets. The piss-pot seemed particularly foul, and I gave it a kick. It was almost 11.00 p.m., and most of the other prisoners were asleep. I was quite drunk, and more than anything I wanted a drink of water. I sat down on the mat and began to think about Suzette. She had been amazingly loyal to me, and she had been weeping when I kissed her goodbye. I began to feel very sorry for myself and I started to sing mournfully in my very uninteresting voice. The other prisoners were soon awake, cursing and shouting at me to stop. The night-patrols came and threatened me with a beating; but I was in a little world of my own and I carried on until, much later, I fell asleep.

I woke up feeling terrible. The realization that I was back in prison did nothing to ease my hangover. My mouth was dry and I was gasping for a drink. My head throbbed and felt as though it had become detached from my body. The guards came and gloated at me through the wire-mesh of the cage, and it was not until late that evening that they unlocked and allowed me to get food and water.

By the next day I was feeling better physically, but the growing realization that it was very unlikely I would get another chance to escape, and the loss I felt at my parting with Suzette, depressed me. Security was very strict. I was moved to another cell-cage, and these moves were to happen frequently during the rest of my stay at the Fort. My court appearances recommenced, and I was taken to Colonel Minnaar's office. He was the head of the prison and he introduced me to a guard called Weideman.

'This is my private "S S" man,' the colonel told me. 'You can't bribe him or con him.'

Weideman was a young man, over six feet tall. He showed no emotion and seemed unaffected by the colonel's description of him.

'He'll see you get what you're entitled to,' Colonel Minnaar went on. 'And he'll be your escort whenever you go to court. You've given me enough headaches already, so please try not to be too much of a nuisance in future.'

I liked Colonel Minnaar. He was straightforward and considered both sides of any issue. He spoke to me quite often whilst I was at the Fort, and on one occasion he got me to sort out a bookkeeping problem he had.

'You know,' he said to me one day. 'I look at you and I realize that I could be in your shoes and you in mine.'

Coming from an officer in the South African Prison Service it was a remarkable comment. He stopped the petty cell searches and twice-daily strips the guards had instituted. He asked to meet Suzette, who telephoned the prison daily to inquire about me – and when he had met her he allowed me unlimited visits at any reasonable time. On other things he was adamant. The leg-irons and chains stayed on. I was to have no visits at court, and I could not supplement the prison diet with private food. So I decided to try another way to get these concessions.

I made application to the Supreme Court for the release of company records seized by the police at the time of my arrest – I needed them to properly prepare my defence in the case involving dishonest sales techniques. The application came before Mr Justice Kuper, who was later to be shot and killed as he sat dining at home with his wife. I found him to be courteous and completely objective. My application was for the documents to be released, made available to me for studying, or that I be furnished with copies of them. Alternatively I asked that at the trial the police be subpoenaed *duces tecum*, so that they would have to produce the documents at that time. As an additional help in preparing my defence I asked for access to a law library. Having no funds for counsel I presented the application myself.

Throughout my short address to the court I stood at counsels' table. I held my notes in one hand and my chains in the other. Having completed my submissions I paused, and in the silence of that moment I dropped my chains on the floor of the court. The resulting noise surprised even me, and those in the court who were taken unawares must have been quite startled. Judge Kuper looked up from his notes and peered at me over his spectacles.

'Are you in chains?' he inquired politely.

'Well – yes, milord. I am.'

'Has that affected you in making this application?'

'Well, milord, I don't want to make a mountain out of a molehill,' I said. 'And, as you are aware, I will be returned to prison from here. I don't want to create any problems.'

He said nothing for a few moments – then he seemed to nod, and he turned to the attorney-general's representative.

'I wish it to be placed in the record that the applicant in this matter appeared before me in chains.' He paused and then went on. 'The applicant has indicated that he does not wish to make a mountain out of a molehill, to use his expression, and has said that he has to return to the prison where these chains were placed upon him. However, in my view, this is a matter that goes beyond the wishes of the applicant. There can be no legitimate reason for him to have appeared before the court in chains. If security is a problem, that can be met by increasing the number of police on duty. To cause a man to appear in chains must inhibit the presentation of his case, and this court will not tolerate the practice in future.

'I direct that a copy of my remarks be conveyed to the head of the prison where the applicant is held.'

He went on to grant my application to have access to the documents I had stipulated, and directed that I be given access under escort to the law library of the Witwatersrand Supreme Court, a privilege that I believe was unprecedented at that time.

After the hearing, Weideman, who had been my escort, took me back to the cells under the court. I was surprised a few minutes later when he opened the door and gave me a cup of tea.

'The colonel's going to love you,' he said, and he was grinning as he closed the door. I thanked him for the tea, but it was only after he had left that I realized he must have paid for it himself, and that he seemed quite pleased at my success. I waited in the court cells for some hours before transport arrived to take me back to the Fort. On the journey back I looked out of the air-vent in the prison truck and a newspaper poster caught my eye.

'PRISONER IN CHAINS – JUDGE ANGRY!!' it shouted.

I counted twenty-two such posters tied to lamp-posts on the route we took back to the Fort. When we arrived I was taken directly to Colonel Minnaar's office. He had a copy of the judge's remarks in front of him – and he was furious.

'I don't know how you managed this,' he said angrily. 'But I've had Head Office on the phone, and you've made a lot of trouble for me. In future you will wear chains at all times except when you actually appear in court. You will wear them on the journey to court, and in the court cells – but not in the dock.'

Surprisingly he took no reprisals – he still allowed Suzette to visit me whenever she could. But he was adamant that I would not be allowed any supplement to my diet.

A few weeks after the chains incident my trial began on charges arising from fraudulent sales techniques. I stood trial with five co-accused, all of whom were represented by counsel; but I conducted my own defence. It looked as though the case would last for several months. I became very involved in the cross-examination of witnesses, and after the long morning session I was exhausted, finding the lunch-time prison meal quite inadequate. I found that I was becoming faint during the afternoon sessions and after a few days I asked the court for an adjournment to allow me to recover. The judge was not very keen and wanted to know what was the matter.

'I'm not getting enough to eat,' I told him. 'I have asked the prison officials for a supplement to the bowl of soup and dry bread I am given for lunch, but I am told that nothing can be done because I am a convicted prisoner.'

'Well,' said the judge. 'What do you want me to do?'

'I am asking that I be allowed to supplement my diet in the same way that unconvicted prisoners are able to when they are on trial. I am willing to pay for my own food, but I cannot do justice to my defence when I am faint from lack of food.'

The judge turned to the state prosecutor.

'Why can't he buy his own lunch?' he inquired.

The prosecutor consulted his junior.

'I understand that it is a prison regulation,' he said a little hesitantly.

'But he is not in prison – he is at court,' said the judge a little testily. 'Can't you make a sensible arrangement for him?'

'We'll go into it, milord, and do what we can.'

That evening as I went back to the Fort I looked out of the prison van and saw that the newspapers had picked it up again.

'PRISONER PLAYS OLIVER – AND ASKS FOR MORE!!' they proclaimed.

Once again I faced an angry Colonel Minnaar. But this time I didn't really care what his reaction was. I was hungry and I *had* felt faint. In my view it was, and still is, grossly unfair to have a system in which the defendant, if in custody, is compelled to eat what is often inadequate, ill-prepared food that he doesn't like, whilst prosecution witnesses and counsel enjoy a proper meal in a proper setting. It is just another part of a system that treats anyone in custody more harshly than if they had been convicted and were in prison serving a sentence. One good thing did come out of the incident. Later when I asked for a table and chair and writing facilities, Colonel Minnaar had me make a list, and then he arranged everything I had asked for. Another sequel to the affair was that the court guards had to cope with ordinary members of the public who arrived with food parcels for me. I never did get any of the parcels and dishes they had brought, but it was gratifying that ordinary people responded in such a practical way.

After the stationery trial had been going on for some weeks, I learned that the judge was anxious to have the case settled as soon as possible. I was serving a nine to fifteen-year sentence, conducting my own defence, and getting one decent meal each day – so I was in no hurry. The alternative was to be locked up in my cell-cage all day, and the dock of Witwatersrand Supreme Court was a much nicer place. So I kept witnesses under cross-examination until they said what I wanted them to say, or until I could think of no more questions. Each evening I prepared a minimum of one hundred questions for the witness under cross-examination, and this with all the subsidiary questions that arose from the witnesses' replies proved sufficient to keep anyone in the witness-box all day. I found that even the most hostile witness became confused and broke or made mistakes if I kept the pressure up long enough. I was enjoying the case, having a lot of success in rebutting prosecution allegations, and saw no reason to change my approach. Counsel representing my co-accused seemed quite happy to leave the hard slog of cross-examination to me. They drew fat fees for sitting down and watching.

Eventually I heard that the judge was becoming agitated. He had booked his holiday for a date that could not conveniently be changed, and he intended to see that the case ended in time for him to take up his hotel reservations. But he discovered that whatever the attitude of counsel for the other accused might be, I was not going to co-operate. He began to harass me. He interrupted – telling me not to repeat myself; but all this led to was a long discussion about what the original question had been that he said I was repeating. I suggested that either he or the court stenographer had misheard the original question, or that it could quite legitimately be put to the witness again in view of admissions made since it was first posed. These interchanges lasted a good deal longer than the original question, and so he gave up interrupting. He could not intimidate me: I was in prison, in chains, serving a nine- to fifteen-year sentence; there was no sanction he could impose which would materially affect me. Under South African procedures I was entitled to conduct my own defence.

As the trial carried on he became increasingly anxious. There was no way it was going to finish in time for him to go on holiday. Then he did what we had all hoped he would do. He stopped the trial and asked to see counsel in his chambers. Of course I was not invited – and I was the one who was holding everything up. So there began a series of toings and froings between judge's chambers and me in the dock of the courtroom. The intermediary was a respected junior counsel.

'It is felt,' he told me earnestly, 'that justice would be done if you were to plead guilty to four of the sixteen charges against you, and you were acquitted on the others.'

He stopped and looked at me speculatively.

'Of course, you would then receive another statutory nine- to fifteen-year sentence, but as the law requires that such sentences run concurrently, you would be no worse off than you are now.'

I was surprised at the directness of the approach.

'What about my co-accused?' I asked.

In the following four hours counsel made many trips to judge's chambers, and it was finally agreed that all conspiracy charges should be dropped, the company should be acquitted with the directors, I would plead guilty to four charges and be sentenced as suggested, and everyone else, including my brother Philip, would receive suspended sentences.

It was after 6.30 p.m., when the judge returned to the court to be informed that we wished to change our pleas. He professed considerable surprise, but quickly agreed when the state prosecutor, who had been with him throughout the negotiations, said that he had no objections. The sentences and acquittals were handed down as agreed. I have no doubt that some of my co-accused ought properly to have been acquitted altogether, but I agreed with them that a suspended sentence was better than risking a capricious verdict and the displeasure of a judge who had missed his vacation. It all confirmed my view that very often justice has little to do with what happens in law courts. The experience left me with a healthy distrust of judicial proceedings, and made me wonder what really goes on behind the trappings of justice the public are presented with. My experience since then, both in South Africa and in England, has done nothing to alter my view that expediency usually takes precedence over any other considerations.

Throughout the long days of those court hearings, and during the two trials that followed, Suzette sat day after day as near to the dock as she was allowed to. We could look at one another, and exchange messages through my co-accused who were on bail, but we were never allowed to speak to one another at court. She visited me at the Fort and wrote to me almost daily. The media discovered her, and for several weeks ran feature articles about the times we had spent together. I remember her with affection; she stood by me despite pressure from the police and the press. She was a real friend and remained loyal to me until, upon my transfer to Pretoria Central Prison, the prison authorities stopped all my letters and visits, cutting off any communication between us and effectively killing any chance of maintaining a relationship.

14

After the sales-fraud case I had been returned to the Fort to await trial on charges of escaping from custody, fraud and robbery. I was serving two sentences of nine to fifteen years; they ran concurrently and so my date of release had not been affected – but in a subtle way I was forced to reassess my position. I had pleaded guilty in the latest case, under considerable pressure from my co-accused, and I realized that it would be very difficult to appeal against that conviction. The sentences I was serving were statutory, so there was no appeal against them.

My belief that the sentences were savage and unwarranted by the quantum of my offending was undiminished; but my two escapes had taught me that life as a fugitive was not the answer to my problems. The way in which my co-accused, including my own brother, accepted the benefits of my conduct at the stationery trial and then deserted me, made me realize just how alone I was. During the whole of the period I spent in prison not one of them was to write or attempt to visit me. Whilst Suzette still wrote and visited me, I knew, even at that stage, that as soon as my trials were over and I was transferred to Pretoria the Prison Authorities would cut off communication between us. My future looked very lonely indeed.

Security at the Fort continued to be very strict. I was now confined to a cell-cage closer to the duty office. I was under special observation, in chains, and subjected to frequent strip searches. For the time being escape seemed impossible, and I concentrated on preparing my defence in the trials still facing me.

I appeared in the magistrates' court at Johannesburg on the escape charge, and took advantage of a confused prosecutor who failed to lead evidence of re-arrest – vital if he were to prove I had been out of custody. It was only after I had closed my defence without calling any witnesses that he realized his mistake. He then antagonized the magistrate by asking to be allowed to re-open his case 'in order to rebut defence submissions'. The rules of evidence were clear – there had been no defence evidence and therefore there was nothing to rebut – one couldn't call evidence to rebut 'submissions'. In the argument that ensued, the magistrate reprimanded the prosecutor for wasting the court's time with an ill-prepared presentation, and for making a patently irregular request. He found me not guilty – as far as I am aware the only time a convicted prisoner has been found not guilty of escape in South Africa.

Later, when I appeared on the cheque-fraud charges, I pleaded guilty to some and not guilty to others. My pleas were accepted and I was sentenced to a third nine- to fifteen-year term of imprisonment with compulsory labour, to run concurrently with those I was already serving.

The only charge still pending against me was the robbery charge – by far the most serious I was to face. When Peter had died as a result of the insulin overdose, the prosecution had promoted me to be accused number one. But before my trial in that matter was heard, the trial of Peter's co-accused in the first robbery of Glenton and Mitchell went ahead. One of the men who pleaded guilty at that hearing was John, and he was now in the same cell block as me at the Fort, awaiting transfer to Pretoria Central Prison. He had been sentenced to twelve years' imprisonment and, in addition, to eight cuts with the heavy cane.

John was a small man, compact, in his early twenties, with a very alert manner and a ready sense of humour. His fair hair had been cropped on admission and the prison clothes hung loosely on him giving him a waif-like appearance. Like most of the men awaiting transfer to the 'Big House', his talk centred on escape. He had been shocked by Peter's death and, quite irrationally, held the criminal-justice system wholly responsible for it.

The cage in which John was held was in a different corridor of the cell block to mine, but as the corridors were divided only by steel grilles it was possible to hear most of what went on in the block. I learned to interpret sounds, as all prisoners do, and it become easy for me to identify individual guards as they patrolled the passageways, locked and unlocked grilles, checked cages and banged the steel-mesh wire with their batons. One man who had a distinctive walk was the guard from whom I had escaped the first time. I would recognize his footsteps as he approached my cage – and frequently he would push cigarettes and matches under my door. He would peer through the wire-mesh and I would thank him with gestures, careful not to let others know what he had done.

A few days before he was due to be transferred to Pretoria, John approached me and said that he had an escape plan. He wanted to know if I would support him when the time came. I didn't hesitate; I assured him of my support and wished him luck. I was very worried about the robbery charge I faced – it was a capital offence, and it was frightening to think that were I convicted the judge had discretion which allowed him to impose the death sentence. It was unlikely that this would occur, as no physical violence had been used by those who committed the robbery, but there was no guarantee that the court would not take advantage of the opportunity to make an example of a well-known criminal as a deterrent to others. Despite my misgivings about escape as an answer to my problems I felt that my previous experience as a fugitive might enable me to take better advantage of opportunities were I to succeed in escaping again. I was not surprised when John did not tell me the details of his plan – I knew only too well how important it was to plan things on a 'need to know' basis. He did tell me that it involved breaking out of the cell block at night.

The involvement in an escape bid lifted me out of the depression I had been slipping into. The excitement of an escape from prison is unique. There is no sense of guilt. The very real sense of shock and frequently of injustice that follows conviction and sentence lends an air of justification to the attempt. Man's innate need to be free, when added to the urge to escape from the inhuman conditions we lived under, was very strong motivation indeed. A prisoner planning escape very seldom stops to think about the consequences of his action. He is caught up in the excitement and the romance of it – reason gives way to fantasy.

Two nights after John had spoken to me I heard the night-patrol come into the cell block. I could hear immediately that it was the guard whom I had first escaped from, and I heard him unlock and lock the grilles as he made his way along the corridors. Suddenly the routine sounds were shattered by a loud cry and the noise of bodies falling to the floor – then there were loud thumps as a heavy object was used to strike a body. The guard began to shout and then, just as suddenly as it had begun, the noise stopped. There was a short pause, then noises I couldn't identify, followed by the sound of the guard moaning as he made his way out of the cell block. Voices babbled in the duty office near my cell-cage. Suddenly the prison siren began to wail, summoning off-duty guards. Confused shouting outside the cell block heralded the arrival of reinforcements. The chaotic noises were broken by the patrol-guard as he re-entered the cell block.

'John,' he shouted. 'I'm coming to get my gun. John, don't shoot me, I'm coming to get my gun.'

I listened intently and heard him proceed cautiously along the corridor towards where the commotion had started.

'John,' he called out again. 'Don't shoot me. I've got to get my gun back.'

'I haven't got your fucking gun,' John suddenly shouted back.

It seemed that that was the signal that the other guards had been waiting for. There was a stampede as twenty or thirty of them rushed into the block. For a few moments it was impossible to decipher the noises as confusion reigned. Then there was a shout and the sound of a cage door being unlocked. I heard the sounds of batons striking a body, and grunts of pain as they landed. The sound of someone being dragged along the passageway drew closer to where I was, and then the steel grille to my section of the block was unlocked and I watched through the steel-mesh wire of my cage as the guards dragged John in. They opened the cage next to mine and threw him in. Two guards stood watching whilst others went to fetch leg-irons and chains. When they returned they fitted the restraints on his ankles, gave him a few gratuitous blows with their batons, then locked the cage door and left him. I could hear him breathing heavily.

'John,' I called to him. 'Are you OK?'

He didn't reply immediately, but then he gave a throaty chuckle.

'Silly bastards,' he said.

The grille to our section of the block opened again, and looking through the wire-mesh I saw Major Gouws, second-in-command of the prison, march in. His swagger stick was tucked smartly under his arm, two guards were in attendance, and a little black-and-white dog scampered along at his heels. One of the guards unlocked John's cage and Major Gouws went in and proceeded to whack John about the head and shoulders with his swagger stick. The little dog became excited and started to bark and jumped at John, pulling at his clothes, trying to bite him.

John's reaction was completely unexpected. He began to chuckle –

and then he burst out laughing. He told me later that he found it incredibly funny that a senior officer could behave like Major Gouws did – and even more funny that he had brought his little dog along to help him.

'So you want to escape, eh?' the major said in heavily accented English. 'What wood do you come from, eh?' he went on in a poor translation from Afrikaans of the question, 'What jungle did you creep out of?'

John laughed even louder, rolling about on the floor in his mirth.

'Norwood!' he answered, naming the suburb of Johannesburg he lived in – and he collapsed in laughter.

The major stopped hitting him and stepped back, and the little dog stopped attacking too.

'Hy's mal!' the major exclaimed, reverting to Afrikaans. 'Sluit hom toe!' (He's mad! Lock him up!)

The guards saluted and locked the cage door; then the little group marched out of the section, the little dog following at the major's heels.

When he had recovered John told me that he had made a hole in the roof of his cage and lain in wait to jump down on the patrol-guard as he made his rounds. He had tried to knock him unconscious with a broom handle, but when he realized who the guard was he had stopped hitting him.

'I couldn't keep on hitting him,' John told me. 'He's such a decent bloke. I just couldn't keep on hitting him!'

John had jumped back into his cage and tried to repair the hole he had made in the roof, but the guard had recognized him. Then when it was discovered that the guard's revolver had disappeared in the mêlée, the other guards had refused to go into the cell block until he had recovered it.

The next night I lay listening as the same guard made his way into the cell block to make his rounds. As he came into the section where John and I were housed I saw that he had bandages about his head. He paused outside my door, and again outside John's door, and as he did so he pushed a packet of cigarettes and a box of matches into each cell.

'He's a bloody gentleman,' John said to me after he had gone. 'Why couldn't it have been one of the bad bastards?'

A few days later John was transferred to Pretoria, and my trial on the robbery charge began. The matter came before the Witwatersrand Supreme Court, and Mr Justice Claassen, an ex-Chief Justice of South West Africa, presided, assisted by two assessors. Although I had requested a trial by jury, which I was legally entitled to, this was refused me – and it was indicative of the disregard for legal requirements that became a feature of the trial. Judge Claassen was not only an arrogant, self-opinionated man, he was also ill-mannered. He ignored proper procedures and made up his own rules. It became clear that he regarded the trial as largely a waste of the court's time, and his prejudgement of the issue before him was so apparent that the proceedings became a farce. In South Africa there was no legal-aid system, and I conducted my own defence – both Charlie and Don Muniz were unrepresented. Judge Claassen interrupted continually during my cross-examination of witnesses, completely destroying the whole object of cross-examination. He queried the relevance of questions, suggested answers to the witnesses, and did everything possible to negate proper questioning.

Charlie had made a confession, and the answers Don Muniz had given to questions he had been asked clearly incriminated him. My stance had always been that I was not present at the robbery, and a denial that I took part in it. I had refused to answer questions, but had made a short statement saying that I was not guilty.

The prosecution case against me seemed to rest wholly on identification. After my arrest at Salt Rock, and whilst I was in custody, detectives in charge of the investigation had held a photographic identification parade. Now at my trial I subpoenaed the actual photographs used. Under cross-examination, despite the harassment of Judge Claassen, it emerged that a dozen passport-size photographs, including one of Don Muniz, who was also in custody, had been arranged on a cardboard mount so that they formed a frame around a photograph of me measuring three and a half inches square – several times larger than the other photographs. Fourteen witnesses had been shown these photographs – no one had picked out Don Muniz, and two had tentatively said that I looked like the man who had robbed them.

I asked for evidence of this photo-parade to be ruled inadmissible. I argued that the disparate size of my photograph was unfair and breached Judges' Rules; the positioning of my photograph was calculated to draw special attention to it, and this, too, was in breach of Judges' Rules. I had been given no formal notice of the intention to hold a photo-parade, although in custody, and so had been prevented from having a legal representative present; this was a further breach of Judges' Rules. I had been in police custody at the time and available for a proper identification parade. A photo-parade in such circumstances constituted the substitution for best evidence of second best, and the court could not allow that in view of Appeal Court rulings.

Judge Claassen ignored all my submissions, and ordered that the evidence of the photo-parade be admitted into evidence.

An identification parade had been held subsequent to the photo-parade, and at the time it was held the police had concealed the fact that the witnesses now being called to identify me had already attended a photo-parade and had been shown a large photograph of me. Had the police been honest about this neither I nor my legal adviser would have agreed for me to stand on the identification parade. The parade was held at the Fort in Johannesburg, in the forecourt of the cell block. It was made up of fourteen men, amongst whom were Don Muniz at five feet six inches, Charlie at five feet three inches, and myself at almost six feet four inches. There were only four other men on that parade anywhere near my height; Judges' Rules required ten. The requirements regarding build, colour and walk of life were also not adhered to. But, incredibly, I was asked to stand on the parade unshaven, with closely cropped hair, and in chains. I had a discussion with my solicitor and we agreed that as I in fact had never been at the robbery scene I had nothing to fear. We arranged for a photograph to be taken of the parade, and this photograph clearly showed that all our objections were valid, and emphasized the fact that Don Muniz and I were the only people on the parade in chains and in unpressed, crumpled clothing.

At that parade no one picked out Charlie, who had been present at the robbery but whose photograph had not been shown to the witnesses. Three witnesses picked out Don Muniz, and two picked me out, only one of whom had picked out a photograph of me.

The photograph of the parade was produced in court, and my submissions based on it and on police witnesses' admissions, took over an hour. I had researched the issue thoroughly and was able to quote several Appeal Court precedents that dealt exactly with the issues. Judge Claassen listened until I had finished.

'Is that all?' he asked a little petulantly.

'Yes, milord.'

'The objections are overruled and the evidence is admitted,' he said.

Under cross-examination the witnesses who had identified photographs or picked me out at the parade all said that they were no longer sure that I was the man who had robbed them. However, the prosecutor, seeing his case begin to crumble, now asked for all the witnesses to be allowed to see if they could identify me in the dock. This was in direct contravention of an Appeal Court directive, and I protested. It was clearly dangerous to hear evidence of such identification when witnesses were in effect being given three looks at the same person, with the inevitable implication that he was the one they ought to pick out.

Judge Claassen ignored the Appeal Court ruling, and overruled my objections.

'The witnesses may have been under strain at the photo-parade and the identification parade,' he said. 'In the calm of this court their judgement may be of more value.'

Two witnesses now stated firmly that I was one of the men who had robbed them. Under cross-examination they stated that although they had failed to make even tentative identification on the two previous occasions they had had opportunity to do so, they were now quite sure. They said that they could not be mistaken and that they had never seen me at any time other than at the robbery. They also said that they worked in the main office of Glenton and Mitchell.

During the course of my sales career I had frequently visited the office in which these two witnesses worked. I had sold both business systems and stationery to the firm, and to do so I would have carried out demonstrations in the very office in question. I had a very strong suspicion that one of them had actually signed one of the orders I had taken from the company, which would have meant that I had spoken to him personally at that time. I accordingly applied for permission to have access to my order books, so that I could prove that the witnesses were mistaken, and they had in fact seen me previously in the normal course of business. Judge Claassen allowed me to put it to them that they were mistakenly identifying me as a robber, when in fact they recognized me from my business calls on their company. They were both adamant that I had never visited their office other than as a robber. The judge then refused me permission to have access to my sales books, which would have proved conclusively that they were mistaken, saying:

'The evidence of the witnesses is very firm. An inquiry into the content of sales-order books would be too remote from the issue of robbery now before us.'

My co-accused did nothing to help me. Perhaps they were afraid of incurring the judge's displeasure. When the case ended Judge Claassen took less than a minute to consult with his assessors. He found all three of us guilty.

I was sentenced first, as accused number one. The judge described me as a dangerous man from whom the public had to be protected. He sentenced me to eighteen years' imprisonment with compulsory labour.

Don Muniz was sentenced next. He had several previous convictions for armed robbery, and was serving a nine- to fifteen-year sentence in respect of two such robberies. The judge sentenced him to life imprisonment.

Charlie received a suspended prison sentence and five cuts with the heavy cane.

15

It was about 7.00 p.m. The prison van made its way down Hospital Hill, around Clarendon Circle, and turned into Jan Smuts Avenue, headed for Pretoria. I looked out and watched as we passed the apartment block where Georgina and I had set up home hardly three years earlier. Two police cars with armed occupants preceded us, and two more followed. The police carried FN rifles in addition to their side-arms – enough firepower to start a small war.

Don Muniz sat on the floor of the van opposite me. We were handcuffed and in chains and leg-irons. Half a dozen other prisoners were also in the van, but they edged away from us.

'Smoke?' Don offered me the butt of a cigarette he was drawing on.

'No thanks.' I shook my head.

We didn't try to speak – we were too stunned to do so. Neither of us had had time to understand the import of the sentences that had been imposed on us. We couldn't. At the court an hotelier I knew had pushed his way past guards to shake my hand before I was taken from the dock.

'I don't know how you can be so calm,' he said.

I had looked at him without answering. The fact was that the words the judge had pronounced had no meaning. They were outside anything I could relate to.

'Eighteen years . . .'

It was meaningless. He could just as easily have said forty years. There is no way that any man can grasp the meaning of such sentences. The mind trips out and cuts off when faced with the unreality of it. My experience has been that the effect of such sentences is to inculcate a bitter sense of injustice in those who receive them, a sense of shock in those members of the public who would never commit crimes anyway, a sense of grim satisfaction amongst those who feed on revenge, and at the same time disbelief and a strange hero-worship in those young people most likely to offend. The sentences seem to ensure rather than prevent recidivism on the part of those who receive them.

Within an hour of our return from court to the Fort, Charlie had received his five cuts. He was now being held in prison whilst Don and I were transferred to Pretoria. The authorities were apparently afraid that I had friends who would try to break me out of prison, and they had mounted a massive security operation which included preventing Charlie tipping anyone off about my transfer to the 'Big House'. They need not have worried – no one had any interest in my movements. The only visits I received over the next twelve years were from two ex-prisoners and a girl I didn't know.

The prison van bucked as it went over a ridge in the road, and we bumped about the floor. I looked at Don and he grinned wryly. The van driver was maintaining a steady high speed, and we covered the thirty-five miles to Pretoria in under forty minutes, despite the evening traffic. As we turned into the private road leading to the prison I looked through the air-vents and saw the crenellated walls of South Africa's premier prison. Here up to seven hundred of the most dangerous white prisoners were held. Here non-white condemned prisoners were housed, and hangings took place with grim regularity on the gallows in B2 section of the prison.

The entrance to Central Prison is like that to an ancient fortress. Two large reinforced doors form the main gates and a heavy portcullis immediately inside the gates, providing additional security, is still in place; but its use has been made redundant by a modern, massive, steel grille set solidly in the granite walls. We were surprised when the main gates to the prison were swung open and the steel grille was rolled back to admit the van. These gates were seldom used. The driver manoeuvred the vehicle into the small courtyard inside the walls, and the gates were closed and the grille rolled back into place. Then the door of the van was opened and the prisoners who had travelled with us were quickly taken out. Moments later Don and I were ordered to clamber out.

I stood up, my chains in one hand, pleased to be able to stretch after the cramped conditions in the van. Lt-Colonel Gouws, newly promoted after attacking John with his little dog at the Fort, was now the officer in charge of Central Prison, and he had stayed on duty to see us arrive.

I grimaced as the chains rubbed against my shins – the whole situation seemed farcical. I had hurt no one, yet I was being treated as a dangerous violent man, sentenced to eighteen years' imprisonment with compulsory labour, placed in chains, and held in South Africa's toughest prison.

A reception guard snapped to attention and saluted Lt-Colonel Gouws, and I flippantly saluted him too. The gold braid on his cap seemed to glitter with indignation as he drew himself up. He was furious.

'Moenie met my speel nie!' he shouted. (Don't play games with me!)

I was tired and mentally drained, and I laughed at him – and Don laughed too. We both knew him for the pig of a man he was – I didn't feel angry: I felt contempt for him.

We stood there for a few seconds, in the evening light. To the left were the prison-administration offices and visiting-rooms; on the right was the hospital dispensary and guard rest-rooms. Then the tableau came to life and the guards hustled us through a heavy steel door into a wide windowless passage leading to the reception office and main hall. Immediately inside the door to the passage we climbed wide steps and made our way to reception. The office had been cleared to receive us and we were quickly finger-printed, given a change of clothing and fitted with new chains and leg-irons. As soon as reception procedures were complete we were taken through the main hall, a huge domed expanse, rising more than fifty feet from floor to curved roof girders. Heavy steel grilles were fitted to all four sides of the hall, and wide, polished steel gates clanged as they opened and closed, giving access to all sections of the prison. On our left was A-section, housing the induction unit, where psychologists assessed new arrivals on the ground floor, and with accommodation for privileged prisoners on A2 and A3 landings. The induction unit was nicknamed the 'Mad House'. On our right as we crossed the hall was C-section – housing the prison's main clothing store and accommodating non-privileged prisoners on its three landings. Directly ahead of us was B-section, and as we walked towards it a prominently displayed notice ordering 'Stilte – Silence' stared down at us.

The ground floor of B-section was taken up with punishment cells in an isolation unit, and the prison's notorious segregation unit. Both of these units were sealed off from the rest of the prison. The floor above was B2, and this, too, was sealed off as a separate unit housing the gallows, cells for condemned white prisoners, and a separate part for non-white condemned prisoners – a unit solely for men awaiting execution by hanging. Above B2 with the condemned prisoners, B3 and B4 landings accommodated still more men – prisoners who were not on any privileges.

Our escorts hurried Don and me across the main hall, and it became clear that the authorities were not going to waste time with assessment procedures in the 'Mad House' for us. We were taken directly to the segregation unit. We had travelled less than one hundred yards through the prison under the escort of four guards, but when we arrived at the unit we were stripped and searched again. Then we were taken to individual cells at opposite ends of the unit – and that was the last time we met for almost two years.

The segregation unit was a prison within a prison; it contained some seventy cells, each with solid steel-plated door and steel grille. When the door was open the steel grille prevented movement in or out of the cell. I stood to one side as the segregation-unit guard opened both door and grille, and then I made to enter when he motioned to me to do so. He pushed me into the cell and the steel grille and door were quickly slammed and locked behind me. I moved more slowly to the centre of the cell and looked around me. I let my chains drop to the floor and they rattled and clinked against a steel ring embedded there.

The cell was quite large – twelve feet by eight, and more than nine feet from floor to ceiling – a very big improvement on the cell-cage I had occupied at the Fort. A window was set high in the wall facing the door and it was closed, covered inside and out by a close-mesh wire grille, effectively cutting off natural light. An air-vent provided ventilation, and it was placed high up the wall alongside the window, and covered with the same fine-mesh wire grille. The walls were painted a dirty brown to a height of some five feet, and the surrounds to the door, grilles and window were in the same depressing colour. Above the dirty brown dado, the walls and ceiling were a discoloured cream, crumbling patterns on them reflecting years of mildew caused by condensation. The floor surprised me. It was of parquet blocks in a pleasant light mahogany, about two inches by six in size. They were warm to the feet, and only later did I discover that the cracks and crevices between them provided ideal homes for bedbugs and fleas.

There was no heating and no furniture. My bedding was the now-familiar thin felt mat and two blankets. There was no bed-board, no trestle, no table, no chair, no locker. I was to sit, sleep and live on the floor. There was no pillow. A wooden spoon, a flaking tin mug, and a

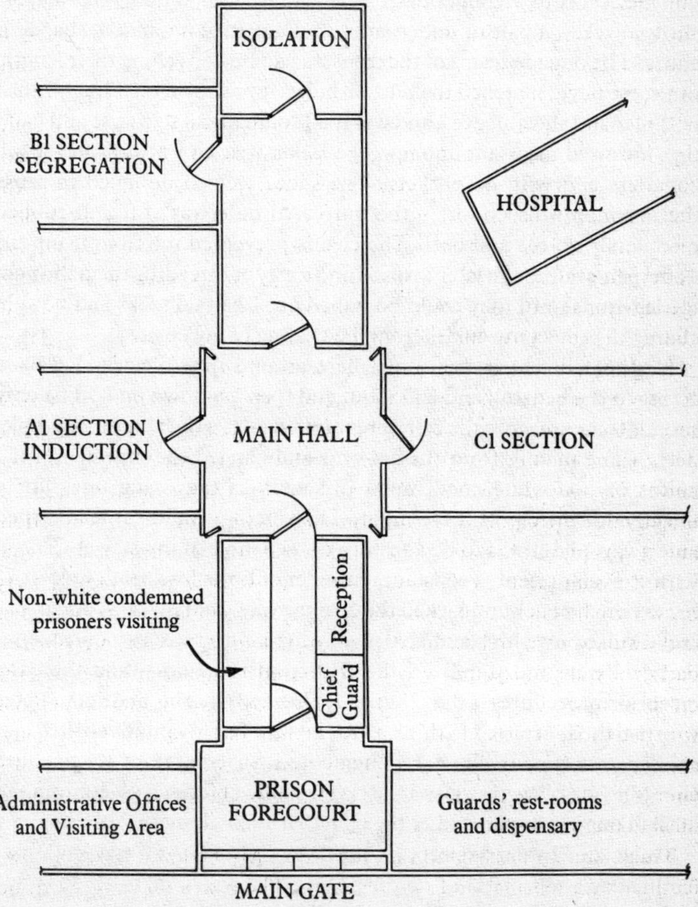

Figure 3 Plan of section of Central Prison, Pretoria (author's impression).

stinking piss-pot were the only articles in the cell other than the mat and blankets. Light was provided by a forty-watt bulb set in the ceiling and covered by a metal grille which absorbed most of its effect. I was to learn that this light was never switched off – it was operated by a switch outside the cell. There was no alarm system at all – the only way to attract attention would be by banging against the door.

The clothing I was given consisted of trousers, split the length of the outside seams to accommodate the chains I wore, a dirty-grey flannel shirt, a jacket, a pair of underpants, and a pair of untanned, shapeless shoes. The outside seams of the trousers had buttons along their length, but these never matched the button-holes opposite them. The shirt had no collar and short sleeves, and was made of material so coarse and hairy that it caused incessant itching. The jacket was several sizes too small, collarless and with no pockets. The shoes seemed designed to cause the maximum discomfort – the untreated hide was stiff and rubbed mercilessly on toe and heel. The chains prevented me from using the underpants, although later I was to find a way of threading them through the leg-irons until they could be pulled on. I had no socks and no shin guards to protect my ankles from the chafing of my chains.

I estimated that it was somewhere around nine o'clock. I walked across to the bed-roll and laid it out and then lay down on it. The only sounds that came into the cell were muffled so as to be almost inaudible. They came mainly from the air-vent and carried the murmur of the voices of non-white condemned prisoners as they sang unendingly throughout the day and the night. The singing would surge and then fade away, and it was to be a feature of the whole of my stay at Central Prison, ever-present, a constant reminder of how close death was.

I lay on my back and kicked the chains away from my legs, cursing as they bruised my shins and ankles. My mind was racing – court scenes flashed before me. I relived the trip from the Fort – and then the reception procedures. I thought about Don and Charlie, and about Peter who had died. I started to think about myself, but my mind rebelled and refused to register. Then I remembered Suzette, tears wetting her cheeks as she blew me a kiss and tried to smile before I was led from the dock. Today I can remember the pain that I felt all those years ago.

Much later I went to sleep.

16

One of the things that I became aware of early in my period in segregation was that I had no mirror. Somehow, if I could have had something that reflected a familiar form it would not have been so bad – but I was completely alone, cut off, isolated.

My cell door was opened in the morning and a tin bowl with a half-pint of rough maize porridge would be pushed in under the grille. A four-ounce portion of dry bread accompanied it, and I had to hold out my tin mug through the steel bars of the grille to receive a half-pint of black, unsweetened, prison coffee. The bread was made in the prison kitchens and it was the best part of any meal. It was baked in small portions with rounded heads, and we called them 'katkoppe', or cats' heads; but it was often so dry that it was hard to swallow without any spread.

I was given a water jug on the morning after my admission, and I was allowed one trip to the recess to slop out the piss-pot, wash under a cold tap, and fetch drinking-water. Later I was given a bowl so that I could wash in the cell. At the time of my admission to the segregation unit, prisoners were allowed out of their cells only one at a time – and so I never saw another prisoner. I found it very difficult to carry a piss-pot, a water jug, a mug and a bowl, whilst holding my chains in one hand, but I learned to do it.

After breakfast the porridge bowl was collected and a low wooden stool was pushed into the cell. The bed-roll had to be made up and standing against the wall throughout the day, from unlock at 6.30 a.m., until the day shift went off duty at 5.00 p.m. I was allowed to sit on the stool during the day, provided I placed it so that it could be easily seen from the spy-hole in the door. In the evenings it was taken away.

Lunch was a stew – mainly of carrots and an indeterminate meat, with mealie-meal thickening. It often looked like dogs' vomit. The bread ration was what made it worthwhile. There was no tea or coffee.

Supper was a bowl of thin soup, either carrot or cabbage. It had little flavour and no substance, but during the cold winter months in the unheated cell it was welcome. It was accompanied by a bread ration and a mug of tea. Normally supper was served at 4.00 p.m., and after that nothing passed through the door until 6.30 a.m. the next day.

On Sundays the diet was supplemented by a one-ounce pat of butter. It was the only spread issued all week – for the rest the bread was dipped in tea, coffee or soup, or simply chewed on until saliva made it possible to swallow. There was no variation or choice in the diet – you either ate it or you starved.

Once a week I was given a clean shirt. Once a week I was allowed five minutes under a cold shower to wash and launder my underpants. Once a week I was given a sealed safety razor and a guard stood beside me as I tried to shave in cold water with carbolic soap and no mirror. The guard neither spoke nor appeared to have any interest in me. He took the razor when I had finished and walked behind me back to my cell, slamming the grille and the door as soon as I had entered.

There was a rule of absolute silence. I was only allowed to speak in reply to a direct question from a guard. In order to make a request I was told to stand to attention when my door opened and wait until I was asked what my request was. After being ignored once or twice I had endless arguments with the guards about this, and I took no notice of that rule. This type of treatment began to embitter me, and I found myself hating the people who were doing this to me.

Most of the guards were Afrikaans-speaking, and I took pleasure in annoying them by speaking English. It made me feel that I was getting my own back a little, and I enjoyed their embarrassment. Many of them had lost grandparents in the Boer War, and they remembered the horrors of the concentration camps that the British invented in that war. I became a sitting duck for their animosity. Sometimes as I sat in my cell I would become aware of the smell of tobacco smoke. All smoking requisites were strictly forbidden in the unit, and the bastards would creep up to my cell and blow smoke through the spyhole, trying to taunt me.

There were regular cell searches. Periodically two guards would burst into the cell, order me to strip, and proceed to search every crack in the floor, every seam in my clothing and bedding. I never left the cell except under strict escort and I never came into contact with any other prisoner. Yet these searches went on. The guards would accompany the search by talking to one another, ignoring me standing to one side in nothing but my chains.

'Die bliksem het dit seker weggesteek,' one would say. (The bastard has probably hidden it.)

'Ja, op sy gat, seker!' the other would respond. (Yes – probably up his arse!)

What they pretended to look for I didn't even care. I don't think they did either. It was just a routine – when they had chucked my clothing and bedding in a heap on the floor, thrown my mug and spoon in a corner, spilled my drinking-water and left the lid off the piss-pot, they would grunt contentedly and leave me to clear up the mess. Had they found me to be infringing any regulations they would have treated it very seriously. Punishments in the segregation unit were the same as they had been at Baviaanspoort Prison. They consisted of deprivation of meals, solitary confinement with spare diet or rice-water and, in serious cases, cuts with the heavy cane.

After I had been in segregation for some months my chains began to create sores on my shins and unprotected ankles. I was given a piece of dry gauze to put on the sore – but nothing to hold it in place. So I began to experiment with the locks of the leg-irons, trying to open them. It took me several days before I found a method of opening them. I knew that the locks were spring-loaded, and I found that by winding a strong thread into the key opening until it caught, I was able to jerk the lock open.

It was very tedious but very rewarding. It was too dangerous to do it during the day shift, but as soon as they had gone off and I knew that the door had been locked for the night, I put down my blankets and took off the leg-irons and the chains attached to them. I knew that if I were caught I could expect to be punished – but this was no deterrent. It was wonderful to sleep without the weight of the chains and leg-irons rubbing against my sore shins and ankles – and there was added pleasure in the knowledge that I was beating the system. I always made sure that they were replaced before unlock the next morning.

For six months I cheated my guards and slept without chains. There was, of course, no legitimate reason to put a man in chains in a doubly locked cell in a prison within a prison. I was a non-violent prisoner, the cell was never opened without at least two guards being in attendance – and so no security factor was involved. It would seem that mechanical restraints were used as a form of punishment, or as a corrective measure. They were imposed arbitrarily without any trial, and, indeed, their use was wholly at the discretion of the prison authorities. In my experience they were used unnecessarily and vindictively. If the intention was to break people, or to make them amenable to authority, then mechanical restraints were a failure. All the prisoners I spoke to regarded them as I did – as inhuman, unnecessary and arbitrary. They induced contempt for those who sanctioned them, and a hatred for the system that allowed them to be used. They were an ever-present reminder of the inhumanity of that system, and, perversely, they came to be regarded by most prisoners as a symbol of a man's refusal to submit to the system – a badge of rebellion.

At that stage of my stay in segregation I never saw another prisoner – but I was not alone. The deprivation I suffered was shared by many others whom I would never meet. Every man in the unit was systematically cut off from any normal contact with fellow human beings. Some of the men were in chains, but every one of them suffered, as I did – silent, unseen victims of an inhuman, hateful regime.

After about six months of unchained sleep I was caught by the night shift without my restraints on. The next day, as soon as my cell was opened, I was taken to the blacksmith's forge in the prison workshops. There the smith forged and fashioned rings of steel to encircle my ankles, and when he had fitted them to me he lifted my feet on to his anvil so that he could rivet them in place, firmly attaching the chains to them.

Back in my cell I cursed my bad luck – but it was not quite finished. Before the dayshift went off duty they came into my cell with a large Yale padlock. They used it to fasten my chains to the steel ring in the centre of the cell floor. Now, between 5.00 p.m. in the evening until unlock at 6.30 a.m. the next day I was unable to walk up and down in the cell. My movements were limited to a two-and-a-half feet circle around the ring in the cell floor. When I tried to move farther than that the chains pulled me up sharply, cutting into the sores that had opened on my shins and ankles.

Day followed interminable day – I became less and less able to relate to what was happening to me. I seemed to become detached from my surroundings, able to stand outside my body and watch myself, my mind refusing to admit that it was me these things were happening to. Each morning the day shift unlocked the padlock that fastened me to the floor, and each afternoon they replaced it before going off duty. Day drifted into night, and night into day. I began to hallucinate – I would imagine myself on a beach, lying in the sun, listening to the surf breaking on the sands. I imagined a seagull wheeling overhead, and a light breeze broke the heat and cooled me. The fantasy became so real that at times I believed I could actually smell the ozone in the air. Hours would pass by as I lay dreaming – then the leg-irons would chafe against a bruised shin, rudely calling me back to reality.

As time passed I found it easier to escape into dreams. I would lie down and relax, consciously slowing down my breathing. Gradually the pain and the tension would leave me – and as my mind began to wander among my memories it found fulfilment for a subconscious need. I would drift away into fantasy and relive the moments my memory had treasured for me.

Perhaps I was becoming a little mad – perhaps this was a good thing. It served to lessen the pain, and it provided an escape from brutal reality.

17

One of the cruellest things that can happen to a man is for him to be placed in an environment that offers no response to, or stimulus to, his senses. The segregation unit was designed to cut a man off from anything his senses could respond to – the drabness of the cell was calculated to bore rather than to stimulate. The sameness of the routine tended to submerge one in indifference, and the almost total silence, hour after hour, day after day, was unnerving at first and then grew into a tension that generated fear. I would feel the tension build up inside me, a hard knot in the pit of my stomach, and I would hold my breath, afraid to break the silence, afraid that in some way I did not understand, to speak would cause me to be harmed. Whilst the silence rule may have reinforced this feeling, my experience was that silence of itself was capable of causing tensions that mounted until my nerves seemed strained and taut – and I wanted to scream my defiance of it, but dared not do so.

The complete absence of sentiment or texture in my surroundings meant that responsive feelings became disused – and as my senses fell into disuse a feeling of helplessness and hopelessness seemed to be born; helplessness and hopelessness that heightened a very real feeling of fear. To escape the pain that attached to these feelings I became more and more detached from my real circumstances. I drifted into hours, days and sometimes weeks of fantasy – and then into deep depression. When I was conscious of what was happening, I hated – and I think that this was the first time that I became aware of hatred in me. It seems strange that the very negativity of my surroundings, the sense of hopelessness and of helplessness, the fear – these things gave birth to hatred.

Whereas before I had viewed the guards with contempt, I now began to identify them as individuals, and I hated them. I would think back over my trial, the sentence and the treatment I was receiving, and I would be aware of a burning hatred for each person who had contributed to it. It is difficult all these years later to recall each of my feelings at that time, and it is painful to relive the torment of segregation; but given the direction that my mind was taking, and my reaction to the negativity and deprivation imposed on me, it was inevitable that at some stage my abhorrence of the system and those who administered it should break out – and it did.

I had been in segregation for about nine months, and my nerves were stretched so that the slightest annoyance made me want to explode. I wanted to shout at the guards who watched me – and in my mind I did shout at them, but months of silence had made speech a rusty vehicle, and I stayed silent. It seemed to me that the cell searches were becoming more and more frequent – I don't know if that was true, or if I imagined it; but certainly I believed it. I hated the degradation these searches entailed; I hated the way the guards stripped me and hurled my clothes and blankets around the cell. They seemed to be consciously trying to provoke me – they were always the same, rude and joking at my discomfort.

'Where have you hidden it today?' they would ask.

I would not respond – I tried to ignore them, hoping that they would get it over with and leave quickly. The senior guard would wink at his partner.

'He's got it up his arse again,' he would say – and they would grunt mirthfully like the pigs they were.

One day they went beyond talk. It had begun in the same way; the same remarks, the same crude jests. But this time the senior guard looked up speculatively.

'We'd better check his arse today,' he said quietly.

There was a short silence, and they both watched me expectantly. I pretended they had not spoken and tried to ignore them.

'Come on, bend over. Let's see what you've got up there.'

The senior guard motioned to his partner and they began to move in towards me. I stood watching them until they tried to grab my arms – and then something snapped. All the anger that I had hidden now seemed to explode inside me – it rose in a thick, black bile of hate. I shouted, cursed and screamed at them, lashing out in mindless anger.

It seemed that I was fighting for ever, but it was probably only for a few minutes. The guards quickly recovered from their initial surprise, and they made use of their rubber truncheons and called on their colleagues to help them beat me unconscious. I was tripped and knocked down to the floor, and I lay naked, stunned by the blows, trying desperately to cover myself, trying to roll into a ball as they systematically beat me. The pain seemed less important than the overwhelming sense of injustice and helplessness. I struggled to get to my feet, but I was knocked down. The hot spewing anger that had raged in me now turned into cold unreasoning hatred. I felt the solid rubber truncheons smash against my head, I felt the shock and experienced the pain. Instinctively I tried to avoid the blows – I was dazed and unable to reason; but before I was knocked unconscious something in me hardened and changed.

When I regained consciousness I was lying on the felt mat in my cell. I was naked – except for a strait-jacket. As I realized where I was and felt my bonds I started to panic. I have suffered all my life from mild claustrophobia, and now I struggled to free myself from the constraints of the strait-jacket – but all I managed to do was to work it up my body, so that it began to choke me. As my position worsened my panic rose, and I began to lose control. I blacked out momentarily and fell back on the mat, and when I came to I was gulping hugely as I tried to get air into my lungs. I tried to calm myself, but the jacket collar bit into my windpipe, and I felt panic take over. I heard the cell door and the steel grille being unlocked and opened, and as though in a haze I saw the two guards standing over me watching me, their rubber truncheons swinging loosely in their hands. Then they bent down and pulled the strait-jacket back into place and tightened the binding. Having done this they left, without a word, and locked the cell behind them.

The next day the strait-jacket was removed – and the padlock that fastened my chains to the floor each night was taken with it. From that day on my cell searches became less frequent and not so thorough. I was able to pace my cell at night, and although the chains and leg-irons remained riveted to my ankles, I had much greater freedom of movement when sleeping.

After several months on the diet issued in the segregation unit, I found that I was losing weight. I was becoming very thin – and I was becoming increasingly hungry. This was especially true during the cold months of winter. The lack of heating in the cell, and the enforced inactivity combined to tire me, and I began to feel weak. I asked a guard if I could have extra food.

'Jy moet die doktor sien,' he said.

So I was taken to an office to see the doctor. There were scales there – and I was weighed. I weighed just under ten-and-a-half stones, five stones less than when I had been admitted less than a year earlier. Standing well over six-feet-three-inches tall, I was clearly underweight. The doctor was a man called Jack van Druten. He said nothing to me; he grunted and made a note in the book in front of him. The guard told me to go back to my cell and two other guards moved in and escorted me back to it, slamming and locking both the grille and door as I entered.

Two days passed and there was no change in my diet. I asked a guard what had happened. He went away to check what the doctor's instructions were.

'You must ask again when you've lost another ten pounds,' he told me.

'If I lose another ten pounds I'll be fucking dead!' I told him.

He just grinned and slammed the door.

The next day I noticed that my bread ration had been increased; everything else was the same – but the bread was the best part of the diet anyway, and I no longer felt so hungry. I don't know whether the diet was wholly responsible for my loss of weight. I sometimes wonder if my metabolism altered under the stress and tensions of conditions in the unit. When I eventually left there, the diet I received was no better – yet I put on weight. So perhaps nervous stress did affect my body functions, and in particular my ability to convert food efficiently.

Each morning the officer in charge of the prison would carry out an inspection of the unit. He was accompanied by the chief guard, and they marched along in fine military style, swagger sticks held proudly under their armpits. They were supposed to hear complaints and inspect prisoners – to make sure that no one had suffered illegal injuries. It is significant that it was officially considered necessary to hold these inspections. Illegal assaults were pretty common and, for reasons I never understood, it was felt that if the officer in charge of the prison carried out an inspection and said he hadn't seen any injuries or assaults, then none could have occurred. No one ever admitted that the officer might ignore injuries, accept fatuous explanations from his staff, or refuse to listen to complaints. All these things were common during my stay in segregation.

When an inspection was due the guards would begin to scurry around to see everything was in order. One of them would stand at the entrance to the unit and peep out of the steel-plated door, to get an early sight of the inspection party. The guards seemed to live in fear of the officers, and I could never understand that. During my time in segregation, the officer in charge was Lt-Colonel Gouws, an inefficient pig. I couldn't understand anyone fearing him. I loathed him and had contempt for him – but I didn't fear him. Yet when the guards saw him coming they would check their uniforms and snap to attention and shout so that the sound carried to most cells.

'Aandag!' they shouted, ordering us to stand to attention.

We were supposed to stand on parade behind the grille in the cell, so that when the door was opened we were ready for inspection. I could hear cell doors being opened and then slammed shut as the officer and his party moved along the unit from door to door. A guard hurried along ahead, opening the cells and another followed behind closing them. I was instructed to stand at attention behind my grille and, when the officer passed, to state my name and number and the reason why I was being held in segregation. I remonstrated that I had not been told either why I was in chains or why I had been placed in segregation – and the guard went to make inquiries.

'Jy het in Johannesburg ontsnap!' he said belligerently when he returned. (You escaped in Johannesburg!)

'I haven't been found guilty of escaping from anywhere,' I told him. 'And I'm not going to stand to attention for that shit, anyway!'

'You'll be sorry,' the guard warned me – and slammed the door.

I held to my position. It was true that I still had to face the second charge of escaping from the courts, but it was unlikely that the state prosecutor would pursue it. My defence tactics made it something the attorney-general would prefer not to bring to trial. I made it quite clear that I was not going to admit to an unproven escape charge just to please Lt-Colonel Gouws – and still less was I going to admit guilt in a matter I had been acquitted on.

The next day my cell door was opened for inspection, and when Gouws appeared he found me standing at ease with my chains lying on the floor at my feet. He pulled up in mid-stride – and then turned away as I met his eyes.

'Hoekom is hy nie op aandag?' (Why isn't he at attention?)

The guard peered in at me.

'I don't know, Colonel,' he said.

Gouws turned to me furiously.

'Why aren't you at attention?' he shouted.

He spoke in Afrikaans and I ignored him, pretending not to understand. The chief guard stepped forward and thumped the grille with his swagger stick.

'Answer the colonel!' he shouted in English.

'I don't understand Afrikaans,' I said slowly. 'And I don't like being shouted at either.'

There was a stunned silence. No one ever spoke like that to officers. The chief guard seemed ready to explode.

'What's your name?' he almost screamed.

'It's on the door,' I shouted back at him.

'What's your number?'

'I don't know and I don't bloody well care,' I shouted.

'Why are you in segregation?'

'Because you are a bunch of pigs!' I screamed at him.

There was another stunned silence. Then Lt-Colonel Gouws found his voice and tried to salvage a little of his wrecked dignity.

'Sluit hom toe!' he shouted.

And the guard slammed the door.

18

The gallows at Pretoria Central Prison were situated not more than forty yards from the segregation unit, and the cells in which condemned prisoners were kept were close to the gallows, on the floor immediately above where I was held. At any one time upwards of eighty non-white prisoners were held awaiting execution, and access to the area housing them was sealed off, forming yet another prison within a prison.

White prisoners under sentence of death numbered not more than five or six each year. They were held in separate cells from the non-whites – and were always executed separately. Apartheid was strictly adhered to in execution procedures, and should it happen that a white man was due to be hanged on the same day as non-white men, then the procedure was that the white man had the dubious honour of being executed first – alone on the gallows. Forty-five minutes later, after the white man's body had been removed, the same gallows would be used to hang the non-white men – this time all together if more than one were to die. The true figures are a matter of public record, and I kept no tally of those grim occasions, but my memory is that some seventy to eighty executions took place on those gallows during each of the seven years I spent in Central Prison.

The gallows themselves were in a large room – over fifteen feet square. The floor was of pine planking, four inches wide and some seven-eighths thick, and as there was no ceiling beneath them, footsteps on them produced hollow echoes. In the centre of the room two wooden hand-rails had been placed two feet six inches apart, and they extended some six to seven feet across the floor. Above the hand rails, and centred between them, a three-inch diameter steel pipe had been secured, and

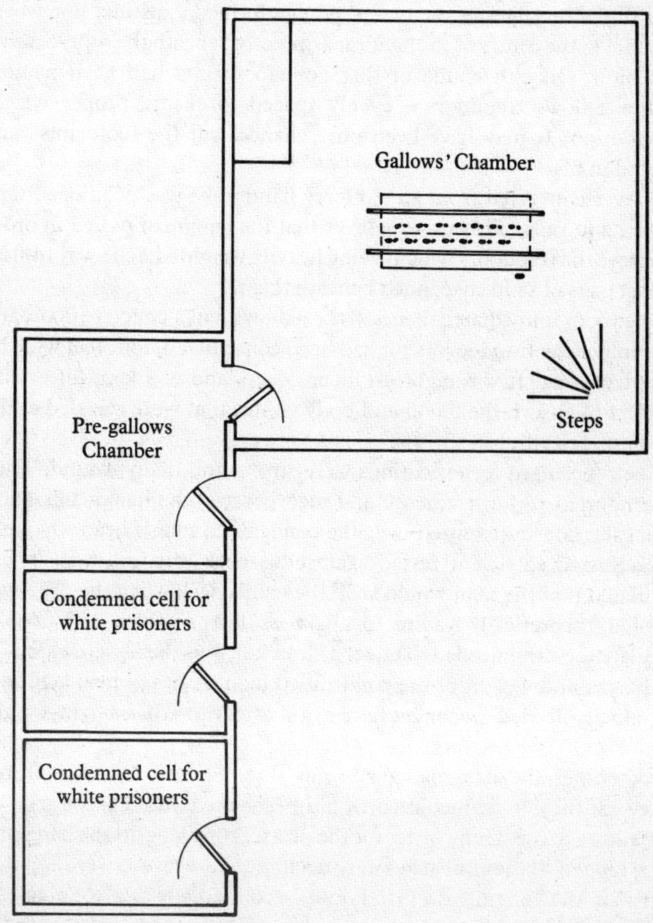

Figure 4 Floor-plan of part of B 2 section in Central Prison, Pretoria – showing layout of white condemned cells and gallows (author's impression).

it served as a stanchion to which the hangman's ropes were attached. The floorboards between the hand rails had been fitted so that they formed two heavily weighted trapdoors. They measured some six feet in length and were each fifteen inches wide. When they were raised they formed a platform level with the floor of the gallows chamber, and small metal staples were set in them so that they could be raised with ropes after use. The edges of the two trapdoors formed a distinct line where they met in the centre of the handrails, directly beneath the rope-bearing stanchion. On either side of that line, footprints had been painted on the gallows trapdoors – evenly spaced to ensure proper weight distribution. It may have been pure chance, but the footprints were painted in black.

A lever converted from an old lorry handbrake was positioned next to the hand rails. This was the lever that the hangman pulled in order to release the trapdoors which, being heavily weighted, fell away to slam against bags of sand suspended beneath them.

The room immediately beneath the gallows had a concrete floor, and in it, under the trapdoors, a pit had been constructed, four feet wide by eight feet long. It was eighteen inches deep, and was kept filled with sawdust to absorb the blood and body wastes that were released at the moment of death.

The ropes used for executions were strong and finely wound. They were knotted to form a noose and incorporated the hangman's knot. When the noose was fitted over the condemned man's head, the knot was adjusted so that it rested against his neck – in this way it was calculated that the knot would snap the man's neck when the drop was arrested, theoretically leading to a painless death. Tables were used to calculate the drop needed to effect a clean kill, and these were based on the height and weight of the condemned man. A heavy man achieved the velocity needed to snap his neck in a shorter drop than a light-weight man.

Sometimes the hangman made mistakes. Sometimes, in multiple hangings, the condemned men would become confused and file on to the gallows in the wrong order for the pre-set rope lengths the hangman had arranged. If these mistakes were not noticed the results were horrific. In Britain the hanging of a man is known colloquially as a 'topping'. In South Africa, a 'topping' had the grisly significance of a miscalculated rope length, which had resulted in the condemned man's head being torn from his shoulders and rolling bloody and hideous beside his

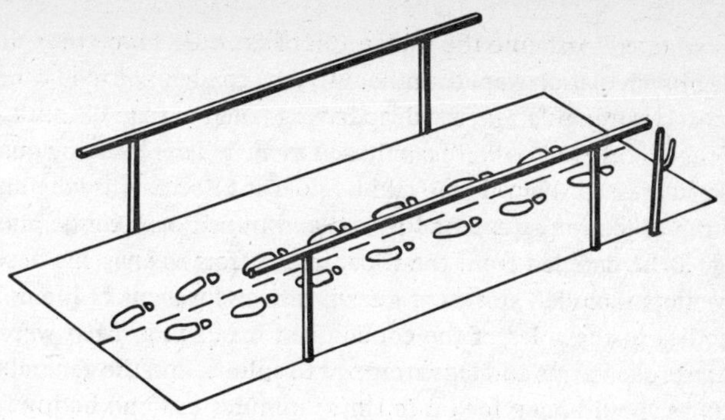

Perspective of the trapdoor

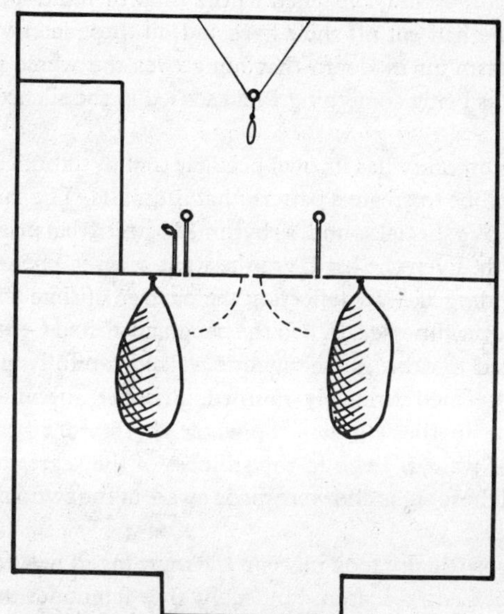

Cross-section of upper and lower gallows chambers

Figure 5 The gallows (author's impression).

decapitated torso into the waiting pit of sawdust. If, on the other hand, the miscalculation went the other way, the condemned man would suffer death by strangulation, the drop having failed to snap his neck. Reports of these occurrences were confirmed to me in later years by guards who had witnessed them. I was told by guards of occasions when members of the execution squad had jerked and pulled on a condemned man's legs as he dangled from the rope, in an effort to snap his neck. Other accounts included stories of guards testing for signs of life by sticking needles in the soles of the condemned man's feet. Men were hanged with broken arms and legs strapped to splints, and the general rule that bodies should hang for up to thirty minutes until all bodily functions ceased was not always adhered to.

In my cell in segregation I could not hear all that was happening, but there was no mistaking the violent thud as the heavy trapdoors were released and smashed against the restraining sandbags. I always knew when a hanging was planned – despite the lack of communication with anyone, I was able to sense it. In later years I saw men led to the gallows chamber and I listened as the thud of the trapdoors told me that the rope had cut off their lives and, in those later years, I recognized the grim air of doom that hung over the whole prison during executions as being something I had sensed in the silence of my segregation cell.

Every community has its own peculiar sounds – traffic, industry and people combine to create a pattern that is unique. The same is true of a prison – it has a special sound, a rhythm, a pattern that prisoners become familiar with. Even the hard, granite walls seem to breathe in a certain way, unyielding and yet reflecting the passage of time and the distress that they have witnessed. When the hangman visited Central Prison the walls seemed to draw in, the guards walked carefully and the ring of their keys seemed strangely muffled. Prisoners became quieter and avoided one another's gaze – the whole rhythm of prison life slowed down – and waited. Even in the stillness of the segregation unit men recognized those signs and were made aware of the awful finality of what was to happen.

Executions usually took place in the morning. The condemned men were held at Central Prison, but legally they fell under the authority of the Sheriff of Pretoria, and three days before they were to die the Sheriff would visit the prison. His duty was to inform the men that their appeals had failed and that the Minister of Justice had signed execution warrants.

The only hope left to the men at that stage was that the Supreme Court would grant a stay of execution – a relatively unusual occurrence.

The Sheriff was a small, wizened man; he had a severe malformation of one foot and a stiff left leg. He walked with the aid of a gnarled stick – a thick rubber cap covering its tip. As he negotiated the steps to the main hall of the prison and crossed it to make his way up the stairs leading to the condemned cells, he dragged his disabled leg along with him. He always wore a plain black three-piece suit. A wide-brimmed black hat added a few inches to his five-foot-three stature. His face was weatherbeaten and red – as though constantly exposed to the elements. Thick grey eyebrows set off his intense blue eyes. To the condemned prisoners he must have represented the bearer of bad news, and amongst many African tribes there was a tradition that the harbinger of evil tidings takes the form of a wild beast or bird – it was not difficult to understand why the non-white condemned prisoners called the Sheriff 'Black Crow'.

On the afternoon before a hanging the death squad tested the gallows. They poured oil on the hinges and greased the bolts. Nooses were prepared and the condemned men were measured and weighed – so that rope lengths could be calculated. The men who were to die were offered the traditional last meal, selected from a fairly wide menu. The prison padre offered them the comfort of his calling, and he would be available to them up to the time they took the final steps to the gallows. At the appointed time they were taken from their cells and led to a room adjoining the gallows chamber. Here they were comforted by the padre as their hands were tied behind their backs and a coarse hood was slipped over their heads. The hood had a flap which was raised so that they would not stumble as they took the final few steps to the gallows.

The singing of the condemned men never ceased in Pretoria Central Prison. It was an ever-present reminder of their presence. Usually it was subdued and came to me as a soft murmur of sound – but at times it would swell, and I would recognize hymns I had heard in my youth. As the condemned men made their way to the gallows they would join in singing a hymn, and a hush would fall over the prison as their voices were raised in supplication. The sound of their voices would ring through the prison, reaching out and stabbing at the emotions of every man there. The padre left them at the door to the gallows chamber and they took the last few steps alone. Guards guided them on to the gallows, lowered the flap of their hood and slipped the noose over their heads, tightening it so that the knot fell in the right position. Other hands bound the condemned men's feet together and, almost simultaneously, the hangman pulled the lever releasing the trapdoors.

The condemned man dropped the number of feet it had been calculated suited his height and weight – and if no one had made a mistake his neck snapped and he ceased to be conscious. His body would still twist and twitch as his heart sought to pump blood through terminally cut off blood vessels, and his lungs strained as they tried to force life-giving air past the constraints of the hangman's noose.

In my cell in segregation I sensed this ritual. I empathized with the men who walked that way and I shuddered as the thud of the trapdoors told me that it was done. Gradually a different set of values seemed to project itself. The horror of what was happening so close to where I lay, the recurrence of it, week by week, month by month, made my own suffering seem less significant. I seemed to become hardened to pain and solitude, indifferent to sorrow – and, perhaps, indifferent even to death itself. I was surrounded by a surfeit of suffering, more, much more, than the human mind could encompass. The mind raised its own barriers and found its own escape from reality – unable to bear the horror and the pain that pressed in on it.

During my stay in segregation I lay and listened as some 150 human beings were hanged. I never got used to it, but I learned to live with it. I never failed to be filled with a sense of the awesomeness of it – and I shall never lose the memory of it or forget the sense of horror I felt each time a hanging took place.

19

During my first year in segregation I had not conversed with anyone. The regulations allowed me one letter and one visit each six months, but I did not use this privilege. I was not allowed to smoke, there was no music, no reading or writing material – nothing was provided to alleviate the silence, the monotony, and the unending isolation. The only sounds I heard were those so loud that they penetrated the closed door – the ever-present sound of condemned men singing, the clash of keys and of doors being slammed shut. Gradually my senses fell into disuse, and as this happened I began to lose the ability to use them. I would hear a sound, but fail to identify it – it had no meaning if it did not relate to my immediate need. The key in the lock meant that it was time to receive food or to slop out – perhaps even to have a shower. But some sounds seemed to lose their meaning. I would hear a voice, but only with an effort was I able to relate it to a guard. I would stand nonplussed when spoken to – unable to register the fact that I was being addressed. I did not hear the words – just a noise – a background sound that did not seem to require my attention.

Sometimes when a guard spoke to me I would smile at him in reply – either not having heard a word or, having heard and understood, replied to him in my mind. My lips and vocal cords were so long unused that they seemed unable to form sounds. I struggled to form words in my mind, and then I struggled again in an effort to activate my vocal cords and break through the barrier of silence. I have listened with deep sympathy to a dumb person learning to speak, or to someone suffering from a speech impediment, and I believe I know something of how they feel. At that time I too suffered a form of speech deprivation akin to dumbness, and the frustration it gave birth to caused a sense of inferiority, a servility, and ultimately the loss of confidence that leads to fear.

My association with the guards changed too. Despite their treatment of me a curious relationship developed. It was not a bond – it was too tenuous for that – it was an understanding, a delineation of areas of yes and areas of no. Parameters developed outside which neither my guards nor I would venture. They no longer insulted me or demeaned me more than their duty required. Gratuitous abuse ceased and I, in turn, ceased to act provocatively. As this understanding continued an element of trust developed – and with that trust came a mutual respect. It may sound incredible that I could ever have developed respect for guards who had physically assaulted me, and who continued to enforce inhuman deprivation – but such are the vagaries of the human mind that it did in fact occur.

As I built barriers in my mind to shut out the pain of what was happening, I developed a fragile toughness, a resilience and indifference to it all. I recognized this same indifference in my guards, and perhaps unconsciously I imitated their attitudes. And so a link, a tenuous point of reference was established between the prisoner and his guards – each indifferent to his circumstances.

At about this time we were suddenly given work to do in the cells. Each morning we were given ten dilapidated mailbags. Many of them were so rotted that any attempt to pull stitches through the material and tighten them simply resulted in the creation of a bigger hole next to the one you were trying to repair. No one ever completed ten bags in a day, but provided you worked steadily no action was taken. Those who refused to work were punished by deprivation of their food. For my part I was pleased to have something to do. It was a change from staring at the walls and pacing the floor.

Another innovation was the introduction of exercise periods; half an hour each morning and afternoon. An enclosed yard had been created next to the segregation unit, and inside it a set of exercise cages had been constructed. The cages were triangular – a spread of brick walls had been built, rather like the spokes of a giant wheel, and wire netting was spread over the walls to form a roof, and the whole structure fenced in with the same material. The result was eight triangular cages, each with its own gate – and they were so arranged that none was visible from any of the others.

Prisoners were taken to the cages singly, so that no one saw anyone else. They were unloaded in the same way. At first it was a peculiar feeling after spending a year in a semi-darkened cell to see the sky again. The six paces along the wall and four paces along the front of the cage seemed too strenuous. But after a few days the pleasure of breathing in air not completely tainted by the peculiar smell that clings to all prisons became a diversion not to be missed.

Looking back it seems strange that as I walked around my cage, my chains in my hand, I felt very grateful for this privilege. Sometimes a bird would settle on the wire netting of the cage, or a butterfly would flitter through the mesh, and I would watch it anxiously, willing it to escape, wondering that such things still existed. The touch of the sun and the warm breeze were things I had forgotten existed, and my senses were reawakened. I was intoxicated by these things, and the flights of fancy that accompanied this re-emergence of feelings were often so real that I dissociated completely from my surroundings.

The segregation unit took up the whole ground floor of B-section. It measured over two hundred and sixty feet in length, and an unobstructed passageway, some twenty feet wide, ran from end to end between the cells. The concrete floor of the huge area this passageway created had been treated with a compound that enabled it to be polished. It shone like a mirror, kept that way by prisoners working in silence with hand brushes and knee-pads. These were prisoners who were soon to leave the unit, and their brushes would tap lightly against the walls and cell doors of the unit as they passed, brushes stroking and polishing this huge indoor hall.

When it rained we were given exercise in this area between the cells. Ten to twelve men were taken out of their cells at any one time and ordered to form a line with twelve paces between each two men. Once this had been achieved to the satisfaction of the guards we were ordered to commence walking. Each man followed the man in front of him, careful to maintain the distance prescribed. We walked in complete silence except for the soft shuffle of ill-fitting shoes on the polished surface.

The names of all the prisoners in the unit were displayed on cards above each cell doorway, and it was forbidden to look at these names. So we walked with bowed heads, watching the heels of the man in front of us. An upward glance was sufficient to invoke punishment – and I discovered this when I tried surreptitiously to see which cell Don Muniz had been assigned to. The guard watching us saw my head move upwards.

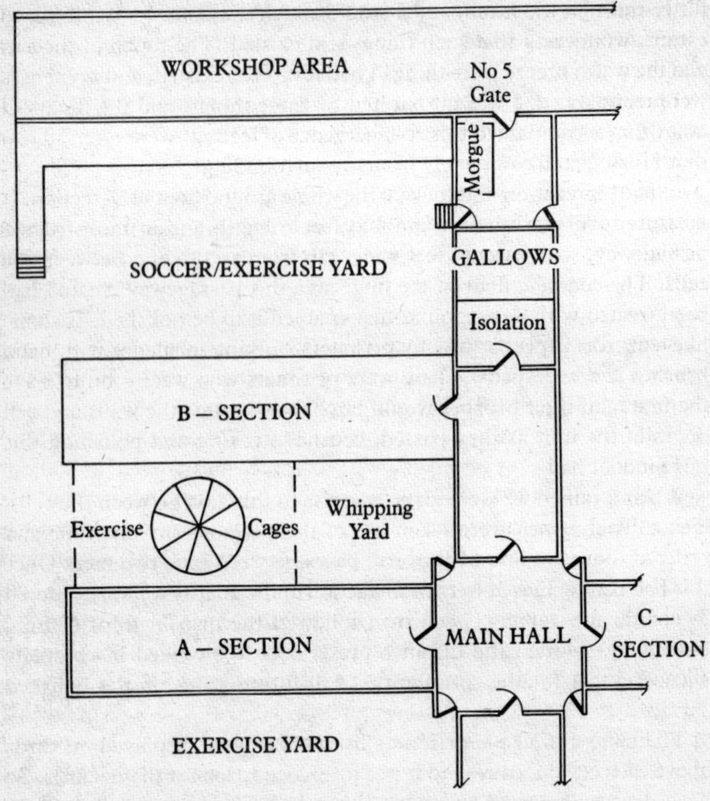

Figure 6 Plan of section of Central Prison, Pretoria, showing segregation unit, gallows and other features (author's impression).

'Jy het gekyk!' he shouted at me (You looked!), and he sounded furious.

I made no reply and after the exercise period returned to my cell in the usual way. The following day I waited for breakfast – but none came. I waited for lunch – but none came. At dinner-time I complained to the guard.

'Stilte!' he shouted at me – and slammed the door. (Silence!)

The next morning my breakfast appeared, and at the same time the senior guard briefly looked in at me through the grille.

'Jy het gekyk, en nou jy het drie maaltye verloor,' he said almost cheerfully. (You looked, and now you've lost three meals.) Then he slammed the door.

I had become so conditioned to confinement in my cell that at first I was ill at ease in the larger area of the unit. It seemed an awful long way to walk almost ninety yards along one side of the unit and then cross over and walk the same distance back again. The sheer size of the area seemed daunting. I had forgotten what it was like to walk so far in a straight line, and I remember that the freedom to shuffle along in that enclosed and segregated prison unit invoked a strange feeling of guilt at having so much space to move in.

A few days after exercise had been introduced, the guards brought me two library books. One of them was *Fame is the Spur*, by Howard Spring, and I think the other was *Fairoaks* by Frank Yerby.

'Julle kry twee elke week,' the guard told me. (You get two per week.)

I found it curiously unsettling to be presented with two books without any warning. At first I just looked at them, a little afraid to read the titles; then I put them aside and carried on with my mailbags. Later that evening, after supper, when the door had been closed for the night and I had put down my mat and blankets, I picked up the first of the two books. It was *Fame is the Spur*, and I didn't open it immediately. I turned it over and ran my hand along the worn binding. The title was blocked in silver letters on the spine with the author's name below it. At the base of the spine a library number had been inscribed. I opened it at the title page and saw that a library record sheet had been affixed there; there were several date stamps on it. I began to turn the pages until I came to the first chapter. Then I realized that I was weeping. There were no sounds that I can remember – but hot, wet tears were falling on to my hands and splashing on to the pages of the book. I cannot explain the feelings or the weakness that made me weep; I only know that I did so. That book was the first piece of literature that I had held in my hands for over a year. In later years I have seen copies of *Fame is the Spur* on library shelves and always, as though drawn by an irresistible impulse, I reach out and touch them. I no longer recall what the book is about, but over twenty years later, as I write these lines, my feelings are stirred by the memory of that moment.

Time passed much more quickly now. The day seemed almost too full of things to do. I had work on the mailbags, two half-hour exercise periods, mealtimes, slop-out and, now, books to read. I had to curb my hunger for the written word. At first I found that I read too quickly and on some days had nothing left to read; so I began to count the pages of the books I was given, and I divided their total by seven, rationing my reading and ensuring that I always had something to read each evening. I recall that I had little concern for the content of the books I received. What concerned me more was whether they were thick books or thin books – with plenty to read. I had no choice, no selection, simply receiving an issue of two books in exchange for those I handed back each week.

Some months after we received the books I was taken to the blacksmith's forge. Once again my feet were lifted on to the anvil – but this time it was to remove the chains and leg-irons that I had worn for so long. At first I found it strange to be without my 'jewellery', as chains were called colloquially, but I slept better, and I had greater freedom when exercising. But, best of all, the sores on my shins and ankles could now begin to heal.

During those months in segregation I had passed from despair to anger, from anger to indifference, and from indifference to a sort of gratitude for the small privileges that came my way. I have said that early in my days of segregation I became aware that there was no mirror in my cell, and one of the consequences of this was that I was unable to retain a memory of my own appearance. Later, when I had access to a mirror, it seemed to me that I was looking at a stranger, so greatly had I changed. Throughout my stay in the unit, the silence rule was so strictly enforced that even speaking to oneself could lead to punishment. Without regular use of organs and senses their normal functions became strange – unused and curtailed in the absence of anything to invoke them. But this does not mean that I quietly and meekly gave up, surrendering myself to the conditions I had been placed in. For many months I fought against the blanket of isolation and the deprivation that it brought with it. Even when my conscious mind had succumbed to the ennui of it all, my subconscious still rebelled and made me aware of bodily needs and wants.

The silence created its own special problems, leading eventually to difficulty in oral communication. The drabness of the cell and the dull lighting tended to depress, and the greyness of it seemed to enter the mind and colour its thinking. The long period of physical restriction in chains within the cell made me afraid at first to go out into the larger area of the unit, and at times I was only content when back in the familiar small greyness of my cell. Even the chains and leg-irons played their part in creating an environment I became familiar with, and therefore strangely at home in. My cell was my own, a place I had stamped with my presence, and having claimed it in this way I became anxious not to be away from it for too long – not to lose it.

I was twenty-seven years of age when I was placed in segregation, a young man, virile and aware of my body. I had known the joy of marriage and the love of a beautiful woman. These experiences did nothing to quieten the natural need for sexual fulfilment. The memory of them caused me a great deal of anguish and frustration – but as the conscious mind became submerged so my subconscious created its own relief. I can remember lying on the hard, felt mat on the floor of my cell, my blankets drawn over me, and becoming aware of the touch of soft hands, conscious of a rounded thigh. In the semi-dream state that mental ennui invoked I imagined that I was once again with a woman. So great was my need to touch and to be touched that my body and my hands responded of their own. In this quite natural and wonderful way, I found relief from the unnatural and cruel deprivation that isolation imposed.

When I look back now at the days and nights of physical and mental suffering, I wonder what the cumulative effect of it has been on me. There is no doubt that ongoing suffering changes the bearing and demeanour of those who are subjected to it. I saw it in the faces of the men around me on those rare occasions when we met. Faces carefully composed to show no emotion – grey faces of grey men, living grey lives within grey walls. Inevitably I became one of them.

The suffering was ever-present, and it deadened the senses and immobilized expression. Behind the mask lay the mind, submerged in a maze of pain, looking out through eyes dulled by the prospect they saw before them. A mind scarred by the memory of events that had long since passed, leaving only the pain behind them. These memories were too private to be shared, and the pain that revelation would bring forbade any impulse to expose them. I took sanctuary behind the wall of silence and I grew to accept the deadened faces around me. Behind that barrier I felt safe.

At times men broke down, and the silence would be shattered by waves of hysterical laughter. The sound of the laughter carried even through the closed doors of our cells. Minds rebelled against the pressures and reached out for the relief that hysteria could give. Sometimes the laughter was so infectious that it spread from cell to cell, from man to man, until the whole unit was filled with the cacophony of half-crazed men, fighting to cling to their sanity, caught up by this moment of relief and freedom from restraint and pain. The guards would shout and bang on the cell doors in an effort to stop the laughter, but neither they, nor the men themselves, had any control over it. It was unnerving and eerie to listen as first one man and then another exhausted his hysteria. The sounds of laughter changed until they were replaced by great sobs of exhaustion. Then even these subsided until the silence was complete again – broken only by a cough, quickly stifled, as though the man responsible realized that he disturbed us.

When the quiet had returned, our minds crept back behind the barriers we had grown used to. The only sounds then were the involuntary cries in the night – the cries of men who tossed on the thin felt mats that were their beds and, in dreaming, relived the moments they tried so hard to forget.

Today, over twenty years later, the memory of that time is still with me. As I write I can feel the pain and the emotions of that experience reawakened. I can feel the tears of frustration and despair, I can recall the anger and the hate, I can hear again the cries of men in distress and relive the moments of hysteria that took me to the edge of madness – and yet, I can be thankful that I am one of the lucky ones. I am one of those who survived the abuse of mind and body that that hateful regime inflicted.

After almost two years in the segregation unit I was transferred out into the general prison community. I was given a single cell, and I was glad of this retreat from the exhausting experience of sight and sound of fellow prisoners. The silence rule still applied, and on those rare occasions when it was possible to speak I found myself unable to do so. I was afraid to use my own voice. I had to relearn the art of speaking.

20

My first labour assignment after leaving the segregation unit was in the stone-yard. It had been set up as a form of punishment for those who rebelled, and I was sent there automatically. There were two sections – one handled the breaking of large granite blocks into smaller pieces of three cubic inches or less in dimension, and the other was where these smaller pieces of granite were broken down into chips.

Men breaking stones were kept apart from other prisoners, and there were about thirty of us at that time. The way the prison was run prevented very much contact between prisoners anyway, but the stone-yard detail was subject to very strict supervision. We left our cells at 8.00 a.m., and made our way in single file through the main hall, out on to the exercise yard, and then on to an area that served as a football pitch for privileged prisoners. Here a line of guards waited to search us. On this occasion the search was confined to a rub-down of each prisoner's clothing, in order to detect any unauthorized articles.

When hangings took place the prisoners making their way to work were often kept waiting on the football pitch whilst members of the execution squad completed their duties. Rows of prisoners would stand in silence facing the blank wall of the gallows building, whilst the sound of hammers nailing down coffin lids could be heard quite clearly. When the grim work in the mortuary was complete, we were marshalled in twos and counted by the stone-yard guards. They signed a register accepting us from the prison guards and, when they were satisfied, we were ordered to proceed. We filed through the gate between the gallows and the morgue, turned left past the morgue building, and out through No 5 Gate, into the workshop area. I was never able to pass through the area behind the gallows without being conscious of what went on there. Sometimes sawdust and splatterings of blood would lie on the steps leading from the gallows – inescapable evidence of what had so recently occurred. Someone had created a small garden opposite the morgue building, and I always found it grotesque that a man could carefully tend plants and create an area of normality in the shadow of the gallows.

We arrived at the stone-yard at about 8.30 a.m. It wasn't really a yard at all, but yet another cage. A corrugated iron roof was set on rough uprights some six feet from the ground, and those of us who were more than six feet tall had to stoop to get into the yard – and remain stooped whilst we were there. The corrugated roofing backed on to an inner prison wall, and the sides and front were enclosed with two-inch diamond-mesh wire netting, with a wire gate to provide access.

In the stone-yard the big hammer took up roughly one quarter of the area. There was only one man working on it and apparently it was a prized job. There was no daily quota attached to it – so long as there were sufficient small pieces of granite to keep the rest of the men busy, the man on the big hammer could pace himself how he liked.

The main working-party was placed in the centre of the yard, with the big hammer to one side and two open toilet-buckets and a water-tap on the other. The stench from the open toilet-buckets became unbelievably foul during the day. Two semi-circles of granite blocks were set out for us to sit on, fifteen blocks in a row, each block some three feet from those next to it, and with a space of some four to five feet between the two rows. We faced towards the front of the yard, and I was allocated a block in the back row from where I had a good view of what went on. The block I was given was twelve inches high – so I had to squat on it with my knees drawn up, or sit with my legs extended in front of me.

The initial break-up of the large pieces of stone was achieved with a fourteen-pound hammer, and the second phase was carried out with four-pound hammers pounding the stone until it was reduced to chips that would pass through a quarter-inch sieve. I was given a piece of one-inch hoop-iron, fashioned so that it formed a circle at one end, the other end serving as a handle. A flat piece of granite formed the base on which I was to strike, and a four-pound hammer and a pair of goggles completed my equipment. The circle at the end of the hoop-iron was about five inches in diameter, and I held the small granite blocks in it while I tried to crush them into chips.

Many types of labour have been described as soul-destroying, but of all those I have experienced nothing can match the breaking of stones. It might be supposed that the chance to dissipate energy and frustration by smashing a hammer into granite would serve as a release for tensions – but this was not my experience. As the hammers rose and fell, a discordant chorus of steel on rock developed, and the sound of it rasped against and frayed the nerves. The hammer, smashing into hard rock, bruised and jarred the hand that held it. After half an hour on the morning I arrived, huge blisters had developed on my hands – but the hand itself had gone numb and so they were not painful. Gradually the numbness advanced through my wrist until it enveloped the whole forearm. Under cover of the numbness, my hand continued to blister until the skin broke, and blood and pus oozed out. I was given no treatment for these sores. I used a dirty rag as a bandage until my hands hardened and calluses formed and took the place of the blisters.

Any change in the tempo of work in the yard, or any break in the continuous ring of hammer on stone, brought sharp, guttural reproof from the guards. They stood in a semi-circle at the front of the yard facing the prisoners, batons swinging loosely in their hands. Outside the wire-mesh other guards stood alert – with rifles to hand.

I joined the stone-yard gang in the late spring – and soon it was summer. The high veld sun was merciless as it beat down on the corrugated roofing, and the metal became so hot that it burned if you touched it. We were dressed in thick, hairy shirts and were not allowed to take them off. Sweat poured off me and saturated the thick moleskin-type trousers we wore. Thick woollen socks and ill-fitting, untanned shoes completed the dress. As the sweat poured off and dried it left a deposit of salt that caked and became hard under the armpits. Gradually this built up, until it began to chafe the skin and combined with the hairiness of the shirt to cause a rash of purulent sores. The granite block I sat on caused sores on the upper thighs and buttocks at first, but after a while these went away and I became used to the hardness of the seat.

The goggles were really simple gauze eye-shields, and these were supposed to protect the eyes from the chips of granite that flew from the hammers. They did nothing, however, to stop the fine dust filtering into sweaty eye-openings; dust that covered absolutely everything. It found its way into shoes, trousers and shirts – it stuck to perspiring skin, and it showed its abrasive qualities when you tried to rub it off, leaving the skin more tender each time. After a little while the dust found its way into the throat. Nostrils began to itch and the throat went dry – men coughed and spat in an effort to get rid of the slime the dust had formed. It was an ongoing irritation, punctuated by the times a big chip would fly off and cut your face, hand or arm. Sometimes a large piece of rock would split under the hammer and smash into your ankle or shin, momentarily numbing, and then raising a throbbing welt.

The quota of chips required of each prisoner was half a four-gallon paraffin tin full per day. This may not sound like very much, but you had to work very hard to achieve it. At times the rock was so hard that it would take twenty or thirty blows to effect the initial split, and it became increasingly difficult to break down as the pieces got smaller. Dust was removed from what you had achieved before your quota was measured and, unlike the mailbag assignment in segregation, every man was expected to complete his quota in the stone-yard. Failure to do so resulted in the familiar system of punishments. It was very hard labour indeed and the guards took pleasure in niggling us and doing what they could to demean and provoke us. This was a punishment gang, and the guards made sure that it stayed that way.

The most common punishment was forfeiture of food – you didn't eat if you failed to achieve your quota, and if you didn't eat you were never able to achieve your quota. As in the clay quarry at Baviaanspoort it was a vicious circle – and the guards knew it and exploited it. It was said that if segregation had not broken you then the stone-yard would. I saw some men rise above the physical pain and abuse – but others were unable to, and I saw them break. Men wept and went mad with despair. I watched one day as a man took his hammer and smashed at his leg in a mindless frenzy, the hammer rising and falling in sickening thuds. He screamed and shouted abuse at the system and at the guards who rushed in to prevent him injuring himself any further. They wrested the hammer from him, and when they had secured it they made sure that he would not do himself further injury by knocking him unconscious with their batons before they carried him off to hospital. Men, desperate to leave the stone-yard, smashed their hands with hammers, or insulted the guards so as to have a day off when the misconduct charge was heard by the prison chief. Some men, unable to bring themselves to inflict injuries on their own person, pleaded with others to break their leg or arm, so that they could get temporary relief through hospitalization.

At times a man would steal chips from his neighbour, and furious fights broke out whenever this occurred – often resulting in both prisoners being taken to hospital before facing charges of misconduct. At other times I saw the guards deliberately kick a man's chips across the dusty earthen floor of the yard, making it impossible for him to recover them. Some time before I arrived one sadistic guard had done this to Johnny, a prisoner well known for his fiery temper. Johnny had completed his quota of chips and had gone to relieve himself at the toilet-buckets when a guard called Groenewald walked over and deliberately kicked his pile of chips all over the floor. The other prisoners saw what had happened and they waited as Johnny returned to his block to sit down. He looked at where his pile of chips had been and realized what had happened. A prisoner who was present told me what happened next.

Johnny looked up at the guards.

'Which one of you sons-of-bitches kicked my stones?' he demanded.

There was silence, and then one of the guards shouted.

'Stilte!' (Silence.)

'Stilte my fucking arse!' Johnny roared back. 'Which one of you mother-fuckers kicked my stones?'

There was a stunned silence – and then the guards began to move in, Groenewald a little ahead of the others. Johnny waited until he was close to him – and then he picked up his hammer and smashed it into his face. He smashed it viciously, again and again, into Groenewald's face and forehead. The other guards leapt forward and overpowered Johnny – they beat him unconscious and dragged him away to the punishment cells. Groenewald lived, but several operations failed to restore his faculties. He lived on as a walking vegetable, unable to speak or think for himself.

I met Johnny some years later, after he had given evidence to the Landsdowne Commission into prison conditions. He was still serving the twelve-year sentence he had received for his assault on Groenewald. I asked him how he felt about it now that time had taken the sting out of the memory.

'He was a bastard,' Johnny told me quietly. 'If it happened again – I think I'd do it again. Groenewald got what he deserved.'

In the heat of the summer, the sweat and dust in the stone-yard combined until it formed a thick film over every part of our bodies. Prison haircuts at that time were short, back and sides, and in the stone-yard we were given a very short crew-cut. Through the protective fine-mesh of my eye-shields it often seemed that I was looking out on a scene from a wild nightmare. Grey figures sat, unspeaking, heads cropped and lowered to look directly in front of them. Arms rose and fell with a complete lack of rhythm or unity. The thudding ring of the hammer crashing against stone sounded discordant and irregular. The dull, hard sounds were pointed by the sharp ring of chips flashing against the hoop-iron. The crunch of stone crumbling and the hoarse intake of breath as men tried to gulp in the hot, dry air – and the occasional sideways glance of goggled faces – all added to the unrealness of the scene.

The very harsh attitudes of the stone-yard guards were reflected in the treatment of prisoners in the prison workshops at that time. Conditions were very bad, and at one time a spate of self-inflicted injuries occurred. Men broke under the mental and physical pressures, inflicting dreadful injuries on themselves. One of South Africa's cleverest safe-breakers, unable to face the conditions, placed both his hands under the blade of a sheet-metal guillotine and held them there while the blade dropped and sliced away the knuckles and fingers of both his hands. I saw young men who had injected themselves with paraffin, the ulcerous sores on their legs and arms open and stinking as they cried out in pain. I saw men whose reason had left them rub human faeces into open wounds, causing terrible infections. Men smashed their feet and hands, their arms and their legs – they cut the tendons of wrists and ankles. Sometimes a man died before proper treatment was administered – others were permanently crippled, maimed and disabled. The actions of these men showed that this was a regime that was inhuman. It had no regard for human needs or values – it was sadistic in its planning and in the way those plans were carried out. It was a regime that drove men to acts of insanity and despair.

In the early days after my release from segregation, discipline was taken to extremes. After a few months I lost my single cell and was placed in a cell seven feet square with two other prisoners. There was hardly room to lay our three felt mats on the floor, and when we laid out our blankets they spilled over on to each other's mats. The bedding was placed directly on to the floor of the cell, and it offered little protection from the hardness of the concrete. We tossed and turned during the night, trying to ease sore hip-bones and shoulders, and quite frequently we trespassed on one another's sleeping area. The only furniture in the cell was a small table, and we placed it at the feet of the shortest man in the cell, so that he slept with his feet tucked underneath it. A water jug, wooden spoons and tin mugs were kept on the table, and a stinking piss-pot was jammed into one corner of the cell. I lived in these claustrophobic conditions for several months before I was again allocated a single cell.

Each exercise period, two guards would stand and hand out tobacco and a piece of brown paper to make a fairly large roll-up cigarette. Cigarette papers were unknown, and the tobacco was harsh, black, Magaliesberg pipe-tobacco. It 'blew your brains out' if you were not used to it. After the tobacco and the pieces of brown paper had been issued, the guards would light a taper from which everyone had to ignite his 'zoll'. All of this was carried out in silence, and as soon as the ritual was over we had to move six feet apart and proceed to walk around the exercise yard in single file, puffing at the 'zoll', and creating clouds of blue-black smoke. If your 'zoll' went out, as many did, it stayed unlit. Any man who tried to get a second light was punished by loss of meals. At the end of the exercise period we had to throw the butts of our roll-ups into a tin provided for that purpose. Under no circumstances were tobacco or any other smoking requisites allowed in the cells.

The standard of cleaning was very high, and any breach of orders about the arrangement of bedding or other cell contents resulted in summary punishment. Some prisoners would use the hours they spent in the cells polishing the floor until it shone like a mirror. The guards would take pleasure in scratching the surface of these floors with their hobnailed boots during daily inspections. I saw them stand and laugh at the reaction of men returning from work to find their cell floor spoiled, their blankets and personal possessions scattered across the cell. There was one guard called Potgieter, who had been nicknamed the 'Black Mamba' because he had a very dark complexion and was an evil bastard. The mamba is one of the deadliest snakes in the world, and to call someone 'black' in South Africa is highly derogatory in 'white' circles – so the nickname was very suitable. Even his fellow guards disliked him. One day he spent hours scratching every corner of the highly polished surface of a prisoner's cell floor with a sail needle. He said that he was looking for a flint which he believed the man had hidden in the polish on his floor – but, in reality, he well knew that the man didn't smoke. His action was typical of his sadistic behaviour towards prisoners – and he knew and exploited the fact that petty niggling and interference was more likely to aggravate than straightforward abuse. Shortly after the incident with the prisoner's floor, there was a rumour that some prisoners planned to kill Potgieter. He was taken off normal duties, and Jack Sanderson, an old-timer, told me what had happened.

A prisoner had been sentenced to serve thirty-five days on rice-water and spare diet in an unheated punishment cell. It was midwinter, and with his resistance lowered by the freezing conditions and lack of food, the prisoner contracted pneumonia. Jack van Druten had examined him and ordered that he complete his sentence there in the punishment cell. When his sentence was complete the man had made his way back to his section from the isolation cells. He was light-headed from enforced starvation and the effect of the pneumonia, and he failed to notice that the top button of his jacket had come undone. Potgieter, the 'Black Mamba', had accosted him in the main hall of the prison, ordering him to fasten the button. As the man did so he became giddy and fell forward, brushing against Potgieter as he fell to the floor. Whilst the man lay stunned at his feet, Potgieter pulled his baton and struck him about the head.

They carried the prisoner to the hospital – unconscious. Two days later he died without having regained consciousness. No one was ever charged with his murder. I have no doubt that Jack van Druten, the prison doctor, certified death from natural causes – like heart failure.

One thing did happen – the 'Black Mamba' was never again allowed to work with white prisoners. The last time I saw him, he was working as a guard in the condemned section, looking after the non-white men sentenced to death.

21

After I left the stone-yard I went to work in the paint-shop. It was whilst I was there that I had the opportunity to visit the gallows. We had been given the job of repainting them, but, for reasons I never did discover, the job was taken away from us after our first visit and given to two guards with painting qualifications. The description I have given of the gallows is based on what I saw at that time. My change of job led to a cell change, too, and I found that I had a little more freedom to meet and speak with other prisoners.

One of the men I renewed friendship with was John. He was the man who had tried to escape from his cell-cage at the Fort and had been attacked by Gouws with his little dog. He had been given a concurrent prison sentence for that attempted escape and assault, but had been sentenced to an additional six cuts with a heavy cane. It was shortly after I renewed acquaintance with him that he learned that his appeals against his sentences had failed, and that he would have to receive fourteen cuts with the heavy cane; six for the assault on the guard during the escape bid, and eight for the robbery he was originally convicted of. The law stipulated that no man could be sentenced to more than ten cuts with the cane at any one time, but the Appeal Court had ruled that the two sentences in John's case had arisen from quite separate offences, and that they were legal. When the court was reminded by counsel that a man now faced a whipping in excess of the maximum permitted by statute, and that to allow a point of law to permit such excessive punishment was a clear breach of the spirit and intention of the legislature's enactment, one of the judges remarked that the appellant had only himself to blame – if he had not appealed he would have received the eight cuts some time earlier, and would now only be facing six. I have no doubt that the ruling would have been different if the judges' own backsides were at risk.

The heavy cane is a solid rod of bamboo measuring anything between ten and fifteen millimetres in thickness ($\frac{3}{8}''$ to $\frac{5}{8}''$). The end of the cane tends to split when it is used, and so it is tightly bound with a fine cord for some three inches at each end – this prevents the cane splitting as it smashes into the flesh. It is approximately four feet long, and being of fibrous bamboo it could be fairly light, but the guards had developed a technique of standing the canes in a specially constructed deep can of salt water. The fibrous cane soaked up the water, becoming a heavy, pliant rod which whipped the flesh, cutting it open like the stroke of a sharp knife. The weight of the cane battered and bruised the flesh surrounding the open wound it inflicted.

To receive this sadistic punishment the prisoner was strapped, spread-eagled on a 'mary' – a heavy wooden tripod. The tripod had two fixed legs to which the straps were attached, and a hinged leg that could be used to lower and raise the prisoner from semi-horizontal to standing positions. Straps bound his hands together above his head and held his feet tightly against the tripod's legs. He was pinioned helplessly to the 'mary', naked, with rough pillows protecting his kidneys and upper thighs, leaving his buttocks exposed to the whippings.

John was a small man, and it was unlikely that anyone could lay fourteen strokes with the cane on his small backside without cutting across a previous stroke, or imposing one stroke on top of another. After the initial terrifying burst of pain the blow of the cane effectively numbed the area assaulted, and for this reason it was considered wrong to superimpose one cut above another – to do so would diminish the effect of the superimposed stroke, so lessening the victim's punishment and suffering.

When the time came John was taken to the whipping-yard, which was sited between A-section and B-section of the prison. He was stripped and strapped to the 'mary'. The prison doctor, the head of the prison and several guards had gathered to witness the caning. Usually a sadistic bastard called Faan Jonker inflicted this type of punishment, but my memory is that a huge guard, ironically called 'Human', was responsible for John's punishment. All the prisoners not employed in the workshops had been locked away in the cells, but none of the usual cell noises were heard. Everyone had stopped to listen, to share John's ordeal with him.

I could visualize the guard flexing the cane in his huge hands, and after what seemed like an age I heard the swish as it cut through the air – and then the sharp crack as it cut into the flesh. I held my breath and waited, expecting John to cry out, but he did not do so. After a long pause the cane whipped through the air again and smashed into the flesh. Still John did not cry out. As stroke followed stroke the pauses between them grew longer. This was a technique used by the guards to extend the agony. Sometimes they would ask the doctor to inspect the damage they had inflicted, and so create a break in the proceedings. All sorts of ruses were used to draw the caning out so that the prisoner suffered not only from the whipping but also from the tension and terror of waiting – not knowing when to expect the next stroke. I have heard men cry out – pleading with the guards to cane them and to end the suspense.

I listened in my cell as eight strokes were administered to John. The guard inflicted them slowly, and yet John did not cry out. I knew that he had to receive fourteen strokes and when the pause after eight grew longer and longer I wondered if he had fainted. If the prisoner fainted the whipping was stopped until he recovered. It was considered wrong to whip a man who could not feel the pain. If the victim died, as some did, then the balance of strokes were not administered. I had heard some guards complain about this. They received a bonus of a few pence for each stroke they administered and, incredibly, they felt cheated when unable to carry out the full quota.

As the stoppage became longer, it was clear that for some reason John could not receive his full quota of strokes. My speculation that he had fainted was not true. The doctor had been asked to inspect his buttocks after eight strokes and had decided that there was nowhere to place the remaining six cuts without superimposing them on those already administered. The whole exposed area had been torn open by the cane, and huge welts were rising rapidly where the flesh had been battered. The doctor decided that John should receive the other six strokes at a later date – after his buttocks had healed sufficiently for him to be able to feel them properly. A hospital guard poured iodine over the torn flesh and pushed a piece of dry gauze on it. John was then unstrapped, handed his trousers and shirt, ordered to get dressed, and then marched back to his cell.

I saw him some two hours later. He was sitting on the concrete floor of his cell, and blood stained the polished surface as it seeped through his trousers.

'John,' I said quietly.

He didn't answer – he sat with his knees hunched under his chin, his arms clasped around his legs as he stared into the corner of his cell.

'John?' I said again.

He did not seem to hear me – he appeared cut off, stunned, and in deep shock. I watched him for a few moments, but he didn't move, made no attempt to look up. I felt tears of anger and frustration building up in me. I tried to keep my voice calm as I called to him again.

'John. If there's anything I can do . . .'

I didn't finish the sentence. I couldn't. John sat quite still and I turned away to move along the passage to fetch fresh water from the toilet recess. Another prisoner emptied his toilet-bucket down the hopper, and I gagged on the stench of it.

'The bastards,' I muttered to myself. 'The fucking bastards!'

Gerry Payne was serving a four-and-a-half-year sentence for embezzlement. He had taken money from the bank which employed him. He had used it to pay for the hospitalization of his aged mother. He was a kindly man – totally bewildered by what had happened. Bewildered by what he had done and by what society's response to it had been. He had a weak heart and prior to his imprisonment received medication for it. Upon admission he was placed before Dr Jack van Druten and he informed the doctor of his condition. The doctor passed him fit and he was allocated to a cell on B4 landing – the top floor of B-section. He was given a job pushing refuse carts around the prison. The carts had been designed to be hauled by a team of two mules, but mules were quite valuable, so six prisoners were allocated to each cart instead.

Gerry Payne lasted just four days. His sedentary job had left him ill-equipped for hard labour – and his heart condition made it inevitable that he would not be able to stand up to the physical requirements of the job and the stairs he had to climb several times each day. He had a heart attack on the fourth day of his sentence.

The prisoners in the cells near to him heard him call for help. There was no alarm system in any of the cells, so those prisoners nearest to him banged on their doors to attract the guards. Soon the whole landing was in uproar, and the noise spread to the whole wing until two hundred men were bashing on their doors with tin mugs and wooden spoons.

The guards had been enjoying coffee in the main hall of the prison, preparatory to making themselves comfortable for the night. Eventually the din became so great that two guards went to see what was happening. They ran up and down the landings shouting and cursing. The response was inevitable – the men simply increased the racket, and in the end the guards gave up and went back to their coffee.

The prisoners did not know what was wrong with Gerry Payne. Those more than two cells away from him did not even know that he had caused the appeal to be made in the first place – the majority of the men just joined in as a way of relieving the monotony. When the day-shift guards opened Gerry Payne's cell at 6.30 a.m. the next morning, he was lying on his face on the floor. His hands were bruised and bloody from trying to attract attention. He had been dead for some nine hours.

Jack Sanderson was an Irishman. It was he who had told me about the assault by the 'Black Mamba' which led to the death of a prisoner. He was over six feet tall and weighed more than fifteen stone. When I met him he was in his early sixties and he had been in prison for more than twenty years. He was the most discontented and irascible man I have ever met – yet I found that I liked him and respected him. He told me that he had fled Ireland at the time of the troubles, and that he had been sentenced to death in his absence. Whatever the truth of the matter he was an unusual man. The guards were heartily afraid of him – he had assaulted a lot of them during his years in prison.

Despite the strict supervision he lived under, at some stage of his imprisonment he had managed to acquire a few oil paints. He had manufactured brushes from human hair and whatever other fibres he could find, and he had taught himself to paint. What emerged was a remarkable talent – his animal portraits were outstanding, and I recall looking at a kudu head he had painted and feeling an urge to reach out and stroke the fur of the animal, so real did it appear.

Those who had known him over the years told me that he had mellowed by the time I met him – but I could often hear him at night, shouting at a prisoner who had broken the silence by whistling.

'Stick that whistle up your arse!' he would storm.

Inevitably, some prisoners baited him, and he would rage as he shouted and cursed the offenders. He hated noise; he had spent so many years in isolation and silence that he could not get used to it. When the cell doors were opened the next morning, Jack would rush up and down the landing trying to identify who had been whistling. He looked comical at times, and several prisoners suffered by allowing their need to laugh to overcome their fear of the consequences. As far as Jack was concerned, the guys who laughed were the guys who whistled, and he didn't worry too much if he made a few mistakes. After giving the offenders a few good thumps Jack felt better, and he retired to his cell, muttering to himself – and then he would settle down and carry on carefully colouring a feather in the wing of a bird he was busy painting.

He was released on licence whilst I was at Central Prison, and so impressive were his paintings that he had received a commission to paint portraits of classic winners in the stables of one of South Africa's leading racehorse owners. He was given a cottage to live in and had ample funds made available to him.

A few weeks later he was re-arrested. He had gone into a local store and stolen a cheap alarm clock and some pencils. He was convicted of theft and sentenced under the iniquitous South African Criminal Procedure Act. Jack Sanderson was sentenced to serve a term of not less than nine years and not more than fifteen years with compulsory labour for the theft of articles valued at less than four pounds sterling. He was then sixty-seven years of age.

He died not many years later.

22

One of the things that I found most degrading at Central Prison was the compulsory strip-search. On our return from work each day we were met by a line of guards, strung out across the soccer yard. The system was that you were directed to a guard and then had to join the queue of prisoners in front of him waiting to be searched. As your turn came near, you were required to strip and stand in line naked, until you headed the queue. The guard took your clothing from you item by item, and after searching it threw it on the ground behind him. When the search of the clothing was complete the prisoner was required to open his mouth, expose his armpits and then turn and bend over, exposing his private parts and buttocks for inspection to show that he had no unauthorized article concealed on his body. The lines of naked men, the rude jests of the guards, and the ignominy of the search, made this a hateful experience. The strip-searches were held in the open yard, and the guards would drag the process out so that, in winter, prisoners stood naked and shivering whilst they waited in the queues.

Another prison routine that caused a great deal of ill-feeling was the Sunday parade. All prisoners, except those attending church or certified medically unfit, were required to stand on parade. Clothing had to be spotless, shoes polished, face clean-shaven, hair short, back and sides, with a crew-cut on top. Buttons had to be in place and the guards conducted the whole thing like a regimental inspection. We were made to stand in lines, dress off and maintain rigid attention. After waiting for up to half an hour the officer in charge of the prison would begin a thorough inspection of each prisoner, back and front. Punishments were freely handed out for dirty shoes, hair fractionally too long, loose buttons and other minor offences. Serious matters such as not shaving or making alterations to regulation clothing often led to solitary confinement and rice-water.

I was told that these punitive inspections were held so that prisoners could complain and report ill-treatment, and so that the officer in charge of the prison could detect injuries and take action when necessary. I saw a man standing with black eyes and with his arm in a sling. Lt-Colonel Gouws took the inspection, and he stopped when he saw the man and asked him what had happened.

'The guards assaulted me, sir,' the man said bravely.

Lt-Colonel Gouws turned to the chief guard who accompanied him.

'Hulle het hom goed gedonner!' he said with a smile as he passed on. (They gave him a good going-over!)

No action was ever taken against the guards.

The hospital was supposed to keep a proper record of injuries, but it was never complete. They very seldom kept a record of injuries that would embarrass the authorities. The doctor was a callous man. Jack van Druten had been a Springbok rugby trialist, but I never discovered where he had studied his medicine – no other doctors I have ever met used his methods.

I knew him from my admission in 1960, until my transfer in 1967. During the whole of that period of over seven years I did not hear him say a single word to a prisoner, and I met no one who had. I wondered if he had something wrong with his vocal cords, but I saw him having quite long conversations with guards at times – it appeared that he didn't consider it necessary to speak to prisoners. At hospital parade the prisoner was marched into his office, where he sat behind a large desk. A water-bottle and a glass were kept filled and stood on the desk beside him, and he would sip from the glass as you recited your problem to him. The guard in charge of the hospital, a lieutenant, stood behind the doctor's chair. Jack van Druten seldom looked at you, but when he did look up he appeared to be amazed that you were asking him to believe what you were telling him. Usually he had a pen in his hand, and as you spoke he scratched hieroglyphics in the report book in front of him.

He was a big man with deep, blue-grey eyes and fierce bushy eyebrows. His hands were large and roughened, and seemed quite ill-suited to his profession. The small finger of his right hand had been dislocated, and he had never had it reset, so that now it stood out and away from the other fingers, bent and deformed and projecting backwards – as though attached to his hand as an afterthought, upside down. It was quite eerie to watch the finger as it moved in directly the opposite direction to the rest of his hand when he wrote. It curled away and stood poised over his hand like a roused scorpion's tail.

The only sound that I heard him make was a grunt, and it was this that first led me to believe that he might have a speech defect. Later I wondered if he thought that speech would have been wasted on prisoners. A grunt is the only way to describe the sound he made – a grunt, just like a pig. Usually the noise signalled dismissal, but occasionally he would take a stethoscope from his desk and, turning in his chair without looking at you, he would grunt. This was the signal for the hospital lieutenant to tell you to go around the desk and stand in front of the doctor's chair, exposing yourself so that he could listen to your heart or lungs, or whatever else he had a mind to listen to. Another grunt would signal that the inspection was over and you were dismissed. You then went and waited outside the hospital office on a verandah that ran the length of the hospital. Later you were called and told what dressing or medication you had been prescribed. More often than not you were simply ordered back to work. Even if one allows that the doctor was visited by a large number of malingerers, I can think of nothing to excuse his callous treatment of the men who sought his help.

Occasionally Jack van Druten would act as the prison dentist, although I suspect he did so in breach of professional codes. He would seat the prisoner in a chair and hold him down with one huge hand as he drew teeth with the other. Sometimes he did this with no anaesthetic. On several occasions his brute-force approach to a difficult extraction left his victim not only toothless but with a broken jaw too.

I visited the dentist twice, and on one of these occasions Jack van Druten was officiating. He grunted and gestured to the chair. I was in a lot of pain, and van Druten stuck his fingers into my mouth, the deformed little finger poking up into my eye. I pulled away and asked what the hell he thought he was doing.

'He's going to pull your tooth,' the hospital lieutenant told me.

'No, he's bloody well not,' I said. 'He's not a dentist.'

'Then you'll have to wait until a dentist visits the prison,' I was told.

I did wait, without medication, and it was only when I went to Cape Town some weeks later that the tooth was attended to.

At that time a prisoner called Green was at Central Prison, Pretoria. He was serving a sentence for manslaughter. He was five feet ten inches tall, weighed some fifteen stone, and had developed his body so that he looked like Charles Atlas. He was tremendously powerful and very fit. He was also totally homosexual.

'Passive, my dear,' he would say.

He soaked pieces of red floor-rags in water to obtain colouring for use as rouge, and he was contemptuous of anyone who regarded him as at all unusual. He would stand at the grille separating C-section from the main hall of the prison and watch out for new arrivals. He scanned them anxiously, looking for a kindred spirit – and failing to find one he would turn his attention to a young man amongst the arrivals who took his fancy.

'T.B.H., my dear,' he would say, and it was some time before I realized that this meant 'to be had'.

It was said that no one refused Green – he simply overpowered them. He had blond hair and a striking Roman nose, and he took pains to maintain a suntan. Quite naturally he was nicknamed 'Blondie', and he accepted the name without apparent embarrassment. Occasionally he had bouts of violent behaviour, and then it took up to ten guards to restrain him. When the 'mood' was on him the guards would never enter his cell – they simply locked the door and used a firehose to fill the cell with water until Blondie was literally half-drowned and stopped raving.

He wrote poems, and those he asked me to read were rambling and incoherent; but you were ill-advised to criticize – and Blondie received good reviews of his poetry from whomever he compelled to read it. He also had visions – visions full of colour and ladders composed of twisted beams of coloured light leading upwards. He said that the visions inspired the poetry, and certainly both were unusual. The dreams left him excited and volatile – dangerously unstable. He said that they left errant stars and spots of colour roaming around inside his head. I was never sure whether he was exaggerating or was genuinely ill, but looking back he was clearly a very disturbed man, and needed proper medical treatment.

He often sought help from Jack van Druten – but the doctor was not receptive. At first he gave no medication at all, but later he issued Blondie with multi-coloured placebos, easing his need to be taken seriously. Like everyone else, Blondie was never given any advice by the doctor – just grunts.

'He grunts at me like a fucking pig, darling,' Blondie told me one day. 'He's not a doctor's arse, my dear. He doesn't care.'

Six months later I attended hospital parade seeking medication for what turned out to be enteritis. I was given a dose of kaolin and returned to work. Blondie was waiting to see the doctor, and I could see that he was tense and a little wild-eyed. Later I heard what had happened.

Jack van Druten sat behind his desk listening to Blondie's tirade. He heard about the flashing lights and the ladders. Occasionally he grunted. He didn't look up, and finally he seemed to signal dismissal with a grunt slightly more terse than the others, and the hospital lieutenant told Blondie to leave. But both had underestimated Blondie's rage at not being taken more seriously. Before either of them could move Blondie had picked up the doctor's water bottle and rained repeated blows on his head. Blood spurted from the wounds as guards rushed in to overpower Blondie. They put him in leg-irons and chains and handcuffs, before dragging him off to the punishment cells. There the guards beat him unconscious with their rubber truncheons.

Despite his injuries, Dr van Druten refused to allow any charges to be brought, and when I saw Blondie some months later, he seemed quite pleased with himself.

'I've just written a lovely poem, darling,' he said in his soft, lazy way, and he pushed it into my hands. I tried to piece the disjointed words and phrases together, whilst Blondie watched me, waiting for my reaction.

'I think this is the best you've shown me yet,' I said firmly.

'Oh, you're lovely,' Blondie cooed. 'Much better than that fucking doctor.'

He walked away, swinging his huge shoulders and buttocks. Then he espied a young admission he had had his eye on – and his walk changed. He seemed quite purposeful as he went to greet his new friend.

Years later I heard that Blondie had successfully set up in business as a beautician. I can imagine how happy he would have been slapping unguents and oils on the parched skin of the society belles who became his clients. A very far cry from the days when it was said that he simply burst out of the strait-jackets guards had used to restrain him.

At about this time I met a man called Joe. He was an Egyptian who had lived in South Africa since he was four years old. He had had several confrontations with law-enforcement agencies, and because of his dark skin and foreign appearance he had frequently been classified as non-white – serving some sentences in non-white prisons. When I met him in Central Prison, he was serving two concurrent nine- to fifteen-year sentences for theft by deception. These extremely harsh sentences seem to have been made statutory by South Africa's legislators in the mistaken belief that if you do not understand a problem it is a good idea to lock it up for as long as possible. The theory appears to be that the problem might miraculously go away, or that you won't be around to deal with it when it is released. Similar silly opinions would appear to govern the thinking of some members of the judiciary and quite a few politicians in Britain today.

After he had received the first of his sentences, Joe had been given one of the infamous blue jackets to wear. When he was later arraigned to face the second charge before Mr Justice Ludorf, he fought the case with some skill, but was eventually found guilty. The judge had then to pass a second mandatory nine- to fifteen-year sentence, but he followed the proper procedures scrupulously.

'Do you wish to say anything in mitigation?' he inquired politely.

'Well, I've already got a blue jacket,' Joe said cheerfully. 'So perhaps you could give me some trousers to go with it.'

Judge Ludorf smiled broadly.

'I'm afraid I can't,' he said. 'You'll have to make do with another "jacket".'

Joe was a man who was always smiling and cracking a joke, but like all of us he suffered under the tensions and pressures created by the harsh sentencing policy and appalling prison conditions. He had a bad heart, and one day I heard that he had been admitted to the prison hospital after a mild heart attack. A few days later I heard that Joe was dead.

Some months after this I was very surprised to hear that Joe had come back to life. When I saw him on the landing he told me what had happened. Soon after admission to the hospital he had suffered another attack, and he had lain in a coma for two days – after which Dr Jack van Druten certified him dead. He was put in a sheet and a wicker-basket – and transferred to the morgue. There he was laid out on one of the slate slabs that were used to accommodate the bodies of executed prisoners.

The morgue was sited directly behind the gallows, and at night the patrol-guard had to pass through the steel door between the gallows and the morgue building when he made his rounds. It was an eerie place at the best of times, and a large owl that had made its nest in the gable of the morgue building added to the ghostliness of the area at night.

At some time during the early hours of the morning following his 'death', Joe had come back to life. He told me that he felt cold and a bit stiff. He couldn't make out where he was and when he sat up he realized that he was naked except for the sheet that had been placed over him. He saw tables all around him with sheets over them, and he gingerly got up and walked across the tiled floor to the table nearest to him. It was dark, and the only light coming into the room was that of the moon outside. Joe said that he pulled the sheet from the table he had approached, and at first he didn't realize what he was looking at. Then, suddenly, he knew. He was in the morgue, looking at the body of an executed black man whose relative had not yet arranged for his burial.

Joe told me that he didn't feel any shock at the time. He was simply puzzled at how he came to be there. He realized that he was alive, and it didn't make sense. He felt cold and he pulled the sheet more tightly around him. Then he heard the patrol guard come through the steel door as he made his rounds. Joe walked to the window and waited until the guard came into his view – then, as he passed, Joe rapped on the window. As the startled guard turned around in disbelief, Joe called to him through the window.

'Have you got a cigarette?' Joe shouted.

The guard stood open-mouthed looking at the sheet-covered apparition in the morgue window. It took him a few moments to realize that this phantom was actually asking for a cigarette – and then he reacted. He turned around and ran. He ran through the door, down the pathway leading to the prison's main hall, across the hall, down the passageway to the forecourt, and straight on out through the front gates.

Two days later the guard was found holed up in a friend's room. At first he refused to talk to anyone. Months later, when he returned to duty, nothing could induce him to accept night-shift work again.

23

Some weeks after I had visited Dr van Druten and refused to allow him to extract my aching tooth, I received an invitation that would in other circumstances have been most welcome. Any break in the harsh monotony of the routine was a relief, and when I was subpoenaed to give evidence in a fraud trial in Cape Town I was in two minds. I wanted to go, but I did not want to miss the dentist when he visited Central Prison. In the end I decided to accept the subpoena and hope to see a dentist in Cape Town.

At that time I had achieved some notoriety amongst prisoners as an expert in the field of handwriting comparison. Whilst preparing my defence against charges of fraud I became familiar with police procedures in presenting handwriting evidence, and I realized that the whole process was wide open to question and error. In general the police used photographs and photocopies of documents as exhibits, and from these, sometimes using enlargements, they sought to show that two exhibits came from the same hand. The technique was to enumerate points of similarity between handwriting specimens taken from the accused and the writing on court exhibits. In the vast majority of cases no technical aid was used other than an enlarger, and I was able to show that no expertise was needed, simply a good eye.

The very nature of handwriting evidence makes it vulnerable to extensive cross-examination techniques, and I attacked the police experts by taking them painstakingly over every point of similarity they had highlighted. I would then point out, and make the expert concede, every point of dissimilarity. Police witnesses tended to confine their examination to the discovery of between sixteen and seventeen points of similarity. I really never knew why this should be considered sufficient, or why the police tended to treat many very common handwriting characteristics as of equal value to the quite rare characteristics that sometimes emerged, and I would point out that characteristics that are common to the majority of writers can never have the same significance as those that are relatively rare. Perhaps the police experts were influenced by the considered opinion that sixteen points of similarity in fingerprint comparisons is pretty conclusive, but there is no scientific basis for transferring that criterion to handwriting comparisons.

I spread my investigation over the whole spectrum of the writing in question. I studied the size, inclination, formation, punctuation, positioning in relation to other letters and in relation to the baseline, and anything else that was capable of comparison. With a little ingenuity my technique enabled me to keep a police expert in the witness-box for a very long time. On occasion I would be able to demolish his claim to scientific accuracy by preparing an exhibit extempore and reproducing in it all the points of similarity he had shown, plus a great many more – at the same time proving that I could not possibly have written the exhibit the prosecution relied on.

An interesting discovery was that the police experts never pointed out significant differences to the court – even when these differences showed quite clearly that the documents were probably written by someone other than the person alleged by the prosecution to have written them. This failure to disclose evidence helpful to the defence was a feature of police procedures everywhere I was subjected to them – including in Britain. The police have never, in any case I have been associated with, volunteered evidence useful to the defence, although they have frequently been well aware that such evidence existed and have frequently concealed it. I do not believe that prosecutors and judicial officers are unaware that this is so; my experience is that they dishonestly pretend that it is not happening or, as happened to me at an Old Bailey trial, actively encourage it by overruling protests that it is happening.

The result of my activities as a handwriting expert was that the overworked police handwriting experts became reluctant to get involved in cases I was connected with. This paradoxically increased my reputation as an expert, and a number of prisoners subpoenaed me to give evidence on their behalf or to assist them in preparing cross-examination of police witnesses. Heinz, the man who had stayed with me at Salt

Rock, was appearing in Cape Town on fraud charges, and it was this appearance that gave rise to the subpoena I decided to accept.

The 1000-mile train journey was incredibly uncomfortable. I was one of a batch of four prisoners who were being transferred, and because of my escapes I was subjected to special security measures. Handcuffs had been clamped tightly on my wrists when we left Pretoria, and throughout the two days and nights of the trip they cut into my wrists. Nothing I could say would induce the guards to loosen them, and my wrists became swollen and angry welts appeared. Once on the train I was shackled to another prisoner, and although he co-operated in trying to find a way to lie down on the narrow railway seat, we never succeeded, and spent the journey sitting up. My discomfort was compounded by my raging toothache, and my jaw became tender and swollen. I spent the trip in great pain, and on arrival in Cape Town I was put in one of the stinking cells at Roeland Street Gaol, water and slime oozing down its walls.

On the morning after my arrival I saw the medical officer, and he immediately referred me to a dentist, arranging for me to see a private practitioner. X-rays showed a festering, badly impacted wisdom tooth. After a course of antibiotics it was cut out. I shudder to think what would have happened if I had allowed Jack van Druten to go ahead and attempt the extraction at Central Prison.

When my arrival in Cape Town became known to the prosecution they withdrew all evidence of handwriting they had proposed to use. I was no longer required to give evidence, but my trip did result in Heinz disposing of a substantial part of the state case against him, and it helped to secure his acquittal on a large number of charges.

Whilst in Cape Town's Roeland Street Gaol, I met a young man called Stevens. He was then almost eighteen years of age, and he was charged with the murder of a woman he had been living with. She was in her mid-thirties, and their relationship had become more and more tempestuous until, in a fit of anger, he had strangled and stabbed her. He panicked, stole money from her handbag, and ran away.

He was very immature – defence and state doctors agreed that he was retarded. The jury convicted him of murder, but stipulated seventeen grounds of extenuation – and they asked the judge to consider these when passing sentence. The judge had absolute discretion in the matter of sentence, and he remanded the young man back to Roeland Street Gaol overnight whilst he considered the matter. I met Stevens that evening in the reception office at the prison. He seemed quite cheerful and told me that he hoped for a light sentence.

The next day the whole prison was stunned to hear that Stevens had been sentenced to death. Mr Justice van Wyk, known as Cape Town's hanging judge, had taken the unprecedented step of completely overriding the jury's recommendation of mercy. He gave as his reasons that were he to send Stevens to prison, he might escape and commit a similar offence, and that if he committed him to a psychiatric hospital the chances that he would escape were even greater. He felt he had to protect the public, and therefore he sentenced the young man to death.

I spoke to Stevens briefly after he returned from court. He was a little wild-eyed, but seemed remarkably calm.

'My counsel says we will win the appeal,' he told me confidently.

I did not recognize it then, but his attitude was that of someone who was unable to take in what was happening to him. I met many men sentenced to death, and in my talks with them not one of them really believed that the sentence would be carried out. They all believed that their appeals would succeed, or that the State President would exercise his prerogative of mercy. Not one of them appeared to be able to relate to what was going to happen to them.

Stevens was transferred to Pretoria Central Prison on the same evening of his sentencing, and some months later, after my return to Pretoria, I saw him exercising in the space behind the prison hospital reserved for white condemned prisoners. He had spent some time in the condemned cell since I had last seen him, living a few paces from the gallows. I called to him and he looked up and smiled at me. But it was clear that he did not recognize me.

He was hanged shortly after his eighteenth birthday.

During my stay in Central Prison, and especially between 1961 and 1965, hangings occurred with depressing regularity. The crowded conditions in the condemned cells caused the authorities to build a new condemned unit attached to, but outside, the main walls of the prison, close to B-section, which housed the gallows.

Condemned men now had a much longer walk to the gallows. They were escorted from the new condemned unit along the full length of B-section, across the main hall of the prison, and up a short flight of stairs to the pre-gallows chamber. It was usual for non-whites to be hanged in groups of four or more, and the journeys these small groups of men made to the gallows affected all who witnessed them. Usually they would sing as they walked, their natural sense of harmony and rhythm lending an awful poignancy to the sound of their voices. At first the singing would be distant, but as they made their way closer to the cell I lay in, or nearer to the library where I now worked, their voices would grow louder until it peaked as they passed by. The fear of death was upon them – and the hoarseness that hysteria breeds made their singing sound strained and urgent. The fervency of the singing made all other sounds recede – it was as though the whole prison held its breath and stayed silent in sympathy with them. As they moved through the main hall and mounted the stairs to the gallows, the voices would grow distant again. There was an air of unreality about it – my mind seemed unable to accept what was happening. I waited with a sense of helplessness until the crash of the gallows trapdoors told me that the moment of death had come – and irrevocably passed.

In the silence that followed those awful sounds my mind would re-emerge from behind the barriers that protected it. Gradually normal sounds would return to the prison – softly at first, and then more openly. The grim greyness of prison life would reassert itself, causing men to forget or bury the horror of the moments that had passed before.

White men were usually hanged singly, but at times in pairs. Their journey to the gallows was made more quickly than that of the non-whites – and they walked in silence, seldom singing. They appeared to be more thoughtful, but the air of unreality was just as strong, and the hush that cloaked the prison was just as real. I met several white men after they had been told they were to die. Some were defiant, some bewildered; some I admired, others I could not relate to. None believed that they would really die.

Jan Schoeman was respected by all the guards. He had been convicted of the murder of a Baron. It was alleged that he had killed his victim at the request of the victim himself – so that a large assurance policy could be realized and the estate saved for the Baron's heir. Despite several stays of execution to enable lawyers for the insurance company to try to get Schoeman to make a statement relieving them of their obligations under the policy, he never did speak about what had happened. He carried his secret to the gallows with him, and the guards detailed to carry out his execution said that he never once flinched, but went to his death bravely.

Duncan had killed his wife, and he did not have Jan Schoeman's stoicism. Guards told me that when he was to be hanged he was unable to stand, so they strapped him in a chair and then placed it on the gallows – and hanged him in it.

Hardly a week passed by without one or more hangings taking place. Yet, despite the awful regularity of them, each execution created its own aura of despair – something so real that the familiarity that stemmed from repetition was never able to dispel it.

Andy suffered from tuberculosis. He was the man who had introduced me to Don Muniz when I had first escaped. He told me of an African who was saved from the gallows by pure chance.

The man had been sentenced to death for the rape of the daughter of the senior chaplain to the prison service. It was quite normal for non-white men to be sentenced to death and hanged for the rape of white women, but I never heard of a single case of a white man being so sentenced for the rape of a non-white woman – indeed, under the present system of apartheid, I very much doubt that any court would believe the evidence of a non-white person where it conflicted with that of a white person – and perhaps that is why so few prosecutions or convictions for sexual assaults on black women by whites ever occurred. It is also significant that at no time did I hear of a white man being sentenced to death for rape of a white woman either. It would appear that there were, and still are, one set of sentences for the whites and a different set for the blacks.

At the trial Andy told me of, prosecution evidence had been that the young white woman, who was well known for her charitable works, had been driving from her home in Pretoria to a non-white township in order to distribute gifts of food and clothing. She told the court that she had been hailed by the accused as he walked towards the township she was to visit, and she had stopped and offered him a lift. Shortly after he entered the car he had drawn a knife and compelled her to drive to a secluded spot, where he had forced her to strip, and then raped her.

The young woman showed very real distress in giving her evidence, and there was open hostility in the court when the man claimed that this pastor's daughter had incited him and asked him to have intercourse with her. He cut a wretched figure, and the public gallery had to be restrained from expressing their contempt for him. The loudest condemnation came from the non-white men and women from the township, who knew the accused man well, and knew, too, that the young woman had selflessly carried out her good works among them.

The man was found guilty, and it was then revealed that he had a previous conviction for a sexual assault on a young black girl, and that he had served a prison sentence in respect of that offence. The trial judge had no hesitation in sentencing him to death.

Two days before he was to be hanged, his solicitor visited Central Prison, to take instructions from him regarding the disposal of his assets after execution. Whilst waiting to see his client the solicitor got into conversation with a colleague, who was waiting to interview another man who was also about to be hanged. They discussed the reason for their respective visits.

'I cannot understand it,' the solicitor told his colleague. 'I've represented many men who faced execution, and almost without exception they have admitted their guilt, or at least their responsibility for what they had done. This man is different. It is almost as though he is telling the truth.'

Later that day, back in his office, the solicitor had a telephone call from his colleague. What he had to say was bizarre and completely unexpected. He said that the story of the alleged rapist's protest of innocence had worried him. He remembered hearing of a case with similar features, and he had been astonished to learn when checking that the same young woman had been involved, and that the earlier offence had allegedly occurred at precisely the same place.

A full investigation was begun. When confronted, the pastor's daughter broke down and confessed that she had lied – and that the black man's account of what had happened was true. She was not prosecuted, but agreed to enter a hospital for treatment. The conviction and sentence of the black man were quashed, and he was freed.

But it was too late to undo the miscarriage of justice that had led to the execution of an innocent man in the earlier case.

One of the scourges of tribal life among a section of the black population in South Africa is the planting, marketing, and the use of dagga – the indigenous marijuana plant. In the hidden glens of the vast Drakensberg range of mountains, small villages spring up whose existence is dependent on this crop. The humid heat of the region makes the plant grow like a weed – it needs no cultivation. Special police spotter planes scour the remote areas where small plateaux make planting possible. The growers camouflage the dagga plants with sophisticated netting, or by planting it amongst legitimate growths of maize and other crops. Police spotters use infra-red devices which are able to identify the illegal plants because they emit significantly more heat than their surrounding vegetation.

Periodic police forays to destroy the crop are routine, and the growers usually desert the area and flee into the mountains, abandoning the temporary village they had built. On one such foray the villagers were heavily under the influence of the drug when the police arrived. Instead of fleeing, they stood their ground and waged a mini-war. Police reinforcements were rushed in and, in the unequal battle between the police armed with FN rifles and sub-machine guns, and the drug-crazed villagers wielding spears, five policemen were killed and the village population halved.

In the days following that confrontation, a massive police force hunted the villagers who had fled after the battle – and eventually twenty-six men were arraigned before Mr Justice Kennedy in the Supreme Court at Pietermaritzburg, in Natal. After a lengthy trial the men were found guilty of murder and sentenced to death.

They were transferred to Pretoria Central Prison and held there whilst their appeals were processed, and I was in the prison when the Sheriff of Pretoria brought the news to the men that their appeals had failed, and that in three days' time they were to be hanged. In the ensuing three days, relatives of the condemned men made the journey from their tribal homelands to visit them and to be near them when the time came. More than 400 men and women gathered near to the prison. Only close relatives were allowed to visit the men and, whilst they did so, the others raised their voices in traditional songs of mourning and hymns.

The solemn beauty of the natural harmony those people created rang out over the prison. Their voices carried across the high stone walls and reached into every part of the prison. They sang with a fervour and a passion which conveyed, as nothing else could, their feelings for the men who were about to die – and the sound of their singing reached the condemned men and supported them in those final hours. Words are inadequate to describe the pathos, the tragedy, the love and the longing that those voices conveyed. At times, when familiar hymns rang out from this great choir of suffering people, the sound transcended normal human experience and carried the prison and all those in it into a realm where normal values had no meaning – where feelings were exposed and laid bare for all to see.

Hardened criminals, with long records of violence, openly wiped tears from their eyes. Guards moved quietly about their duties. No one could escape the effect of those days of mourning – the sound of so many people raising their voices in harmony seemed to exorcize the prison and make it for a moment a great cathedral, in which every man's thoughts were irresistibly drawn to the awful contemplation of his own helplessness in the face of death. We spoke in hushed tones – and only when necessary. Each man seemed to withdraw a little into himself, and the realization of the insignificance of our own suffering beside that of the men condemned to die made us feel humble.

The hangings began at 8.00 a.m. The black men had to wait whilst a white man went to the gallows before them – alone. I listened and heard the gallows trapdoors crash open as the law took the revenge that society had demanded. After the white man had been taken down from the gallows the procedure continued. Four more times the trapdoors crashed open and signalled the end of the lives of men society had decreed should die. The non-whites were hanged in three groups of six, and one of seven – for on the morning before the hangings one man had been granted a stay of execution.

By 10.30 a.m., the hangman had completed his job. One white man and twenty-five black men lay dead upon the tables and floor of the prison mortuary. At 12.30 p.m., I stood in line in the main hall of the prison with my tin bowl in my hand, waiting for lunch to be brought from the kitchen. I was not hungry – I joined the queue from habit, and once in line I was required to stay in line.

The side gate to the main hall opened. It led from the hospital and the mortuary, and a number of chattering and laughing medical students, wearing white housecoats, spilled into the hall. Two of them carried a white painted wooden box between them. It had rope handles attached to each end and it swung slightly as they walked across the hall. They passed within feet of where I stood, and the box they carried left drops of a liquid in a trail behind it. When I looked more closely I saw that it was blood. The students had been cutting specimen organs from the bodies of the dead men – and the blood dripping from the box they carried had, until a few hours earlier, beat in the hearts of the men who had been hanged.

I turned away, no longer able to face any food, but the guards curtly ordered me to stay in line.

The names of the twenty-six men condemned to die had been published in a Johannesburg newspaper. A white businessman had run his eye idly down the list of names, and he had recognized the name of his chauffeur, who had gone on holiday some months before and had failed to return. He made inquiries and established that the man condemned to die was indeed his chauffeur. He had been positively identified by four policemen as being the man who had stabbed one of their colleagues to death in the drugs raid.

Further investigation by the businessman had led to a stay of execution being granted. It was later established that the chauffeur had in fact been in Johannesburg, 500 miles from the scene of the drugs raid, at the time the offence had been committed. No one had believed his story – his own counsel had not even bothered to check his claim to have been working in Johannesburg when the crime was committed. Had it not been for the blind chance that his employer had spotted his name in that single newspaper report, he too would have been hanged.

The female section of Pretoria Central Prison was completely cut off from the section housing males. It was much smaller – and condemned female prisoners were kept in a special cell there. They were comparatively few in number and, when their appeals had failed, they were executed on the same gallows as the men. In order to reach the gallows the women had to walk from the female unit through the whole length of C-section, into the main hall, and up the stairs to B2 landing before reaching the pre-gallows chamber. On the two occasions that women were hanged whilst I was at the prison, they were hanged alone. As with all executions, the prisoners not in the workshops were confined to their cells for the time it took the hangman to complete his task.

There can be nothing more poignant than to listen to the progress of a lone woman, escorted and supported by her guards, as she made her way through the prison, singing a hymn, on her way to die. The women did not have fellow-condemned to lend support – and I shall always remember the fear and the pain in those voices as they grew louder on nearing my cell, and then grew fainter as the route to the gallows took them away from me. On occasion the voice would break, and uncontrolled sobs would be torn from the heart – and then, in a supreme effort of willpower, the sobbing would end, and the singing would begin again, a little weakly at first, and then more strongly as courage returned. The sheer volume of executions may have created a pattern I grew to recognize – but those two women, completely alone in the time of their greatest need, have left memories that shatter equanimity and revive the shock and horror of that time.

24

During 1963, I was given a job as a landing cleaner on B4 landing – the landing on which Gerry Payne had died – three storeys above the segregation unit, and two above where the condemned prisoners had been housed. The new condemned unit had recently been completed, and the men had been transferred to their new quarters. I was talking to a landing guard called Lategan one day. He was a pleasant young man, and as we were talking sirens began wailing, whistles blew, and we heard the sound of gunfire. Lategan hesitated a moment, and then he handed me his landing keys and ran off to see what had happened.

I was so taken aback by his action that at first I didn't know what to do. The landing was empty as all the prisoners were at work, and I put the keys in my pocket and went down to B3 landing to get closer to where the noise was coming from. Someone shouted that the condemned prisoners were rioting, and the sounds of fighting and shouting continued for almost half an hour before things began to quieten down. It was some two hours before Lategan returned. I handed him his keys and he grinned at me.

'I knew you'd look after things,' he said.

I did not know what to say. I realized that the urge to escape had gone. For the first time since my admission to prison I had been trusted by someone – and I had not even thought of letting him down.

Lategan told me that Wanka, a white prisoner who had been sentenced to death for killing a policeman, had managed to have a pistol smuggled into the condemned unit. He had unlocked the non-white condemned cells before trying to break out and escape in the confusion. The non-whites had been blocked from following him, and a furious battle had ensued. One group of non-white condemned prisoners saved two white guards from certain death during the fighting, and they were later rewarded with commuted sentences.

Wanka had managed to get out into the road leading away from the prison, but he was spotted by an officer and brought down with a rifle shot through the buttocks – but not before he had shot and seriously wounded the man who apprehended him. Captain Fourie had been shot in the chest, but still managed to detain Wanka until help arrived.

The behaviour of some guards proved very interesting during the riot. Most of the bullies were nowhere to be seen when fighting broke out. One loud-mouthed guard, on duty in a turret overlooking the condemned section, had simply abandoned his rifle and run away as soon as the shooting began.

After a few days of excited discussion, Central Prison was rudely reminded that it was a grim penal institution. The Sheriff visited and three days later a new batch of executions took place. The new condemned unit was considered no longer safe, and the men there were moved back inside the main prison on to B2 landing. Once again the sound of men singing as they awaited execution became part of everyday experience in the prison. The low murmur of singing would rise at times and echo throughout the prison – and on those long, dark nights before an execution was to take place, the singing rose and fell continuously until dawn.

At about this time I met Jack 'Babyface' Goodwin. He was considered South Africa's leading confidence trickster, but I knew him as a man of high intelligence, softly spoken, and as devious as it is possible to imagine. I liked him – in more ways than one we were two of a kind. During the 1960s, Jack had been sentenced to imprisonment for fraudulently selling counterfeit import permits to businessmen. He had very little money, so together with a man called Claude he devised an escape plan that was, and still is, unique.

Jack somehow managed to obtain two blank copies of bail warrants from the magistrates' courts in Johannesburg. He had them completed by a master forger, complete with rubber stamps and signatures. Then, together with his friend Claude, he began to pester the guards with questions about their bail. After a very few days everyone knew that Jack and Claude were waiting for their bail to be posted so that they could be released pending appeal.

Now Jack implemented the second phase of his plan. He arranged for a friend to telephone his solicitor to say that bail was about to be posted, and to request that the solicitor take the bail warrants to Central Prison, in case there were any snags. A fee was agreed and the solicitor undertook the task. The forged warrants were now delivered to the solicitor's offices, and he took them to Pretoria Central Prison, never imagining that they were anything but genuine.

Jack and Claude were released, and it was only several weeks later, when detectives visiting Central Prison about another matter casually asked how Jack was getting on, that the truth came to light.

Claude had made good his escape to South America and has not been heard of since – but Jack 'Babyface' Goodwin was different. He travelled to Israel, Switzerland, Paris and, finally, to Los Angeles. At the height of Interpol's search for him he sent a South African national newspaper a large photograph of himself endorsed, 'Fugitively yours, Jack Goodwin!' He received the front page billing he obviously hankered for, but shortly afterwards he was arrested on Sunset Boulevard, and eventually he was returned to South Africa to serve his sentence – but not before the American solicitor he employed had been jailed for stealing from Jack all the money Jack had stolen from other people!

It was in 1964 that a change of emphasis in the treatment of prisoners in South Africa first became clear. During the 1950s, the Landsdowne Commission had investigated and reported on several instances of brutality – and the Commission's recommendations had slowly worked their way through the maze of government bureaucracy. Prison conditions had been exposed, and the study of criminology alongside sociology and psychology became common. The affluent society produced people with time and resources to devote to what were previously unacknowledged social needs. The University of Pretoria, and the University of South Africa, were both sited close to Central Prison. Students of criminology, sociology and psychology were attracted to the prison service by offers of commissions and generous study arrangements. When account was taken of the opportunities such employment provided for research and practical study projects, the attractions were considerable.

The trend towards educated prison personnel brought an entirely new breed of men into the service – and with them came changes in attitudes that were to alter the whole prison system. Imprisonment *as* punishment and not *for* punishment became the new theme – and men like Lt-Colonel Gouws had to alter their attitudes or face posting to the far outposts of South Africa's huge prison system. General Steyn, a dedicated Christian, became Commissioner of Prisons, and he shared with his wife a genuine desire to improve the mess he inherited. Young undergraduates joined the service, and they included men like Fourie, Otto (now Commissioner of Prisons in South Africa), Reitjies, and others, who were to stamp their attitudes on every facet of prison administration. Rehabilitation of offenders became the new aim of the department.

None of this happened without opposition. Guards brought up in the days when their word was law were not happy when arbitrary punishments were phased out and they were ordered to speak to the prisoners civilly. Some left the service, others took early retirement – but most gradually adapted to the new regime.

In some areas changes were dramatic – in others they took a long time. The silence rule was abolished, the harsh discipline was relaxed – sport, recreation and study facilities were introduced. Dietitians moved in and prepared adequate menus. Restrictions on visits and letters were relaxed to enable reasonable contact between the prisoner and his family to be maintained. Remission was dramatically increased to encourage good behaviour – and, eventually, parole was introduced. Celebrations of the founding of the Republic of South Africa were used to give amnesty to almost all categories of prisoners, relieving the overcrowding at a stroke, and making the implementation of progressive policies possible.

In the midst of the relative excitement that these changes created I met a man called Don Martyn. He was the Anglican priest at Central Prison, and he interviewed me in the prison library, where I was working at that time.

'Are you studying?' he asked me.

'No. I haven't the funds.'

'You can take Senior Certificate subjects free,' he pointed out. 'And if you get the required number of passes, I'll get you a sponsor for a degree course.'

I had hardly spoken to him before he made this approach – but this man was so genuine in everything he did that I accepted what he said without hesitation. So at the age of twenty-nine, I went back to school.

Working in the library, I was able to find books on Commerce, Economics, Bookkeeping, English and Afrikaans. I obtained copies of the relevant syllabus and worked out a study programme. Eight months later I passed English, Commerce, Economics and Bookkeeping at the required level, and I applied for and received a certificate of admission to a degree course with the University of South Africa, with the proviso that I pass Afrikaans and a science subject at senior certificate level within three years. Tuition was to be by correspondence, but the proximity of the prison to the University allowed me to arrange tutorial visits if required.

I took my certificate to Don Martyn – I was proud of it, it was the first school certificate I can remember obtaining, but I was very much aware that the four subjects I had passed were unlikely to arouse much enthusiasm in a sponsor. Don Martyn congratulated me and made me fill in an application form for a degree course. I selected a Bachelor of Commerce (Law) degree, and later I wished that I had chosen something easier. Don Martyn merely suggested that I plan things over at least four years, and then he took the application form with him.

'I'll see what I can do,' he said.

Ten days later I received notification from the University of South Africa that my fees for the first year had been paid and that the lecture notes would be forwarded in due course. Don Martyn had gone directly from the interview with me to see Mary Oppenheimer, daughter of Harry Oppenheimer, the Anglo-American Corporation chairman. She had authorized sponsorship for three years, dependent only on genuine study effort, and had included an amount to cover the cost of textbooks and stationery.

During the years that followed I got to know Don Martyn well. I had always had, and still do have, a distrust of people who make a career out of their faith or cause. Don Martyn is the only minister of religion I have ever met who made me forget my prejudices and accept him for what he was – a man who lived what he preached. I began to attend his services, and I found him as robust and honest in his preaching as he was in his dealing with individual prisoners. He helped anyone he could, regardless of their faith – or lack of faith. After two years I was confirmed in the Anglican church by the Bishop of Pretoria. I had no real commitment to the creed, although nothing in it seriously conflicted with my childhood beliefs. Looking back I now believe that I joined the Anglican communion because of Don Martyn. I owed him so much – the studies he had introduced me to helped me to regain some of my self-respect, and saved me from the stagnation that threatens all long-term prisoners. Joining his church was a small token of my appreciation.

Fred was not a member of Don Martyn's congregation, but sometimes he attended services in order to avoid the hated Sunday parades. When Fred was due for release it became known that he had nowhere to go. On the morning that he was discharged he found Don Martyn waiting for him outside the prison gates. Don took him into his own home, gave him a bed in his son's bedroom and, with his family, did everything he could to make the transition from prison easier for him.

A few days after Fred had been released, well after midnight, Don Martyn received a telephone call from the police. Fred had been arrested for having sex with a black girl – an offence which, under South Africa's race laws, could carry a penalty of seven years' imprisonment. Don Martyn contacted Mr Justice Rumpff, a Supreme Court judge, and the police were persuaded to drop the charge. It was suggested that the privations imposed by imprisonment had made him unable to control his sexual urges. As soon as he was released Fred was taken back into Don Martyn's home, and efforts were begun to obtain employment for him. Before this could be finalized Fred decamped – taking most of Don Martyn's personal possessions with him.

Some weeks later Don Martyn received a telephone call from the police in Johannesburg. Fred had been arrested and faced serious robbery charges. He wanted to know if Don Martyn would try to arrange legal representation for him. As soon as Don Martyn put down the telephone he got into his car and drove the thirty-five miles from his home to Johannesburg to see Fred.

'I gave him a jolly good dressing-down,' he told me later. 'And then I got him a solicitor.'

'But why?' I asked him. 'Why? He didn't deserve it.'

'I know some people say I'm a fool – but he needed help. If I am to be a Christian, as I ask others to be, I must forgive and give help whenever and wherever I can.'

Whether Don Martyn's philosophy is right or wrong, there will always be those who take advantage of kindness. I remember him as a man who gave help to a great many men – without any preconditions. He lived more closely to the basic tenets of Christianity than any other man I have ever met.

Many prisoners viewed the new official attitude with considerable distrust. Years of petty tyranny and deprivation had developed attitudes that were not capable of changing overnight. Just as the guards experienced difficulty in coming to terms with the new era, so the prisoners had to feel their way into the new environment that progress brought with it. At first I felt a little cheated that the guards whom I used to hate were no longer there. The new guards did not act in a way to provoke anger or hate. There was no longer a legitimate excuse for dispensing choler and the gratuitous abuse I had grown used to giving expression to. I began to recognize that not all guards were the same. I transferred my frustrations to the bad ones, and grew to tolerate and occasionally to respect the others.

The stone-yard was closed down. Workshops now gave opportunity to acquire artisan qualifications in sheet-metal working, carpentry, fitting and turning, welding, and painting and decorating. A rebuilding programme within the prison system provided work for men nearing the end of their sentences, and enabled them to gain practical experience and develop ability in the trades they had trained in.

I was a prisoner serving multiple sentences, the effect of which was to make me ineligible for amnesty or parole in the foreseeable future. The operative sentence was the eighteen-year term, and I was not aware then, as I am now some twenty years later, of what was actually happening to me. My sentence was too painful for me to face – I could not bring myself to contemplate the future whilst it contained an unending period of imprisonment. In my experience very few prisoners serving a term of more than five years are able to relate to it. Prison, 'even the best-regulated prison', to employ Winston Churchill's expression, is a very painful experience. Where the duration of the sentence makes the pain more than a man can bear, the mind erects barriers enabling that man to retain his sanity. One of those barriers is erected to prevent contemplation of the future. Where the future holds the prospect of ongoing imprisonment, and therefore the prospect of ongoing pain, there is a point at which the mind rejects consideration of it. I was in that position – I had no future that my mind would allow me to see.

The strain of coping with my sentence had made me negative – it made me hate the system that had devised my punishment and, by extension, the forces of law and order who, representing society, enforced it. It effectively drove me further away from acceptance of a normal role in society – it was society who had authorized and who permitted such a savage response to my misconduct. The improvement in prison conditions did not change that basic attitude. What did happen was that I was able to exclude people and groups of people from the blanket criticisms I had formerly employed. Don Martyn is an example of one who, although he made a career out of his faith, was so genuine that I had no difficulty in excluding him from my blanket censure of priests. 'Henna' van Niekerk, a long-serving Head Guard at Central Prison, so named because of his red hair, was another man who even during my days in segregation had, on the rare occasions when we met, always been fair and straightforward.

My studies proved a great help in dealing with my sentence. They were demanding and drew on the energy I might otherwise have used negatively. The courses I had selected were more difficult than I had imagined they would be – and like a great many before me and since, I discovered that the jump from 'O' level study to university standards was a very big one. Whilst the studies helped me to deal with my sentence, they did nothing to disperse the hate and the anger my prison experiences had left me with. Just as I had buried the hurt and the pain of my rejection by the Plymouth Brethren and my family, so now I became embroiled in my studies and, submerging myself in them, I evaded the feelings that studies diverted me from. I was not aware then that the attitudes shaped by those feelings would later re-emerge and have very serious consequences for me.

As part of my study programme I became *au fait* with current events in South Africa. In the years between 1964 and 1967, whilst tension may have diminished in Central Prison, Pretoria, the political scene in South Africa erupted again and again as black aspirations burst through legislative barriers and spilled over into violent demonstrations. The agony of Sharpeville was to shock the world. The Rivonia trial, and Nelson Mandela's defiant speech when facing the death sentence, left a deep impression on me. Here was a man who was prepared to die for his beliefs – or to further the welfare of his people.

No one I met condoned the action of John Harris when, in 1964, he placed a bomb on Johannesburg's main station and it exploded, killing an elderly lady and frightfully injuring innocent men, women and children standing by. His action, and those of other white terrorists, only served to harden the attitudes of the ruling white community – and probably did much to injure the cause of black advancement and equality of opportunity. I met no one who was sorry for him when he was hanged, early in 1965.

In general, white communist sympathizers appear to have been accepted by black activists under sufferance – as opportunists who could be used and then put aside when the black community achieved self-determination. Black nationalism values the freedom it aspires to far too much to allow it to be enslaved by international communism. South Africans made, and still do make, the mistake of interpreting political unrest among the non-white population as the work of outside agencies. It is not, and it never has been. It is the response to oppressive legislation and reaction to the exploitation of the indigenous population by the white minority. The movement towards the fulfilment of black aspirations in South Africa will succeed. Its progress may be slow and perhaps it will be bloody – but it is only a matter of time before the minority are overthrown and the natural order is restored – with the black majority determining their own future. The time-scale is unpredictable, because this is Africa – a vast continent where time has less impact on traditional ways of life than it does in highly developed countries. Yet it is a violent continent, and the possibility of sudden, savage confrontation and upheaval is never far below the surface.

Whatever the tragedy or excitement of life outside the prison walls may have been, and however diverting an analysis of events may have proved, there was no way I could escape the reality of day-to-day experience. Despite the new attitudes and facilities that a new administration had introduced, prison life remained what it always will be – a violent act by society which deprives fellow human beings of freedom, shatters family units, and leaves jagged wounds in the fabric of society itself. In spite of my preoccupations, I was always conscious of the tension the abnormality of prison life imposes. Whilst the expression of my disapproval might have been tempered by a better understanding of the problems involved in running the system, nothing could diminish my rejection of a system that subjects human beings to violent deprivation of normality and, after imposing abnormality on them for arbitrary periods of time, then throws them back on to the street, expecting them to act normally. Of course, very few do act normally – and those that do, do so despite the system, not because of it. The current concern in Britain, amongst those close to the problem of overcrowded and undermanned prison establishments, is not very different to the concern I felt all those years ago – that it was all purposeless, a huge waste of public resources. Just as at that time, so today, no one seems to give sufficient consideration to the question: what is the purpose of prison?

An example of the forces society casually allows to develop in the abnormality of prison is the case of Steve Grobbelaar. This man had served many years of an indeterminate sentence, and had been given a trusted job as a prisoner. He had permission to move in and out of the prison whenever necessary in order to carry out his work as a draughtsman on new building projects. He was due for release, and accommodation and employment had been arranged for him by the Public Works Department. They had monitored his work as a draughtsman and he was to continue in that capacity when employed by them. Three weeks before his date of release he went to the prison gate and greeted the guard whom he knew well. The guard opened the gate to let him out, and Steve grabbed the guard's revolver before running off and stealing a car to make his escape in.

Later he robbed a newsagent in Braamfontein, near Johannesburg, callously shooting the man down when he resisted. He was recaptured, tried, sentenced to death by hanging, and executed on 7 July 1966.

As far as I am aware no one ever asked the question: was Steve Grobbelaar the product of years of penal violence? Society had taken him as a young man and claimed his adulthood in payment for a single act of misconduct. He was subjected to a regime as brutal as can be imagined – where physical, sexual and psychological torment were the order of the day. He survived those experiences and, later, he was allowed to study – and then given responsible work to do. But it seems that no one considered he needed help to recover from the years of violence he had been subjected to. He was a product of the system, and I can think of several others like him who, after years of violent treatment, were allowed to study and, later, against all expectations, committed mindless murders and were hanged.

What is frightening is that despite ample evidence of violent behaviour by those subjected to regimes indifferent to suffering, society continues to sentence men to serve terms of imprisonment under conditions that breed violence – and then appears surprised that the violence so carefully nurtured should manifest itself. No real consideration is given to the fragility of a man's mind – or how careful we should be before we subject it to stresses that we do not fully understand.

During 1966, I was surprised to receive a letter from a girl who professed to know me. She asked if she could call and visit me and, as I had had no visits for several years, I wrote welcoming the suggestion. Some days later I was called for a visit and I found that my visitor was young and that I had never seen her before. She seemed a little frightened, and I was soon to discover why.

The visiting-room consisted of a row of stools on each side of a double steel-mesh partition, designed to prevent contact or smuggling with visitors. Through this partition my visitor told me that a man called van Biljon had undertaken to act for a consortium of Johannesburg newspapers in making contact with prisoners in Central Prison. The newspapers had been charged with knowingly publishing false information about prisons, and it was hoped that I would agree to give evidence for them in support of the stories they had published. The stories were largely accounts written by journalists and political detainees about prison conditions in 1965 and 1966. I had read the accounts and, so far as Central Prison was concerned, they created an untrue picture of conditions at the relevant times.

Whilst I sympathized with anti-prison sentiments, and still do so, I felt that I could not do what I was asked to do without being dishonest. The accounts the newspapers had published were part invention and part exaggeration. Van Biljon had only recently been released from Central Prison, and I knew him as an unscrupulous man – I wanted nothing to do with him. I felt no sympathy for the journalists concerned – or for their newspapers. They had only themselves to blame. Instead of printing the truth about past conditions and the pressing need for further improvements, they had elected to make up a series of stories riddled with hyperbole piled upon hyperbole. It seemed that for once their reckless pursuit of headlines had come unstuck.

I told the girl that whilst I had suffered very real abuse under past prison regimes, and intended to publicize it should a proper opportunity present itself, I could not support the untruths the journalists had published regarding conditions in 1965 and 1966. She left a little unhappy, but said that she would write to me again.

I later received a letter from her saying that it was the intention to call me as a witness anyway. I resented this arrogant assumption that I could be used by the newspapers' defence team, and I took steps to stop it. I wrote explaining my position and also made a statement to the prison authorities setting out the facts and asking that any further visits or letters be intercepted.

I continued to study and began to take an interest in the organization of sports and recreation. Under the new regime we were allowed to arrange competitions – and I won the chess tournament, played goalkeeper for one of the soccer teams, and helped to organize boxing tournaments. But despite these activities the strain of being confined in Central Prison began to affect me. My examinations taken for the year, I found myself becoming increasingly irritable and, on impulse, I went to see the chief guard.

'I feel I'm going mad,' I told him. 'I need a change of prison. I don't know how much more I can take.'

'Leave it with me – I'll see what I can do,' he told me.

Two months later I was transferred to Vooruitsig open prison at Kroonstad, in the Orange Free State. A new phase in my prison experience was about to begin.

25

The Vooruitsig prison complex at Kroonstad is 165 miles south-west of Pretoria. I made the trip in a closed prison lorry with ten or so companions. We were in handcuffs and leg-irons, and the heat built up throughout the journey. There were no seats in the lorry, and we bumped about on the floor. I was glad when we arrived.

We had travelled for almost four hours when, at Vooruitsig, we drew up in front of a single-storey modern building. A small man came down the steps as we arrived, wearing the insignia of a chief guard, and later I learned that he was called Breytenbach.

'You can take those off,' he said to our escorts when he saw the handcuffs and leg-irons. 'We don't use them here.'

He seemed very casual, and he chatted to the escorts as we clambered out on to the roadway and the restraints were removed. When we were all unshackled, Breytenbach looked us over and turned to go back up the steps.

'You lot had better follow me,' he said.

We followed him into the building and down a corridor, arriving at a small, paved courtyard in front of the reception office.

'Hang on there,' said Breytenbach – and he disappeared into an office.

The first thing that I noticed was that there were no guards anywhere that I could see. Then a prisoner came out of a room opening on to the courtyard – he wore standard prison khaki trousers with tennis shoes and a sports shirt. He introduced himself as Chris, and told us that he looked after the prisoners' sports interests. He made a note of what we felt we would like to take part in – and then he disappeared.

After sitting around in the sun for half an hour we were called into the reception office and quickly processed. We were given fresh clothing and allocated to our living quarters. I found that I was to be sent to A-camp within the prison – the section reserved for those with maximum privileges. When I arrived I found that the camp was arranged in quadrangles, so that the buildings themselves formed the perimeter walls. The accommodation was in single-storey blocks, modern, clean, and with areas of well-tended lawn between them. I had been met by a prisoner who told me that he was the camp monitor, and he added that if I needed anything he would see what he could do to get it for me.

'We try not to worry the guards more than necessary,' he told me.

I followed him into the cell block and looked in the cell I had been allocated. It measured eight feet by seven and had a steel grille and sliding door. The windows were narrow and rectangular – designed to make bars obsolete. It was freshly decorated and had a bed, soft rubber mattress, locker, table and chair. The block contained forty such cells with ample toilet and shower facilities under the same roof.

'The grilles and doors stay open,' the monitor told me. 'They are only locked in emergencies.'

'What about at night?'

'They stay unlocked. But we have to keep to our own cells after 10 p.m.'

Later that day I met Brigadier Fourie. He was the same man who, as a captain, had been shot by Wanka during the condemned prisoners' riot at Central Prison. He called all the new admissions together to tell us about the prison.

'In this prison you will be given every chance to show that you can behave responsibly,' he told us. 'We believe in a healthy mind in a healthy body. You will find that the emphasis is on work during work periods, and on active participation in sport during leisure periods.

'You may have noticed that apart from the grille-gates between the camps, there are no bars in this prison. This is because we believe that if we want you to trust us, we have to demonstrate our trust in you. Some of you may want to escape, but if you do so you will be returned to a closed, secure prison when you are recaptured. Please do not make holes in the walls, or damage the windows or roof. If you want to escape go to the front gate and ask the guard to let you out. He has instructions to do so.'

We laughed, a little embarrassed by this dramatic change in the treatment we had grown used to, but, as I was soon to learn, I would be allowed out of the prison at any reasonable time to visit the playing-fields – which were sited over half a mile away. These new areas of freedom required getting used to, and when I met men whom I knew from Central Prison, and others who had heard of me, I was surprised by the willingness they showed to share whatever they had to make me feel welcome. The relaxed atmosphere seemed very strange after the years of tension – the only time I saw a guard was at breakfast parade and at 5.00 p.m., when a head count was taken.

Meals were taken in a large, modern mess-hall – and the food was very much better than that at Central Prison. Free association offered opportunities to organize a full sports programme. Active sports committees represented each sport, and a six-man committee monitored all activity. Everything was organized and carried out by the prisoners themselves. Donations from inmates' private cash largely covered the costs involved, but these were supplemented by official grants.

When I arrived I had been asked if I could referee a soccer match, and a few days later I was called to reception and asked to go and officiate at a match in the 'black' prison. I was given a watch, a whistle, a pair of training shoes and a sports shirt – and told to see the lieutenant in charge of the 'black' prison when I arrived.

'Where is it?' I asked.

Breytenbach took me out into the road in front of the prison and pointed.

'If you go along there, you'll find a sports field on your left,' he told me. 'Then you just keep going – straight past the sports field – and the prison is about half a mile further on, on your right.'

I thanked him and set off. It was a Saturday morning, about 8.30 a.m. The sky was a clear blue and, early as it was, the sun was already getting warm. I walked along that road completely alone. It was a very strange feeling – and I realized that if I wanted to do so I could simply disappear. Then I realized something else – I didn't want to escape, I was tired of running away. I had been trusted and I was being treated humanely – I had been given back self-respect. It took me about twenty minutes to walk from the white prison to that housing non-whites, and in that twenty minutes I decided that I liked being trusted. When I arrived at the non-white prison I was greeted by a white lieutenant.

'Are you the ref.?' he asked.

'Yes – that's right. They said to come up here to ref. a match.'

'If you go down there,' he pointed. 'The induna will find the teams for you.'

I went down to the wire gate of the camp he had indicated, and I was greeted by a black prisoner with a monitor's badge. He quickly rounded up the two teams and about a dozen spectators – and the induna opened the camp gate to let them out.

'Where do we play?' I asked.

'Over there, baas,' the induna pointed to playing fields outside the wire fencing to the prison.

I took the two teams and the spectators back with me to the front gate of the prison, and the induna there let us out. The lieutenant was standing outside his office watching us.

'Make sure they all come back,' he called out to me with a grin.

'I'll do my best,' I responded.

In order to reach the playing-fields we had to walk around the fence surrounding the prison. I don't remember much about the game – except that some of the players showed a high degree of skill, and that they were adept at handling the ball when heading it. It is very hard to see a black hand alongside a black head in the heat of contest for the ball, and it was a little while before I realized just how quick and sneaky some of them were. One thing I do remember – no one argued with the referee – the match was played as a game with just as much laughter as friendly abuse. I enjoyed it and, after we returned to the prison, I agreed to come again whenever they needed me.

The lieutenant thanked me for coming, insisted I have a cool drink from his office stock, and waved goodbye as I went out of the gates to make my way back to the white prison. It was less than a week since I had left the austere regime at Central Prison in Pretoria and, although the administration had changed before I left, Central Prison was still a closed environment, housing long-term prisoners at odds with themselves and society. The tensions in such an environment, exacerbated by the continual hangings, were something that I had grown used to. At Vooruitsig, within days of my arrival, I had enjoyed more freedom, more trust, and felt more relaxed than I had imagined possible in a prison environment.

The labour board allocated me to work as a clerk in the reception office of the black prison, and during the next six months I walked to work each morning and back each evening. During that time I came to realize that not all white guards were kindly disposed towards non-white prisoners. I never saw an assault by a guard on a black prisoner at Vooruitsig, and there was none of the pillaging and theft of prisoners' property I had witnessed in other prisons. There is no doubt in my mind that this was entirely due to the influence Brigadier Fourie wielded. Of course, as in all prisons, I heard of assaults, but the only injured non-whites I saw had been injured in fighting amongst the prisoners themselves. Although I saw no assaults, there were some white guards who regarded the non-whites as little more than slaves. They treated them with no regard for human dignity or fairness. Applications for letters, visits, work transfers, and similar matters, were at times dealt with without regard to the legitimacy of the application. Outside the offices I heard that some guards goaded their work-parties and worked them beyond the regulatory requirement. I found the non-white prisoners to be mainly passive in their acceptance of a role they had been brought up to – they accepted the conditions they lived under – but occasionally they rebelled. I worked in the reception office of the black prison with another white prisoner, and one day he pointed out a white guard to me.

'There goes Seven-up,' he said.

'Seven-up? Who's he?'

'The guard in charge of the garden working-party.'

'Why is he called Seven-up?' I asked.

He told me that a few years earlier this guard had treated his work party so badly that one day they attacked him. They bundled him into the tool-shed allotted to the gardening party. There, whilst others kept watch, seven of the non-white prisoners had buggered him.

The non-white prisoners at Vooruitsig were mainly from rural and tribal areas, and most of them were in prison for the first time. They were accommodated in single-storey dormitories, like army-style huts. There were always some problems arising from tribal rivalries which, in Africa, run very deep; but most of the problems arose from the smuggling of tobacco, money, food and dagga. Dagga presented the most serious problem, both because it was illegal and because it was part of the tribal way of life many prisoners had grown up with. Serious assaults occurred because of dagga – sometimes because of quarrels in dealings in it, but often because of the intoxication the drug induced.

Another feature of life among non-white prisoners was that homosexuality was never far below the surface. The dormitory accommodation lent itself to liaisons, and the non-white prisoners who had secured positions as monitors and in the better jobs around the prison, did not hesitate to use their position to secure sexual favours from the younger, more vulnerable men. Squabbles arising from infidelity were common and were accepted as a part of prison life. The indunas seemed to be indifferent to them, and sometimes I got the impression that some indunas were equally guilty of sexually abusing the youngsters under their control.

Despite the difference in the attitudes of some staff to those adopted in the white prison, Brigadier Fourie's influence was clearly seen in the sports and recreational facilities the non-whites enjoyed. They had their own sports committee, an annual concert, boxing tournaments, and properly organized sports programmes. In addition to these facilities some of the non-white prisoners were given the opportunity to work as waiters and catering staff in the messes attached to the Vooruitsig prison complex, and others were taught building and agricultural skills.

One of the least desirable features of non-white imprisonment was the scheme under which short-term prisoners were hired out to farmers. The farmer paid a small sum to the prison, part of which was credited to the prisoner. The farmer agreed to provide clothing, food, work supervision and proper, secure accommodation. The scheme was wide open to abuse – and it was constantly taken advantage of. The prisoners represented a source of cheap labour, and a study of statistics showed a trend of increased arrests and convictions of non-whites for minor breaches of the race laws during busy agricultural seasons. The large number of prosecutions of farmers who ill-treated non-white prisoners hired out to them under this scheme is a matter of record. Those prosecutions include cases of multiple homicide caused by whipping, malnutrition and overwork. Significantly no white farmer had ever been sentenced to death for murdering a non-white prisoner. The longest sentence I ever heard of was one of twelve years' imprisonment – imposed in respect of six murders the farmer had been convicted of. That sentence was reduced on appeal.

At Kroonstad, where the scheme involving the hiring-out of non-white prisoners was operated, a check was kept on the way prisoners were treated by the farmers who employed them. I heard of several instances where Brigadier Fourie struck a farmer's name off the list of those approved by the head of the prison – but not many prison chiefs were as dedicated to the care of prisoners as he was.

After six months working in the reception office of the non-white prison, the labour board re-allocated me, and I was given work as a bookkeeper in the main prison-administration building. I became the *de facto* internal auditor for the prison members' recreation club, an organization that catered for the domestic needs and service requirements of several hundred men and women and their families. The club also met the needs of 7–800 recruits inducted annually into the prison-service training college, which was part of the complex.

Whilst I was at Vooruitsig, Brigadier Fourie's influence dominated staff attitudes and prison policies. In some ways he was a tyrant, but his aims were genuinely humanitarian, and it would be an ungenerous person who did not acknowledge this. He worked tirelessly to help the men in his care. He waged wars with prison headquarters in Pretoria about the policies he wanted to implement – and won a large measure of autonomy in the process. He lectured groups of insurance men and business chiefs, urging them to give released prisoners employment and opportunity as the logical way of eradicating the economic motivation for many offences. He invited groups of social workers, churchmen, policemen and politicians to visit Vooruitsig and see for themselves what had been done to change the attitudes of convicted men and staff alike. During my stay at Vooruitsig I came to know a great many men who owed their non-return to crime to this man, and to the policies he instituted.

In common with every prison I have been in, Vooruitsig had problems with prisoners smuggling unauthorized articles into the prison. A pretty benevolent attitude was adopted towards food, tobacco and small items which simply enhanced a prisoner's comfort. The one thing that was not tolerated was dagga. The plant grows wild in many areas of South Africa, and it presents a real control problem. It has some social acceptability amongst those who are prepared to break the law and who claim that it is no more harmful than tobacco or alcohol. It was smoked widely amongst those sent to prison in South Africa. It is a cheap, plentiful intoxicant – and easy to conceal. At Vooruitsig it was an endless source of trouble.

The use of the drug was not compatible with Brigadier Fourie's rehabilitation programmes, and it was difficult for him to obtain concessions from head office in Pretoria when statistics showed a high incidence of drug usage in the prison he commanded. Periodic abuse of the comparative freedom we enjoyed resulted in cutbacks in the facilities available to us, and on many occasions this had its origin in drug usage.

Drug-takers in prison tend to be more assertive than other groups of prisoners, and they generate and promote the fear of reprisal being taken against anyone who acts to stop their drug trafficking. Like drug users in the community at large they tend to gravitate towards one another, forming well-knit cliques, and opting out of responsibility towards the full community. Many different ways are devised to avoid detection in smuggling the drug, and during my time at Kroonstad I saw men train pigeons to fly the drug in – one man trained his cat to carry it for him. But by far the commonest means of smuggling the drug was the insertion of packets in waterproof wrapping into the rear passage. Incredibly I saw an exhibit in a charge against a non-white prisoner at Kroonstad which contained over six ounces of dagga, crammed into a small cocoa tin, which the man had then forced into his anal passage. So common was this practice among dagga users that the anal passage was colloquially known as the 'suitcase'.

I hear and read a lot of rubbish about marijuana or 'pot'. How it is a safe drug, non-addictive, and ought to be legalized – how it is less harmful than alcohol or tobacco. The people who promote this myth of harmlessness are either dishonest or ignorant of the degradation and physical harm the drug can cause. People smoke 'pot' in order to get stoned – to get a 'high'; if it had no intoxicating effect it would not be used at all, and the fact that it does intoxicate makes it a dangerous drug. If one looks at the physically demeaning practices adopted by 'pot' users, it becomes clear that we are dealing with something that has a very strong lure – that causes people to act in quite filthy and degrading ways. It is common for users to swallow small quantities of the drug, suitably wrapped, and to recover them later from their excrement, after they have passed through the body. It is common to insert packets of the drug in the rectum. It seems astonishing that anyone can suggest that a substance which can cause a man to poke about in his own shit to recover it, or causes him to hide it in his anal passage, does not have a very strong hold on the person it so degrades.

No doubt there are strong-willed or psychologically secure people who do smoke 'pot' without it ruining their lives – but I have seen young men degenerate from healthy, alert people, to become punch-drunk uncoordinated wrecks purely by smoking dagga over a number of years.

I have seen pleasant courteous young men become aggressive, selfish degenerates, because dagga took over and controlled their lives.

I have also seen a very large number of men who smoked pot socially, without any thought of becoming addicted, who, because of pot, have gone on to use amphetamines, cocaine, morphine and heroin. These men ruined their lives because of where pot led them. Those who say that it is safe ignore the catalogue of crimes committed to feed addiction to it; ignore social and domestic tragedies caused by dependence on it; and ignore the physical wrecks it is responsible for.

At one time I smoked pot socially. It gave me a buzz; helped me to escape reality for a while. At the time I was most likely to develop dependence on it I was placed in segregation, and couldn't get it. When I left segregation I looked around me and saw what it had done to men I knew, and I resolved never to use it again. There may be good grounds for arguing that there ought to be stricter controls over both alcohol and tobacco, and that both are a genuine health hazard. I can think of no grounds to justify the legalization and free distribution of marijuana.

After I had been at Vooruitsig for a year I was called to give evidence in the case against the Johannesburg newspapers. I was asked to confirm that I had been approached by van Biljon whilst I was at Central Prison, and I confirmed that I had been. The statement I had made whilst at Central Prison was put to me, and I confirmed the contents of it. My examination and cross-examination was confined to the period of 1965–6, and it was strange to find myself defending a prison system I heartily disapproved of. I told the truth; my own experiences of ill-treatment were outside the time-span covered by the trial, and were therefore inadmissible as evidence at that hearing.

26

Sporting programmes at Vooruitsig were highlighted by the visits of several famous sporting personalities. During 1967–8 we were treated to displays by leading trampolinists, including the reigning world champion. Tennis stars, Bob Hewitt and Frew MacMillan, accompanied by Evonne Cawley (then Evonne Goolagong) and Margaret Court, visited the prison complex. Hewitt and MacMillan were the reigning Wimbledon Doubles Champions at that time, and I was one of the prisoners who played a few games against Hewitt on the tennis court in A-camp at the prison. Needless to say I didn't win a game, but I did manage one snorting return of service that surprised us both. The speed and reflexes of these two great players were amazing.

Later, Ray Reardon, then the World Professional Snooker Champion, visited Kroonstad, and I played an exhibition match against him on one of the tables in the prison. Gary Player visited the prison, and this great athlete and golfer spoke to us about the attitudes that had made him the champion he was. Cricket and soccer teams from as far away as Johannesburg travelled to the prison to play matches against us. We arranged regular games of snooker, table-tennis and cricket against the staff, and there is no doubt that this involvement in healthy pastimes did a great deal to create the degree of co-operation between staff and prisoners that was so pronounced at Kroonstad.

Another regular event was blood donating. On one memorable evening we broke the South African record for the number of pints donated at any one session. We achieved over three hundred and eighty pints, and it was only when someone mentioned the number that I realized that there were only three hundred and seventy-odd men in the prison.

A quick check showed that some prisoners had got so carried away by the enthusiasm we had whipped up for the project that they had donated two pints. One young man was turned away by the doctor when trying to donate a third pint. He had successfully donated two pints by asking technicians to draw blood first from his left arm, and then from his right arm – concealing the first puncture from the second technician. At his third attempt he was spotted by the doctor as having puncture marks in both arms, and turned away with a stern warning not to be silly and endanger his health in this way.

We broke the record on a Friday evening, and it was past 11.30 p.m. before the trolley-loads of blood had been packed away and loaded on to the Blood Transfusion Service vehicles. The next day was Brigadier Fourie's birthday, and at 8.00 a.m. I went to his home with another prisoner to wish him many happy returns on behalf of the prisoners, and to tell him that we had broken the record. His house was quite a way from the prison, and when we arrived he greeted us courteously, insisting that we go into his home whilst his wife made us coffee. His interest in every facet of life in the prison he had inaugurated was clear, and he was very pleased with the news of the achievement the previous evening.

'That is a special birthday present,' he told us, and as we left he shook our hands and urged us to convey his thanks to all the men in the prison.

That afternoon I refereed a soccer match, and the young man who had been caught trying to donate three pints of blood the night before was playing. He seemed none the worse for his escapade – he scored three goals!

One of the most rewarding experiences I have had occurred at Vooruitsig. The men were encouraged to write, produce, direct and stage an annual concert. But this was a prison concert with a difference. It was held in the prison officers' club hall, which could seat some six hundred people, and had full stage facilities, lights, sound, refreshment kiosks and box office; and these were handed over to the prisoners for the duration of the concert. During my stay at Kroonstad the show ran for an average of ten days each year, covering some fourteen to sixteen performances. We ran the show for the prisoners themselves, for the prison staff, for the trainees in the prison training college, a matinée for children of the staff, and then performances for the general public.

Prisoners were encouraged to invite their friends and relatives, and the concerts were attended by people who had sometimes travelled hundreds of miles to be there. What never failed to surprise me was the amazing support the local community gave to the shows. An admission charge was made, programmes sponsored by local advertisers were sold, and a very brisk trade was conducted at the kiosks. All the profits went to the prisoners' own recreation funds, helping to buy new equipment and to pay for films and the replacement of expendable sports items. During my time we managed to help several men with the cost of advanced study courses too.

I first became involved with the layout of the programmes, and soliciting advertising revenue – but soon I was asked to help with production and direction. I began to write scripts and devise stage effects. For the next three years, when the concert came around, I became fully involved. I got to know the pressures of co-ordinating the efforts of a cast of some twenty-five prisoners plus ten to fifteen stage-hands, liaising with prison staff, and doing the hundreds of things necessary to get a show open on time. I loved it. I can think of nothing I have done that required more sheer hard work and taxed all my abilities so completely – and I can think of nothing to compare with the reward of standing at the back of the hall on opening night and watching a prisoner who has fought his inhibitions and lack of expertise deliver a performance that brings spontaneous rounds of applause from a packed audience.

I never ceased to be surprised and moved by the sheer magic of the rapport between the audience and the performer. I knew the cursing and the shouting that had gone into rehearsals – I knew how many times the man had wanted to give up – but now, on stage, the memory of tough practice sessions disappeared and a magic moment of entertainment emerged, often from the most unlikely material.

For two years I had the task of devising the complete show, and auditioning as well, and I soon discovered that any show requires firm handling of both cast and helpers – so much depends upon the efforts of everyone, even the least public stage-hand. As an example of an unforgettable experience during that time I remember an insignificant young lad who came to me and asked if he could join the rock band. I listened to him play his guitar piece – and he was terrible. There was no way I could see him improving to anything like the standard required, and I told him as kindly as I could that he was not good enough.

'Why don't you practise something from the Shadows?' I suggested.

'And when you've got it together come and see me. But you'll have to be quick because rehearsals start in ten days' time.'

He was obviously disappointed. He went away and I didn't expect to see him again; but ten days later he was back, and he asked me to listen to him again. He strummed a few chords on his guitar and then settled down to play. He had chosen 'Apache', a smash hit by the Shadows. He wasn't bad, but I doubted he could improve enough in the time we had for rehearsals. I was impressed by his persistence and, as I was about to tell him that I was sorry he couldn't join the concert group, I noticed that the fingers of his left hand were discoloured and had plaster on them.

'Let's look at your hands,' I said on impulse.

I took his left hand and gently pulled back the plaster on his middle finger. He winced – and so did I. He had practised until he had no more skin on his fingers – they oozed blood beneath the plasters.

He became a star in the show. No one in the audience knew the effort he had made, and no one knew that apart from 'Apache', and the short encore I had made him learn, he could hardly play at all. On stage he looked like a lost waif, with immense appeal, and his playing of 'Apache' was infectious and precocious. The audience loved him – and I got a lump in my throat every time I watched him perform – I remembered how close I had come to rejecting him, and I could never forget those bloody fingers.

The total commitment of all the men I worked with in those shows made it possible for us to pull in full houses every night we performed for the public. The sheer determination to succeed made the men perform far beyond anything they had believed themselves capable of.

One of the special memories I have of those shows is of the evening we entertained the folks from local old people's homes. We hired coaches and fetched them from the residences. Each one got a front-row seat, a programme, a small gift, and refreshments; and as the show ended with old favourites like 'Danny Boy' and 'Bless this House', I saw many a tear wiped away from the eyes of these lovely old people.

The concerts were a very special experience for me and for all those connected with them. They did more to break down the barriers between law-abiding citizens and those who had offended than any other exercise I know of.

Soon after my arrival at Kroonstad, Brigadier Fourie was promoted to a newly created regional command, centred on Vooruitsig. His place was taken by Colonel Otto, who followed the same enlightened policies. Two years later Colonel Otto was transferred and Colonel Loubser replaced him. I came to know Colonel Loubser better than his predecessors. He was a man who admitted to me that at times he had acted cruelly and wrongly in the past, but at the time I knew him he was a man with a very real commitment to the policies he inherited. I liked his straightforward approach to the problems that landed on his desk each day. He had a genuine sense of humour – and, at times, he needed it. I worked closely with him on matters related to prisoners' needs, and he later allowed me to travel from prison to Johannesburg, where I helped to negotiate the purchase of two full-size snooker tables and a pair of 35 mm projectors for weekly film shows. I remember conspiring with Colonel Loubser to get the snooker tables delivered over a weekend when the Brigadier was away – because we both felt he might veto them as unsuitable recreation. And I remember Colonel Loubser's quiet pleasure when, on an inspection of the prison some time later, the Brigadier asked him,

'Waar die donner het julle hierdie gekry?' (Where the devil did you get these?)

'Die inwoners het hulle aangekoop, Brigadier,' the colonel replied very casually (The inmates bought them, Brigadier).

I was asked to help in the sale of advertising space in a diary published by the prison command – in order to raise funds for an Olympic-standard swimming pool at the prison training college. I went to Johannesburg with another prisoner, and for two weeks we canvassed support, arranged printing and publishing, and got the project off the ground. During those two weeks I lived in an apartment we rented for the purpose. A young guard spent some of the time with us, but he was recalled suddenly when his father-in-law died, and from then on we were on our own.

We had hired a car to enable us to canvass efficiently, and one morning as I drove towards the city centre I saw a young woman whom I thought I knew. I drew up and offered her a lift. It was Dawn, who had helped me so often as an escapee some ten years earlier.

'Jesus Christ!' she exclaimed. 'Not another escape?'

I laughed and explained my reason for being in the city. We had coffee together and she told me she was staying with 'friends'. She had changed very little and we agreed to meet later that evening after I had finished work. She waved goodbye as we parted – but in the evening I found that the address she had given me was a false one. The young couple who lived there had never heard of her. Perhaps she found me less attractive as a legitimate parolee than I had been as an escaped habitual criminal.

During the two years that he was in charge, Colonel Loubser allowed the prisoners at Vooruitsig a great deal of freedom – but not all my experiences at the prison were pleasant. The complex incorporated a unit for young offenders and this unit, approved by Brigadier Fourie, was run on the so-called 'short, sharp shock' principle. Young men were subjected to a daily routine of crushingly hard labour and very strict discipline. The compulsion necessary to enforce this policy made it inevitable that abuses would occur – and they did. On several occasions I protested at the treatment the young men received, but Brigadier Fourie would not be moved. He believed in the idea of a short, hard experience as being deterrent and rehabilitative. I did not share this belief at that time – and my experience since all serves to confirm my view that such systems are counter-productive. My view is that punishment, which is what a short, sharp shock is, has to be immediate, certain, consistent and equitable, if it is to either correct or deter. No custodial regime at present meets these requirements. Custodial sentences are not immediate – they last too long – they drag on for days, weeks or months, and in so doing they cease to be related to the offence for which they were imposed in the mind of the recipient of them. They evolve an identity of their own, quite separate from the concept of 'immediacy' which would make them effective. Nor are custodial sentences certain or consistent – the belief that the offender will not be caught next time eliminates any element of certainty, and detection statistics prove that in fact the young offender is more probably certain not to be caught, and strengthens the belief among young offenders that punishment is a consequence of being caught and not of offending. Disparate sentencing eliminates consistency and creates feelings of resentment that negate the effectiveness of the treatment – and at the same time disparate sentencing policy, which tends to penalize the poor and the unemployed, has never been equitable. This trend is current in Britain today, resulting in sentences that are often too severe – occasionally too clement.

The records show that, in every country it has been tried in, the short, sharp shock regime breeds callous and uncaring attitudes in those required to enforce it – and a sense of injustice and resentment in the majority subjected to it. The incidence of recidivism amongst those who passed through the juvenile unit at Vooruitsig was several times greater than amongst young offenders who had more caring treatment.

When Colonel Otto left Kroonstad, he took up the post of officer commanding Groenpunt prison, a prison farm near Vereeniging in the Transvaal. Some time after he had left I was called to Colonel Loubser's office and told that I was to be transferred. I was very surprised until the colonel explained that Colonel Otto had asked to borrow me for a few days – to sort out an accounting mess at his new prison. Two days later Colonel Otto arrived, and I travelled to Groenpunt with him, his wife and two small children, in his private car. At Groenpunt I shared an army-style hut with three other prisoners.

As soon as I began work on the books of the prison members' club it became clear that no proper records had ever been kept. I had a meeting with the club's auditors and got them to approve a plan to consolidate previous accounts, and I then opened up a new set of books for the current financial year. When I had completed the work we found that the club's wet canteen showed unexplained losses. Subsequently I showed that a chief guard had embezzled the money, and he was disciplined.

On my return to Kroonstad, another officer who knew me, a Major Stoop, asked to borrow me to install a new accounting system at the prison he had recently been transferred to, and I spent some time there teaching staff to operate it.

In 1970, a Major Snyman took over the white male prison at Vooruitsig. From the outset he made it clear that he disapproved of the policies that Brigadier Fourie had instituted. He was unhelpful when approached regarding prisoners' needs, he was frequently untruthful, and he quickly lost any respect his rank might have inspired. Colonel Loubser was transferred and his place taken by another colonel, a small man whose name I can't remember. His nickname was 'donner en bliksem', which is an idiomatic expression which roughly translates as 'bloody hell', but the Afrikaans is somewhat stronger. He was arbitrary, unhelpful and usually unapproachable. Both he and Major Snyman were dedicated Afrikaners, and they made their dislike of me as an Englishman quite plain. I found it increasingly difficult to work with them, and eventually I resigned the head monitor's post I had held, and asked for a job in the library.

One of the effects of the change was that the studies, that I had given up when transferred from Pretoria in 1967, now had a greater appeal to me. My registration with the University of South Africa had lapsed, but the Department of Education agreed to accept the credits I had acquired towards my B. Com. degree for exemption purposes in respect of the National Diploma in Commerce. In 1971, I completed this diploma, and I received my certificate with a sense of achievement. I was thirty-seven years of age, and I had found the discipline of study difficult – now I was glad I could relax and take part in sport again. Whilst working in the library at Vooruitsig I also began to give evening classes for prisoners taking 'O' levels in accounting, economics and business economics, and I found a great sense of satisfaction when those I had helped were successful in passing their examinations.

27

The arrival of Major Snyman and the new colonel meant the end of Vooruitsig as Brigadier Fourie had envisaged it. The emphasis shifted gradually away from rehabilitation to containment. It surprised me that the introduction of old traditional attitudes was permitted by those higher up in the chain of authority, but perhaps there was little that could be done once these two men were in charge at Vooruitsig. It must have been painful for Brigadier Fourie to have to watch as he saw a regime he had devoted his life to undermined and broken down by the type of men he had had to overcome in order to establish it. Prisoners no longer had such free access to sports facilities. Fund-raising schemes to improve and maintain equipment were discouraged, and the prisoners' sports inventory began to show signs of wear and tear. One thing the new officers could not do was to cancel the annual concert – it was a privilege written into the prison regulations – but they did so much to obstruct it that it headed for disaster. I had opted out of the overall arrangements, and confined my efforts to producing a good quality pop group.

Three days before the show was due to open the first stage-rehearsal was held, and one of the officers asked me to go and watch it. I did so and, when asked for my opinion, said it was a shambles. It had been interfered with so much by Snyman that it had no continuity, not a lot of enthusiasm from the performers, and a general air of despondency about it. I was asked to put it right as the 'top brass' were coming from Pretoria to see it.

Working through the days and nights left to us, a new show emerged.

Scenery was altered, two new backdrops were painted, lighting sequences were reorganized, and the major part of the show rewritten. I sat in front of the stage with a typewriter and wrote the script as we rehearsed. Fortunately the programmes had been designed for just such last-minute alterations, and a new centre page was printed and bound into place. It was an incredible experience. Everyone worked extremely hard and a new enthusiasm seemed to emerge from the pressures placed on us. We became determined to show that, provided prisoners were left alone to get on with it, they could achieve very high standards.

The show was a success. We played to full houses for ten days – and the funds we raised did much to restore the fortunes of the prisoners' sports committee.

A few months later I was transferred to Zonderwater prison, close to Baviaanspoort where, as a young man, I had undergone such brutal treatment. Zonderwater was an open prison and the administration was quite liberal. Accommodation was in dormitory-type huts, and I was sent to work in the paint-shop. Shortly after we arrived my bedside locker was searched in my absence and I was charged under the prison regulations with being in possession of unauthorized articles. The articles were a pair of underpants several sizes too small for me, and a small pair of socks which didn't fit me. I was told that I had forfeited three meals, and I was locked up in the segregation cell for one day to make sure that I didn't get any food from my friends. Upon my release I discovered that the man responsible was the same chief guard whom I had proved guilty of embezzlement at Groenpunt some years earlier. I immediately approached the major in charge of the workshops and, within hours, I was transferred from Zonderwater back to Central Prison, Pretoria.

When I arrived and looked at the high walls, I relived some of my experiences inside them. The architecture was the same but, when I got inside, I found a different atmosphere. A long-serving guard in the reception office recognized me, and I knew one or two of the prisoners – but, apart from that, the whole prison seemed to have changed. Everything was much more easygoing than I remembered it.

I was assigned to a cell on A3 landing. It was next door to the one I had occupied some nine years before. For two weeks I was given no work to do, and I spent my days in the exercise yard and my nights in the cell, thinking about the way life had brought me a full circle, back almost to the same cell I had occupied in 1963. It was April 1972, and by a strange coincidence, Colonel Otto, whom I knew from Kroonstad and Groenpunt, was now the officer commanding Central Prison.

Executions no longer took place in the prison. A new unit, complete with gallows, had been constructed almost on the top of Vulture's Hill, directly behind Central Prison, and condemned men no longer walked and sang through the main hall on their way to die. The day after my arrival I had gone to the main clothing store in C-section, and there I met John Bradley, who had been sentenced to die for his part in the murder of Waldeck, a director of a mining company. The prosecution case had been that Bradley met a man at Jan Smuts airport outside Johannesburg, and took the man directly to Waldeck's home, waited while Waldeck was shot on his doorstep at point-blank range, and then drove the man directly back to the airport. By the time the police found out what had happened, the man was safely back in Britain. Whilst Bradley was in the condemned cell at Central Prison, London detectives had visited him and, in recognition of the help he gave them about London gangs, his death sentence was commuted to one of life imprisonment. When I met him I found him to be arrogant and self-opinionated.

Jeff was another man I met at that time. I had known him for a number of years. He had conducted a homosexual affair with a highly intelligent, well-educated young man called Raymond. They were exact opposites, Jeff being rough, uncouth and of low intelligence – but they were fatally attracted to one another. One day Raymond was found dead in A-section. The door of the cell he was found in was locked, as was the security grille inside it. Raymond had suffered extensive stab wounds, many of which he could not possibly have inflicted on himself. At the time Jeff was in a hospital ward some four hundred yards from the cell Raymond had been killed in. Everyone believed that Jeff was responsible for the murder, but in order to have committed the crime he would have had to leave his hospital bed, pass through at least three manned and locked steel grilles, and then open Raymond's cell door and grille. He would also have to have returned by the same route. There was no way he could have done it without the help, albeit unwitting, of the guards – and the guards said that they had seen and heard nothing. As far as I am aware the mystery remains unsolved.

After I had been in Central Prison for two weeks, I was called to an office on B2 landing, where the old condemned cells had been. A young clerical guard, whom I had never met, asked me if I had any clothing.

'Yes, I've got an outfit in reception,' I told him.

'Good,' he said, quite pleasantly. 'Does it need pressing?'

'I should think so,' I replied. 'But what do I need clothes for?'

'You're going into town tomorrow to have your photograph taken.'

'What do I need a photograph for?'

'For your passport,' he said. 'You're being deported in three days' time. Hasn't anybody told you?'

That was how I received the news that after more than fourteen years in South African prisons I was to be released and sent back to Britain. I made my way back to my cell on A3 landing in a daze. I didn't yet believe that it was true. There had been no warning, and under South Africa's remission laws I still had more than five years of my sentence to serve. The news found me completely unprepared and, for the first few hours after I had been told, I was unable to relate to it at all.

'I'm going to be released,' I told anyone who would listen.

'Good luck to you,' they replied, and then carried on with whatever they had been doing. I looked at them and then realized that I didn't even know the people I was talking to.

'I've finished twelve years,' I said to a man I hardly knew.

'Jesus! I'll bet you'll be glad to get home,' he said as he made his way to get some hot water for his tea.

No one seemed to understand.

What followed was like a dream. My photograph was taken; the British Consulate issued me with travel documents; I signed numerous release forms; and all the time I tried to believe that it was really happening. On the morning I was to leave I was taken to the reception and handed my belongings. I dressed in a sort of daze. A head guard whom I had known came in and shook my hand.

'Totsiens. Alles van die beste!' he said as he wished me goodbye and good luck. I looked around the reception office and recognized neither the guards nor the prisoners there. They were all strangers. So much had changed since my admission to the prison. I had been a celebrity then – one of South Africa's most wanted men, according to the media. Now it was 1972, twelve years on, and those years had swallowed up my reputation. Attitudes had changed – now I was just another prisoner for discharge.

'Teken hier,' a reception guard pushed a property and private-cash record towards me for signature. 'Het jy alles?'

'Yes, I've got everything.'

It was only 7.30 a.m., but already the heat of the high veld sun was finding its way into the office. Contrary to all my expectations I suddenly felt very tired. I had waited so long for this moment, and now that it had arrived I felt a little afraid. The faces I had grown used to over the years had changed and I was being processed by strangers. I felt a little resentful that they did not recognize who I was. They were too impersonal. I had grown used to insults and abuse in this prison – and now, in a strange way, I missed them. The discharge procedure itself was strange and unfamiliar. I was about to leave an environment that had provided me with food, clothing and accommodation – I was apprehensive about leaving, afraid of the world I had forgotten and I was now being returned to.

Over the years I had considered this moment, but never as anything real. Now that it was actually happening it found me unprepared. It brought with it a new set of tensions and fears to take the place of those I would leave behind me in prison. I was thirty-eight years of age, and I was about to be deported to a country I had left as a child of fourteen. From the prison I was to be escorted to the airport and put aboard a Boeing 747 of South African Airways. I would be accompanied by two members of BOSS, the notorious Bureau of State Security. Their duty was to see that I did not leave the plane en route to London.

It was all unreal – the sort of thing you read about in books – and I found it very hard to accept that it was actually happening to me. The reception guard handed me over to my escorts and, a few minutes later, I was standing outside the gates of the prison. I climbed into the unmarked car that had been provided, and my escorts settled in on either side of me. As we pulled away I looked back and saw the sun shining on the weathered red brick and grey stone of the prison walls. The prison gates closed and it looked just as it had many years earlier when I had first seen it. But it was not the same – this time I was leaving.

I looked ahead and the car pulled out into the main stream of traffic, turning right and heading up the hill leading out of Pretoria. On the left stood the imposing new buildings of South Africa's Open University, the largest of its kind in the world. A little farther on, dominating the hill on which it stood, towered the Voortrekker Monument – not just a memorial to the courage and endeavour of Afrikaner pioneers, but a symbol of Afrikanerdom itself – with its ox wagons drawn up in laager formation, a rallying point for the old and the young of a beleaguered nation.

A civilian jet-liner passed overhead, slim and shining against the clear blue of the sky. I realized that it had just taken off from Johannesburg's Jan Smuts International Airport, where we were headed. I tried to remember what it had been like to travel by air before I had gone to prison. The planes then had been old Dakotas, Skymasters and Constellations. The Vickers Viscount, the whispering giant, had been quite new.

Now I was going to travel by Jumbo jet. I looked around at the countryside we passed through and I realized, with surprise, that I did not feel tired any more.

28

The flight from South Africa to London was fairly uneventful. We flew first to Salisbury in Rhodesia, now Harare in Zimbabwe, and milled around in the small transit lounge at the airport while mechanics tried to repair a faulty lock on the rear door of the aircraft. From Salisbury we flew to Luanda in Angola, where a new lock was fitted whilst we took refreshments in the air-terminal buildings. Security was very tight, the military was very much in evidence and armed soldiers guarded every area in the airport complex.

By the time we had taken off and were on our way again I had celebrated my release with a few whiskies, and as we flew around the bulge of Africa I watched an in-flight movie until I fell asleep. I woke briefly when we refuelled at Las Palmas, and then I dozed until we came in over the English Channel, early in the morning, locked into the flight-pattern that would guide us to Heathrow Airport.

The two BOSS agents had virtually ignored me throughout the flight. At Heathrow they arranged for me to leave the plane before the other passengers, and I was met by the British police. They quickly established that I was not wanted for any offence in Britain, showed me where to find a taxi, and bade me farewell.

One item of clothing I found I needed was a belt to take up the slack caused by weight loss whilst I had been in prison. Sitting down in the plane it had not presented a problem, but now I got the taxi driver to take me to a men's outfitters, where I purchased a belt and a few other items I needed. I found a small hotel in South Kensington and, as I booked in and paid a deposit on the room, I knew for the first time that

I was really free. I lay on the bed after the porter had deposited my luggage and I began to consider my position.

I was a complete stranger in a country that was strange to me. I would have to get a job and arrange accommodation a good deal cheaper than the hotel I had booked into. But, although I knew these things had to be done, for the time being my mind rejected consideration of them. I was in no hurry to exchange the euphoria of my new-found freedom for the mundane constraints real life imposes.

I had spent almost my whole adult life in prison, and neither my childhood nor my prison experience offered me much help in coming to terms with life as a free agent. I had given as little thought to what I was going to do after release as I had to what I would do after I escaped on previous occasions. The pattern was the same. I was inadequate in social skills, and had forgotten much of how to earn a living and set up a home. The years in prison, despite the enlightened regime at Kroonstad, had left deep psychological scars, and these now began to make themselves known. Years of silence had created a mental block that returned in times of stress, making speech difficult, seriously affecting my ability to communicate freely. A very real sense of guilt about my background began to emerge, leading me to avoid anything except casual conversation. But these things were to become apparent later – now I lay on the bed in the safety of my hotel room and tried to get used to the idea that I was free.

That evening I left the hotel and ventured out into the streets of South Kensington. I had found it strange to be able to open the door to my room and simply walk out. I was very self-conscious, and I imagined that the hotel porter was keeping an eye on me, and I curbed a strong desire to go and tell the night porter where I intended to go. One of the things that stopped me doing so was the fact that I had no idea what I was going to do. Outside it was already dark, and the sight and sound of the traffic and of pavements filled with bustling people frightened me at first. I kept well away from the kerb. I could see the speed and sensed the purposefulness of this mass of humanity, and slowly I came to understand that I had no objective, I had no reason to hurry. As I watched them I wanted to retain my independence, to put off the time when I would have to become one of these people, one of the hurrying masses.

I was to learn that I was not a normal man – in many areas of normality I was not functioning at all. In dealing with the problem of my new-found freedom I would have to relearn how to respond to normal situations, I would have to proceed carefully, for I had largely forgotten how people in a free society were supposed to treat one another. It was the first time I had ever been in London at night, and as I walked along towards Knightsbridge I began to feel more confident. I stepped towards the edge of the pavement and hailed a taxi.

'Piccadilly,' I told the driver.

The lights, the jostling crowds, the noise and, above all, my freedom to go and do what I pleased, were intoxicating. I moved carefully, not yet sure of myself, still learning to accept that I was free, that it was not a dream. I registered at Charlie Chester's Casino and remember a mild irritation when told that I must wait forty-eight hours before I could gamble. I wandered along Shaftesbury Avenue looking at the theatre lights. I had two pints of lager, finding the brand names strange and unfamiliar.

Well before midnight I hailed a taxi to take me back to the hotel. I was not used to late nights and, quite irrationally, I was afraid that I would offend an unseen authority if I over-indulged on this first night of freedom. I had met no one, I knew no one – and as I returned to my hotel, somehow the excitement and pleasure I had experienced seemed a little devalued – I began to realize that I was alone.

I had arrived in London with approximately £200 sterling. This represented money saved from the gratuity paid to prisoners in South African prisons each month, part of which they are compelled to save. It had taken twelve years to accumulate and a few days after my arrival in Britain I went to Epsom racecourse. I lost almost every penny.

I felt a sense of panic. I was shocked at what I had done and yet I felt that it was not my fault – I was quite unable to accept responsibility for it. I blamed the bookmakers, the jockeys, the trainers, the horses – anyone but myself. Fortunately I had paid for my hotel room in advance, and I had two days in which to solve my dilemma.

For twenty-four hours I did nothing. I hid in my room – emerging only at mealtimes. Gradually the shock of my loss faded and I began to rationalize that I had done nothing illegal – that I ought not to be angry with myself. I realized that I was not going to be punished by any higher authority, and I began to feel a little more clever and cocky. I fantasized that I was a man of the world – a man who had survived tougher things than the loss of money. It was a hiccup, I would make it up. One thing it did do – for the time being I was scared to place a bet. I had no one to confide in, and so I told no one about my loss. I bought a newspaper and found a job as a live-in barman.

I was to remain in this type of work for the next eighteen months. I was competent and my employers found me reliable. After I had settled into my first job, I began to gamble again. One of the regulars at the bar was a bookmaker with a betting shop almost opposite the pub, and I used to place small bets with him. On my days off, I would travel into London and spend time in the casinos, but, at this stage, my betting was kept within the limits of what I earned. The unsocial hours that bar staff work in Britain gave little opportunity for social activities, and I made no friends. I was afraid to let people get too close to me – afraid that I would let slip something about my past. I had hidden my criminal record from my employers, and the need to maintain secrecy about it made close friendships dangerous – I avoided them. After eighteen months working as a barman, I obtained work as an estimator for a glazing company.

Gambling had by now become a part of my life. It relieved me of any need to expose myself to others. Gamblers do not ask questions of each other, and bookmakers and casino operators are not interested in the problems of the people they lure. Gambling is a solitary pursuit, and the crowds that gather at racetracks and in casinos are largely composed of individuals, each pursuing his or her individual objective. They form part of a community where each is competing against the bookmaker or the casino, but individually, not as a group. Secretiveness is part of the ritual a gambler embraces, and it spills over into other parts of his life. It fitted in very neatly with my fear that my background would be exposed, and it made me careful in my conversation. Gambling itself provided temporary relief from the need to have friends, to form a satisfying relationship – and I sought that relief more and more as my loneliness became more pronounced. At first I restricted my wager to amounts that I could afford, but gradually the self-control I had exercised fell away, and I began to find myself without funds to meet my commitments. On several occasions I found myself penniless, and had to walk the eight miles or more back from the casino in Piccadilly to Crystal Palace, where I was working. I borrowed money from my employer, telling him lies about a sick relative to justify the request. I arranged a small bank overdraft and I took out a loan with a finance company. But these were only stop-gap measures, and as my involvement in gambling grew, so did the need to find the money to feed the involvement.

One evening in 1974, I had been to the casino and lost all my money. I walked along Piccadilly, preparing to walk back to Neasden, where I was then living, when I bumped into a man coming towards me, and turned around to apologize. It was Jack 'Babyface' Goodwin. We were both momentarily stunned, and then we recovered and I wrung his hand as I remembered where we had last met – in a labour gang rooting out trees in Central Prison, Pretoria, more than 6,000 miles away.

Jack looked very prosperous. He was visiting London en route to Canada. He invited me to dinner and we renewed acquaintance over Châteaubriand and a bottle of Chambertin. It was an unforgettable experience for me. Over the previous two years I had hidden behind a façade of respectability, careful not to reveal my background. With this man I was free to talk, free to discard pretence without fear of criticism. It was as though a dam had been breached, and I felt the pressures flow away as I told him about my experiences since leaving South Africa. I told him about my gambling losses and he gave me enough money to meet my immediate needs and promised to keep in touch with me. That night as I lay in my bed I felt that my life was about to change. I had met someone whom I regarded as a friend, and for the first time in two years I had spent an evening without barriers, without fear, and without inhibition.

My life was about to change. I was about to be drawn back into the world of fantasy I had lived in before my imprisonment in 1960. I would make half-hearted attempts to resist, but already I had begun to identify with the glamour of the world Jack 'Babyface' Goodwin had reminded me of. A few days after he left for Canada, Jack telephoned me at my place of work. He was speaking from Montreal and invited me to join him there. My financial position was again desperate. I had made no friends in Britain. I had no reason to remain in London, and so I accepted his offer. I left my job without giving notice, wrote letters of apology to my bank and the loan company, collected the return air ticket Jack had arranged, and flew to Canada.

I might have been less enthusiastic had I known that the ticket I was flying on had been obtained fraudulently.

29

I stayed in Montreal for only six weeks. During that time I discovered that Jack Goodwin was engaged in an attempt to sell shares in an off-shore finance company to United States citizens. I was not sure of the legal position, but I knew that the Securities Exchange Commission frowned on this type of operation. I had a healthy fear of arrest and imprisonment and so I decided to leave. Whilst I was in Montreal, Jack had introduced me to a lifestyle more befitting a millionaire than someone in my position. Through his Nassau-based company, he arranged credit-card facilities for me and, on my return to England, he arranged a hire car and hotel accommodation for the first few weeks. I accepted these gifts from him and returned to London with a full wardrobe and over one thousand dollars in cash.

My association with Jack worried me – I sensed that what he was engaged in would bring trouble to everyone connected with it. I knew that he would probably arrange a way of avoiding payment of his bills, including those arising from the credit facilities he had arranged for me; so shortly after my return to England I adopted the name George Thompson and, hiding behind my new identity, cut off any links I had with Jack's Canadian operations. Before I did this I had exhausted all the credit facilities Jack had arranged for me, and quickly lost all my cash in the casinos I visited. Gambling again became a factor influencing my behaviour. I sold my camera, my few personal possessions, and eventually most of my clothing, in order to feed what had become a serious compulsion.

Using my new identity I obtained work as a live-in barman in Notting Hill Gate and, despite my fears that continuing to associate with him would get me into trouble, I contacted Jack through an acquaintance called Jack Baker. When Jack Goodwin returned from Canada, having abandoned his scheme, I met him with Jack Baker and, together, they outlined a scheme they had worked out to enable South African citizens to transfer funds out of that country, bypassing normal monetary controls. The premium South Africans were prepared to pay to exchange rand for pounds sterling made the scheme very profitable. The South African regulations at that time allowed the transfer of money to pay for business services without control, and I agreed to join them in exploiting this loophole in South African legislation.

We decided that a British company, providing business services, was needed, and it was agreed that this should take the form of a mailing-list service. I was asked to register a company for this purpose, and I did so – using the name George Thompson to do so. I then proceeded to set up a service that would provide the cover the scheme needed. The intention was to provide a South African company, Prestige Services of Johannesburg, with invoices for the supply of direct-mailing lists and, by inflating the fees and issuing bogus invoices, to create an apparently legitimate reason to make substantial payments to the British company.

Not having the funds to hire premises or take on permanent staff, I advertised for home-workers to address self-adhesive labels, commonly used in direct-mail operations, and made preliminary arrangements to obtain copies of electoral rolls from which names and addresses could be copied. I required home-workers to furnish a small deposit to cover the cost of the labels and lists I would send them, and I was inundated with letters taking up the offer of work. I banked all the monies I received, issued receipts, and informed the applicants that the work would be forwarded to them within ten days. Five days later, whilst collecting mail, I was arrested by City of London police, who told me that they believed my intention was to defraud the home-workers by stealing the deposits I had been sent.

I was in a dilemma. I was a party to a conspiracy to bypass South African fiscal controls, and to explain the whole scheme to the police would inevitably have led to them informing South African authorities – and to the arrest of Jack Goodwin, who had returned to Johannesburg. As far as I am aware I had contravened no law which warranted either my arrest or my subsequent trial, but my reluctance to explain the whole scheme to the police left a great many questions unanswered. Police suspicions hardened and, I believe, my unwarranted arrest now had to be justified – so the police set to work to prove that their allegation was true.

I was held without bail, incommunicado, refused permission to use a telephone either for a solicitor or a friend until I had made a statement. Any illusions I may have had about the honesty of British policemen were soon dispelled. They continued for weeks to tender spurious reasons to the court for objecting to bail, and they did so in order to bring unlawful pressure to bear on me to involve other people in the matter.

'Tell us about Jack Baker,' they said. 'And we'll let you go.'

They falsely pretended that I was wanted by the police in other countries, and it was only when they were shown to be unable to produce any evidence whatsoever to substantiate these allegations that the magistrates lost patience with them and allowed bail. Whilst holding me in custody the police raided my room without a warrant, despite the protests of the landlord, and removed all my belongings – including all the documents I needed to show exactly what I had been doing. Later they were to claim to have lost my contract with the South African company, vital to my defence, and so deprived me of evidence which would have shown conclusively that I had been acting in good faith.

Despite my clashes with the police and prosecution in South Africa, I had always believed the myth that British policemen are fair and impartial. My experience at the hands of the City of London police left me in no doubt that the truth was of less interest to them than the preparation of a watertight case. Irrelevant facts were twisted to fit a preconceived theory and then slotted into a one-sided framework of evidence – and relevant facts, not susceptible to distortion or misinterpretation, were omitted or concealed if they did not fit into that framework. I am not surprised by recent convictions for corruption in the City of London police force, or by the allegations that the corruption was widespread. The cynical, dishonest attitudes I experienced were entirely consistent with those that gave rise to recent corruption charges.

I had been held in conditions that are an affront to any civilized society in Brixton prison, awaiting bail. Both staff and prisoners are subjected to disgusting, overcrowded conditions, and when I left there, having been released on bail, I left with a deep resentment of the treatment I had received, contempt for the police who had lied at my court appearances, and apprehension about the forthcoming trial. If the rest of the

British justice system was as bad as that I had so far experienced, I saw no chance of my receiving a fair trial.

I returned to the public house I had been employed at prior to my arrest. The licensee told me that he had been refused permission by the City of London police to visit me, and that they had warned him not to re-employ me upon my release. Despite this he very kindly provided me with a room and board until I could find my feet – he did all he could to help me. He, too, had been shocked by police tactics – they had ignored his protests and searched my room without permission or a warrant, removing documents and personal possessions without giving a receipt for them.

My fear of prison, which I believe had prevented me from actively engaging in crime up until this time, was now submerged in the resentment and sense of injustice I felt. I found a room, but the police had effectively cut off my ability to earn a living. It may sound incredible to anyone brought up in the welfare state, but at that time I had no idea of how to go about claiming unemployment or supplementary benefits – nor was I aware that I was entitled to them. There hadn't been state handouts in South Africa. I was in rebellion against authority, and I identified very strongly with the criminal sub-culture my brief stay in Brixton prison had introduced me to. I was ready to listen when Jack Baker and a friend of his offered me the chance to earn money with stolen credit cards and cheque books. Under their guidance I quickly learned all there was to know about this type of fraud.

Jack Baker provided me with a car and with references enabling me to obtain a flat in Artillery Mansions, in Victoria Street, Westminster, directly opposite New Scotland Yard. My bail conditions required me to report regularly to Paddington Green police station, and whilst doing so I was engaged almost daily in 'fronting' for Jack Baker and his friends with stolen credit cards and cheque books. There was a certain perverse satisfaction in doing this from an address opposite New Scotland Yard.

I prepared my defence against the charges I had been bailed on with some care. I had several interviews with my solicitor and a long, full consultation with counsel. The full amount of the money I had received from job applicants totalled £192, and this was lodged with my solicitor, who advised me that to return it to applicants prior to my trial could be construed as acknowledgement of guilt. During my talks with solicitor and counsel I did not tell them the whole truth; I continued to shield

Jack Baker and Jack Goodwin – the first because he had stood bail for me, and the second because he was liable to arrest by the South African police if I did not do so.

On the morning my trial was to commence at the Old Bailey, I was met at the court by a barrister I had never seen before. I was surprised, but he reassured me, saying that he had only stepped into the case because the barrister I had had consultations with was tied up in another case. He said that he had read the brief, was *au fait* with all the facts – and then asked me to plead guilty!

'We don't want to upset the judge,' he said.

I have since discovered that the fear of upsetting judges controls the actions of a large number of solicitors and barristers – and is the prime factor in determining what line of defence to pursue, irrespective of the merits of the case. One is left with a picture of irascible and intolerant judges, and kowtowing, sycophantic court officials. This must say something about the barristers, or the judges – or both. Another practice that I now know is common is for barristers to accept briefs and then pass them on when they are unable to meet their commitments in respect of them. The result is that very often an accused is represented by counsel who knows little or nothing about the case he is presenting. The prisoner has no complaint, or any chance of proving that he has become a mere 'football' in the scramble for legal-aid payments by these barristers.

I explained to my new counsel that I didn't really mind if the judge did get upset, suffered from indigestion or had boils – what I was interested in was an acquittal, based on the fact that I was not guilty. The barrister scratched his head beneath the wig he was wearing, said that he had read and understood the brief and, on reflection, thought we had a good case.

'It will be up to the jury,' he said, and then he fairly flew into the courtroom, wig awry, gown flapping, and proceeded to completely mess up what had been a good, simple defence. It soon became clear that he had neither read nor understood the brief – nor did he believe in my plea of not guilty. It was not so much a trial as a débâcle. The police lied about the contract they had taken possession of when searching my room – saying it did not exist – and lied about what I had said to them when they first approached me. The judge refused to subpoena documents that would have proved conclusively that one of the state witnesses was lying. The court's bias is best shown in interjectory remarks made whilst I was giving evidence. My counsel had asked me what steps I had taken to ensure that no monies I received as deposits went astray.

'I opened up a set of books,' I replied.

'What system did you use?'

'The normal double-entry system,' I said.

'Double entry,' the judge interjected, turning to the jury to emphasize his point. 'That sounds highly suspicious.'

Whether the interjection was intended as entertainment or not, it had the effect of belittling my evidence and possibly casting doubts on my honesty in the minds of jurors not familiar with bookkeeping practice. Of course, I should have dismissed the barrister for his incompetence – but I didn't. It was my first appearance in a superior court in Britain, and I was a little overawed and complimented that it was at the Old Bailey. The air of theatre in the courtroom seemed to make what was happening less real, and I could not bring myself to believe that anyone could be as bad as the man who was defending me – I kept waiting for his 'master-stroke', his attack on the state case, but it never came. Despite the fact that I began to believe the man was a fool, he was a good actor, and I was curiously reluctant to dismiss him. The whole thing appealed to my gambling instinct – legal proceedings are frequently decided by pure chance, and as the risk of conviction grew and the odds against acquittal lengthened, I became more and more detached until I seemed to be watching the proceedings as an uninterested party. Were I ever to meet that barrister again I would not let him defend my dog.

When the defence closed I realized that the case was lost. Whatever reasons may have motivated me, my failure to explain some matters, my barrister's clear disinterest, and the judge's bias, must have left the jury with little option but to convict. It was a Friday afternoon, and the judge remanded the matter without beginning his summing up. He allowed my bail to stand, and I returned to my flat opposite Scotland Yard with a weekend to look forward to a return to prison.

'Four years, I should think,' my barrister told me quite cheerfully.

My memories of prison in South Africa now came flooding back. They were very vivid indeed, and my experience of British prisons at Brixton had done nothing to dispel them. I had a little money and I decided to have dinner and go to a casino. I did so – and I won several thousand pounds. There was now no reason for me to stay in England. Jack Baker had been paid back the amount of his bail surety many times over as a result of my credit card and cheque frauds. I had no ties, no friends; and so, on the following Monday morning, I obtained a passport and left the country. At about the time the judge was inquiring where I might be, I was having a quiet drink on the Champs-Elysées in Paris.

Later I learned that the trial continued in my absence. My conviction was a formality in view of my non-appearance. My barrister had been right about not upsetting judges – the trial judge took exception to what he regarded as my wasting the court's time, and to the fact that I had estreated bail.

For convictions involving one hundred and ninety-odd pounds sterling, I was sentenced to seven years' imprisonment, *in absentia*.

30

For the next eighteen months I lived as a fugitive, and my first impulse was to get as far away from Europe as possible. I remained in Paris for only a few days – then I flew to Canada, staying a little while in Montreal before renting a car and following the trans-Canadian highway across that vast country. My route took me to Toronto and then, skirting Lake Huron and Lake Superior, to Winnipeg, Moose Jaw, Medicine Hat, Calgary, and on over the Rocky Mountains and down into British Columbia – and Vancouver. I had travelled over 3,000 miles by car from Montreal and I was glad to relax and enjoy the unhurried way of life Vancouver offers. I took the ferry to Vancouver Island, stunned by the incredibly beautiful scenic route. I discovered cosy bars, good restaurants, and friendly people. I met a showgirl from Las Vegas and she moved in with me for ten days whilst she waited for money to arrive from her home town. Then I discovered trotting. The racetrack was just outside the city and I spent several nights there losing whatever money I had.

When I left London I had taken with me several stolen credit cards and false identities, and now I added to these by obtaining a Canadian passport. Once I had lost all my money gambling at the trotting-track I began to use these stolen credit cards to live on – and this meant that within a short time I had to leave Vancouver, or risk arrest. Using the new Canadian passport I crossed over into the United States, taking the coach from Vancouver to Seattle. There I rented a car and drove down the western seaboard until I came to San Francisco, crossing the Golden Gate Bridge and finding my way to Nob Hill, booking into the prestigious Fairmont Hotel – ironically one of the hotels used by John Stonehouse when he staged his disappearance. During the day, I visited the beaches and watched the tram-cars as they climbed incredibly steep hills all around where I was living. I spent my evenings visiting restaurants and shows but, inevitably, the lure of the casinos in Nevada proved irresistible.

I had spent some of my time accumulating resources with the aid of my stolen credit cards, and now I travelled to Reno and in two days exhausted whatever funds I had. I gambled morning, noon and night – it was a new experience to have the dice table opened up especially for my use at 8.30 a.m., so that I could have a little action before breakfast. My cash exhausted, I made my way back to San Francisco, stopping at Boomtown on the Nevada–California state border to get rid of the few dollars I had raised by selling my watch. Continuing on my way to Sacramento I was stopped by the Highway Patrol as I crossed the Rocky Mountains. I was taken into a mountain village where I was arraigned before a Red Indian judge, and charged with speeding. He fined me twenty-five dollars, and I had to ask for time to pay – explaining that I had lost all my money in Reno. The judge smiled and told me to post it to the court within ten days.

I stopped for an hour in Sacramento and used my credit cards to buy a camera and a new watch, and then I carried on to San Francisco. There I sold the camera, abandoned the car I had been using and, after one night in a Hyatt Hotel, where the service was lousy, I rented another car and set off to drive across America. Once again I crossed over the Golden Gate Bridge, looking down at the shipping a long, long way below. I recrossed the Rocky Mountains, drove across Nevada and on into the vast flatlands, heading for Utah, and Salt Lake City. I stayed there for two days, amazed at the lush green landscaping of the university complex – a startling contrast to the arid plains in which the city lies.

From Salt Lake city I travelled on, through Denver, Colorado, Kansas and Kansas City, until I reached St Louis, Illinois. The sun was shining as I drove into the city and the huge crescent of the Spirit of St Louis shone like burnished gold. It was an amazing sight, and it soared overhead as I crossed the river looking for an hotel. I had driven some 6,000 miles in a few weeks, and my shoulders and neck muscles were feeling the strain. As I booked into the hotel I inquired where I could get a massage. The reception clerk referred me to a salon not far from the hotel, and after a shower and a change of clothing I took a taxi to the address I had been given. The establishment proved to be on the tenth floor of an office block and, when I arrived, I was shown into a room by a young lady and told to undress.

'I'll be with you directly,' she told me.

The room she had shown me to was quite large. Plush red curtains draped three of the walls and the only furnishings were a low, double divan-bed, and a small table with a collection of oils and powders on it. The bed was not more than ten inches high, and it was set in deep-pile, wall-to-wall carpeting. I began to undress, placing my clothes carefully on the floor beside the bed. As I stepped out of my trousers I stumbled and fell against the curtains, falling through the drapes and bouncing off the plate glass. I recovered my balance, but not before I heard a loud crack, followed by sounds of glass smashing on the sidewalk below.

A few minutes passed as I waited for the girl to return, and then I heard male voices in the corridor outside the room. The door was thrust open and two policemen, their hands on holstered revolvers, stood looking at me through the doorway. I felt a bit foolish standing there in my underpants, but after they had established that I was all right they wished me 'good evening' and left. Not long after they had gone the girl came and asked me to move to another room. She helped carry my clothes and explained that I had smashed the plate-glass window, and that the police had insisted the room be closed until the window was repaired.

The new room was almost identical to the one I had left and, after leaving me for a few minutes, the girl returned in a dressing-gown. She asked me to strip off and lie down, and when she discarded her gown I saw that she was naked. She had a trim, young figure, her breasts standing out pertly as she approached the bed. She knelt beside me and placed the towels she had brought with her next to the bed.

'Do you prefer oil or powder?'

'Oil, please.'

'Would you like a hand massage or a body massage?'

'Which is best?'

'Most clients prefer the full body massage,' she said with a smile.

'I'll have that then.'

She poured oil on to her hands and rubbed them together – then she leaned over and spread it across my shoulders. She lightly teased the tensed muscles around my neck and smoothed the oil over them.

'My name's Lucy; what's yours?'

'I'm George,' I said with a chuckle.

'Well, you relax, George, and let me get rid of that tension.'

It was easy to comply, and I felt the muscles begin to loosen under her fingers. Her hands moved down my spine, teasing the muscles that driving had tightened up. She moved down and worked the oil into my feet, legs and buttocks.

'You can turn over now.'

I turned on my back and looked at her kneeling beside me. She grinned at my embarrassment.

'My goodness, you're a big man,' she said playfully.

I was very conscious of her nudity and, as her hands worked oil into my arms and chest, she leaned over so that her breasts brushed against my cheek. Impulsively I turned my head and kissed them. She chuckled and made no effort to remove them. Her hands worked on the muscles of my stomach, deftly brushing and then avoiding my erection as she worked down thighs and legs until she reached my feet. Then she turned to me and smiled as she began to run oil over her own thighs. Moving up the bed until she was beside me, she held out the bottle of oil.

'Would you mind putting it on?'

'Where do you want it?'

'All over, please.'

I sat up and poured a little oil into one hand, and tentatively began to rub it on her shoulders.

'No, not like that,' she said. 'You have to use both hands.'

'Then you'd better lie down so that I can do it properly,' I said.

I spent the next fifteen minutes making sure that I hadn't missed anywhere on her body. She was relaxed and appeared to enjoy it as much as I did. When I had finished she sat up and told me to lie down on my stomach. Then she began to massage me with her body. It was one of the most sensuous experiences I have had. She used her breasts at first, caressing me with them, and then pressing them firmly against me as she worked over my body. Later she used her stomach and the insides of her thighs to massage me. Her skin seemed incredibly smooth and soft, and when she told me to turn over, I lay on my back as she began to work on my stomach and thighs. She was unable to avoid my erection, and she stopped and looked up at me.

'Would you like me to?' she asked.

I nodded, not wanting to speak. She smiled and turned away, her soft hands encircling and then gently stroking me. Then she lowered her head and her hair fell forward on my groin a moment before her lips brushed me. I tensed as I felt her tongue playing on me; and then she opened her lips and I felt the warmth of her mouth envelope me as she lowered her head still further and I involuntarily rose to meet her.

Afterwards she sat back on her heels and carelessly played her hands over me, no longer avoiding any contact. She turned to me and saw that I was smiling.

'Satisfied?'

'Thank you,' I said, nodding.

'You're welcome,' she said.

The route I had chosen took me to Chicago, and I stayed there for two days before heading for Cleveland, Ohio, and then on to New York. Entering the city I lost my way and somehow finished up in the Bronx. I stopped at a gas station to inquire where I was, and a pretty black girl in a white, convertible Cadillac solved my problem by driving ahead to show me the way I wanted to go. I booked into the Lexington Hotel, behind the Waldorf Astoria, and when the reception clerk advised me to put all my valuables in the hotel safe I knew that I had arrived.

In the evening I walked down towards Broadway, crossing Fifth Avenue and pausing to wander round the fountains in Rockefeller Center. Having reached Broadway, I made my way up to Times Square, but I found it disappointing – not at all what I had imagined it to be. Retracing my steps I found my way to Dempsey's Bar. The great man was there, posing for photographs, and protected from everyone by his wife. I sat next to him and we posed together for photographs. I chatted with him and asked him what he had been thinking about during the long count in his fight with Tunney.

'Nothing really,' he said. 'I just wanted to finish it off.'

'You mustn't ask questions about his career,' his wife intervened.

After a few drinks, I wandered on down Broadway. I noticed a lot of people going into a doorway – and no one seemed to be coming out. They all seemed quite respectable, so I thought I would go in too. The doorway proved to be an entrance to a passage that led into a large room. A big man stood at the entrance to the room.

'Good evening,' he said. 'That will be two dollars, please.'

I paid him and went in. There was a bar set up in one corner of the room, and a number of people were drinking there. At first I didn't realize what struck me as strange about the people, and then I saw that there were no women in the room. As I made my way towards the bar I noticed another doorway opening into another room, in which I could see men and women mixing together. I went over, and a big man stood just inside the room.

'Good evening,' he said. 'That will be five dollars, please.'

I paid him and went over to the bar and ordered a drink. Looking around I realized that all the women were with partners and, when the bar tender set up my drink, I asked him if there was anywhere I might find some company.

'Why don't you try next door,' he suggested, pointing to yet another room entrance. I thanked him, finished my drink, and went over.

'Good evening,' the man at the door said. 'That will be ten dollars, please.'

I paid him. I reckoned that if the price was anything to go by, I was beginning to make some headway. I was not disappointed. I quickly made contact with a small brown girl. She had huge brown eyes set widely apart in a pretty face. She had a pert little nose and a happy smile.

'I'm Glory,' she told me.

'Gloria?' I queried.

'No, Glory,' she said. 'Like in "Glory, glory hallelujah".'

We had a drink together and I asked her if there was somewhere more private that we could go.

'Sure, honey,' she said cheerfully. 'We can have our own room if you like.'

'I'd like that,' I told her.

She got up and took my hand, leading me to a doorway that opened into a hall. I could see a flight of stairs beyond the hall, but first we had to pass yet another big man.

'Good evening,' he said politely. 'That will be twenty dollars, please.'

'For two?' I asked him.

He grinned.

'That's right, bud,' he said.

Glory led the way up the stairs and along a corridor until she showed me into a large room. She closed the door behind us and I looked around. The room was dominated by a huge circular bed. Mirrors covered two walls and had also been fixed to the ceiling.

'The jacuzzi is over here,' Glory said, as she led me to a recess fitted with a circular, sunken bath, a toilet, bidet and shower.

'Is this OK?' she asked as I looked around.

I nodded, and she seemed pleased that I was satisfied. She went over and bounced lightly on the bed.

'What do you want to drink?' she asked me.

'Can we get champagne?'

'Sure, honey,' she skipped off the bed and caught my hands. 'Can I have some, too?'

'Of course you can. You can have whatever you like.'

Her eyes sparkled as she began to loosen my tie and unbutton my shirt.

'Gee, you're swell,' she said. 'I think I like you.'

We shared two bottles of champagne, and Glory offered me a joint from the pot she had brought with her. I declined: I was already a little drunk and I didn't want to miss out on what was to come.

It was past midnight when we made our way down the stairs to the hallway, and the same big man guarded the door as we left.

'Good evening,' he said, and I paused beside him.

'No charge?' I asked him.

He grinned at me as I turned to go out the door.

'Wise guy,' he said.

The rooms were more crowded than when I had arrived, and it was about 2.00 a.m. when I finally made my way out on to Broadway. I decided to walk the few blocks back to my hotel, and set off along the sidewalk. It was fairly chilly, and the steam escaping through gratings in the sidewalk made the deserted streets seem a little strange and eerie. I felt relaxed and quite pleased with myself as I walked along. A black man stood in a doorway and eyed me as I approached; then he stepped out to block my path.

'Let's have your bread, man,' he demanded belligerently.

'Fuck off, you bastard!!' I screamed at him.

He flinched and seemed shocked at my anger. Then he backed off and turned to shuffle back into his doorway. A little further on two large shadows loomed up, one on either side of me. I looked around and saw that they were New York policemen – their long night-sticks swinging loosely in their hands.

'Good evening,' one of them greeted me. 'You're out late?'

I explained that I was on my way back to my hotel.

'You're British,' the cop said, recognizing my accent. 'It's really too dangerous for you to be out alone at this time. D'you mind if we see you back?'

They walked along with me, one on either side. I felt a little strange being escorted by two policemen, but when we got to the hotel I thanked them.

'Have a nice stay,' they said as they strolled away into the night.

Later I realized that I had left the photographs of myself with Jack Dempsey beside the bed in the room I had shared with Glory. It was much too late to go back to get them – and the next morning the doors leading into the place were securely locked.

The continual use of stolen credit cards meant that I had to leave New York, and I decided to make my way back to Montreal by coach. I knew that I could not stay there long without risking capture, and within days I flew back to Paris, and then returned to London.

31

Prior to my leaving London, and whilst I had been on bail, I had met a young woman called Karen. She was an Iranian student, and we had had a brief affair – now, on my return to London, I renewed the friendship. Karen was twenty-three, many years younger than me, but we enjoyed a very high degree of compatibility. The difference in our ages never seemed to intrude.

Settling back into the pattern of life I had lived before fleeing to Canada and the United States, I made contact with men who offered me the opportunity to cash a parcel of stolen travellers' cheques. I did so, and after I had lost half my share gambling, Karen persuaded me to take a holiday in the South of France. We travelled by air from Gatwick to Le Touquet, and there we boarded the little yellow train that takes air travellers into the Gare du Nord in Paris. A taxi took us to the Place de la Concorde at the foot of the Champs-Elysées. We spent the first night in the Sheraton Hotel, and in the morning I rented a car and we moved into a smaller hotel – a little to the east of the Arc de Triomphe.

We remained in Paris for several days, visiting Notre Dame and the Louvre, and drinking coffee at pavement cafés, watching tourists and *Parisiens* pass by. Karen tried to persuade me to go up the Eiffel Tower, but my fear of heights proved stronger than her pleas, and we bought a souvenir model of the tower instead. At night we went to the Moulin Rouge, the Lido and the Crazy Horse, enjoying the special vitality that makes Paris night-life unique. But the pleasure we found in the evenings' entertainment was only a prelude to the happiness we shared when, hand in hand, a little drunk, we returned to our hotel room in the early hours of the morning. Karen was a caring and responsive lover – slim and with a dusky eastern beauty, she never failed to excite me. She had huge brown eyes which reflected her moods, and I responded to her pleasure and her anxieties as with no one I had known before. I learned again what it was to love and be loved, and as my reserve fell away my happiness grew.

Leaving Paris we headed south towards Nice and Monaco, taking the route through Lyons, Grenoble, Digne and Grasse. We passed by the monastery where Chartreuse is still made, and high in the French Alps we sampled wines sweet with the flavour of honey – the bouquet of mountain flowers still trapped in them. When we arrived in Nice, we chose an hotel on the seafront and spent several days doing nothing except bask in the sun. We visited Cannes, and in the evenings we wandered between pavement bistros, sampling wines and food, happy in each other's company. At night we returned to the hotel and fell into contented sleep – close together – satisfied with our lovemaking.

From Nice we moved on to Monte Carlo, booking into a small hotel at the bottom of the hill overlooking the harbour. I was conscious that however idyllic our holiday might be, I would have to return, at some time, to the criminal way of life I seemed to be locked into. My past actions had made it almost impossible for me to pursue any normal career without risking exposure and arrest, and the ease with which the banks made their facilities available to all and sundry made the type of crime I specialized in very profitable. For the time being, however, I put that problem to one side and determined to enjoy this holiday to the full. The grey skies we had left in London quickly became a distant memory.

I lay on the bed in the hotel suite and listened to the sound of Karen showering through the open bathroom door. The shower was turned off and Karen padded barefoot into the bedroom, clutching an enormous bath-towel around her. She moved to the full-length mirror and smiled at her reflection, dabbing at the drops of water that glistened on her skin. She stopped as she felt me watching her, and then she turned and came to me. She leaned down and kissed me gently, a wet strand of her hair falling down and lightly playing against my cheek. I put my arm around her shoulders and drew her down beside me. Gently I loosened her fingers and put the towel to one side. We embraced, and I shivered a little as she pressed her still damp body against mine. She looked up at me, her eyes searching mine, and then she kissed me again.

'I want you,' she said, almost in a whisper.

Later, we slept, nestling close together, the warmth of the evening making bed-clothing unnecessary. When I woke Karen was sitting up on the bed beside me. She was watching me and gently ruffling the hair on my chest. The after-scent of our lovemaking hung faintly on the air, and she smiled as I pulled her close and kissed her.

'I'm hungry,' she said.

We had dinner looking out at the lights of the harbour. I watched as the waiter placed a flaming Zambouki in front of Karen. She studied it before gently lifting the glass. The pale blue flame flickered and the coffee beans hissed softly as they roasted. She blew the flame out carefully and then sipped the clear liqueur, then replaced the glass gently on the table and, reaching over, she placed her hand over mine. Neither of us spoke – we didn't need to.

Leaving the restaurant we moved slowly towards the casino. Palm leaves rustled softly overhead, and strings of coloured lights swayed gently in a warm breeze. Below us the lights of the yachts bobbed and twinkled at their moorings in the harbour. Across the water, the palace of the Grimaldis stood floodlit on the promontory guarding the principality. It was breathtakingly beautiful – like a scene from a fairy tale.

In the casino we moved into the inner gaming-rooms, and for a little while savoured the atmosphere, watching the roulette tables. Karen fingered the betting chips I had given her, running her fingers over the '1000' printed on them.

'How much are they worth?' she asked me.

'It doesn't matter,' I told her. 'Tonight nothing matters.'

Impulsively she placed two chips on the red diamond and stepped back, watching anxiously as the wheel spun. There was a tinkle as the small white ball fell into a division.

'Trente-six. Rouge. Pair,' the croupier called. He added two chips to those Karen had wagered, and she hesitated and then let it ride. Again the wheel spun and the white ball whirled until it was finally trapped. We looked anxiously to see where it had fallen.

'Dix-huit. Rouge. Pair,' the croupier called.

We watched as four more chips were added to Karen's stake. She shook her head as the croupier looked at her inquiringly. The wheel spun again, as though it would never stop. Finally the ball tumbled into a slot.

'Cinq. Rouge. Impair.'

Eight more chips were added to Karen's pile, and she made a preparatory move to collect them; but then she shook her head and stepped back. We tensed as the wheel spun and the white ball became a dotted streak. Then it lost momentum and fell, rattling over the divisions at the wheel base. There seemed to be a pause before the number was called.

'Cinq. Rouge. Impair,' the croupier chanted, his voice expressing no emotion. There was a small sigh from the spectators as sixteen more chips were pushed over beside Karen's stake. Again she hesitated, and then she shook her head. There was a low buzz of excitement as the other players placed their bets. Karen now had thirty-two thousand francs piled on the red diamond. Then the wheel was spinning again and the ball became a blur. As the wheel slowed, the small white ball tinkled against the metal dividers. It seemed to hover for a moment before turning over and nestling into a notch. There was a little silence as we all strained to see where it had fallen.

'Sept. Rouge. Impair,' the croupier announced, and an audible sigh went up from the spectators.

Karen moved to the table to collect her winnings. She could not hold all the chips, and I helped her to carry them over to the cashier's cage. Together with those I had given her, there were sixty-seven chips. The cashier checked them and then counted the money out carefully.

'Soixante-sept mille francs,' he said finally.

I gathered up the banknotes and gave them to Karen, but she pushed them back to me.

'You look after it,' she said. 'It's nearly seven thousand pounds.'

I carefully pocketed the money and put my arm around her waist as we turned away from the cashier. She leaned against me and I realized that she was trembling.

'What's the matter?' I asked her.

She looked up at me, and then she grinned.

'I might have lost,' she said quietly.

We made our way into the bar lounge and found a table against a wall. A waiter came over to take our order.

'Madam? Monsieur?'

Karen looked at me, and we both laughed.

'Dom Perignon,' I said.

We left Monaco the next day and stayed for a few days in Cannes. Then we slowly made our way back to Paris. We lingered there, reluctant to bring the holiday to an end.

When we did return to England it was from Calais. It was only when I saw the white cliffs of Dover that I realized that I had been to Monte Carlo, visited the casino, and had not placed a single bet.

Back in London I leased an apartment near Portman Square, and began to develop my contacts. I found that I was able to obtain stolen cheque-books and cheque-guarantee cards quite freely, and I spent several months commuting between London and the capitals of Europe, cashing stolen commodities I had obtained.

Karen was unaware of my true occupation. I told her that I was a commodities dealer, and beyond inquiring whether I had had a successful day, she never pried into my affairs. I would leave the apartment at 6.30 a.m., in order to catch an early flight to Paris or Amsterdam, spend the day cashing cheques in the city I had selected, and then return to London on a late afternoon flight. Occasionally Karen would ask me where I had been, or I would bring her a present from the city I had visited, but she expressed no surprise at my travels, regarding them as part of my normal work pattern.

Our friendship had developed into a warm and rewarding relationship. In December 1974, Karen left to spend Christmas and New Year with her family in Tehran. I saw her off at Heathrow, and we both looked forward to her return early in January of 1975.

Once Karen had gone, my need to gamble seemed to increase. Money was easy to come by – I was offered more commodities than I could handle. I found that I missed Karen terribly, and I began to gamble recklessly. As my gambling became more impetuous so did the rest of my behaviour. I forgot the rules I had made to safeguard myself against re-arrest. I began to revisit places I had avoided, and it was in Charlie Chester's Casino, ironically the first casino I had ever joined, that I was re-arrested by detectives from Snow Hill police station.

After a brief visit to the police station, I was taken directly to prison to begin serving the seven-year sentence that had been passed at the Old Bailey in my absence. The shock of my re-arrest and committal to prison was severe, but it was as nothing compared with my feelings at my separation from Karen. The strength of those feelings came as a complete surprise to me and, perhaps for the first time in my life, I was made to realize just how much my years in prison had cost in terms of personal relationships. During the early days of my sentence I became very depressed, and a probation officer at Wormwood Scrubs prison seemed to sense my feelings, helping me through the first few difficult days, and arranging for me to be allowed to telephone Karen in Tehran. When I spoke to her I managed to contain my own emotions, and I told her not to return on my account – but she insisted on doing so, and she visited me regularly until I had settled down, and then, as we had agreed, she left me.

After my re-arrest I faced trials in respect of the offences I had committed as a fugitive and whilst on bail. The Scotland Yard detectives who dealt with those matters acted with propriety at all times, and I had no complaint about the way they handled an inquiry that proved to be quite complex. Eventually I received a further three years' imprisonment for all the offences I had committed whilst on bail and as a fugitive – and I asked the courts to consider 876 offences other than those I had been charged with.

After that hearing I was returned to prison to serve a sentence which now totalled ten years' imprisonment.

32

The prospect of long-term imprisonment was daunting. Although, in general, I found the regime in England less onerous than in South Africa, my sentence represented a long, dark tunnel which, at times, I was unable to see the end of. The environment in prison is depressing, and is seldom conducive to the promotion of good habits. There are many reasons why this is so. There are the disgusting conditions of overcrowding and undermanning in many prisons. There are the groups of prisoners who neither recognize, nor have the desire to change, habits that bind them to crime. It is unfortunately true that prisons are so organized that these groups influence the treatment meted out to all prisoners – in a way that is inimical to reform or rehabilitation.

Despite this I tried to reassess my life. I had not at that time acknowledged that gambling had played a very large part in influencing my behaviour – but I was aware that if I wanted to stay out of prison I had to alter my ways. Upon my conviction and sentence, everyone except Karen had deserted me – and when she left me I was completely alone. I became determined to manage on my own, to do without help.

I remembered the genuineness of Don Martyn in Central Prison, Pretoria, and I began to attend church regularly, hoping to recapture some of the basic honesty I had lost; hoping to rediscover some of the moral discipline that I had abandoned after being cut off from the Exclusive Plymouth Brethren. I was unfortunate in that I failed to meet any churchman in British prisons who was not a servant of the Home Office first and a Christian second.

Imprisonment is by definition non-voluntary, and the violence inherent in the coercion necessary to enforce it causes resentment and antagonism. My past experience had taught me how easy it was to become embittered and twisted, and many of the failings in the British prison system promote just such tendencies. Committal to any prison is a thoroughly degrading experience. The shock of the verdict, the sentence, and the separation from loved ones, is compounded by the way personal dignity and self-respect are encroached upon. There seems to be an indifference to human needs. Upon admission all the convicted prisoner's personal effects are taken from him. He is stripped and issued with prison clothing. Bureaucratic regulations mean that the man who has thoughtfully provided himself with toilet and smoking requisites finds most of them confiscated. Private clothing is packed away, valuables and money held for safe-keeping – and when the formalities are complete the prisoner is given a number and told not to forget it. The number identifies him within the prison system and helps to strip him of his former identity.

Allocation to a prison wing brings the prisoner into contact with what prison life really is. In Britain today he is subjected to a daily routine that erodes self-respect, denies initiative, and is often physically nauseating. The physical aspects of having to use plastic toilet-buckets in communal cells is demeaning, and the queues at morning unlock to perform the disgusting slop-out procedures are unacceptable by any civilized standard. Wash-hand-basins where prisoners wash, shave, clean teeth and wash up the plastic plates and utensils used for meals, are sited in the same area as open toilet-cubicles, urinals, and the hopper into which toilet-buckets are emptied. These facilities are usually used at the same time as one another – so that a man may be cleaning his teeth at a wash-hand-basin whilst, less than three feet away, another prisoner is emptying his toilet-bucket. Meals are taken in cells where the smell of the previous night's use of toilet-buckets often lingers, and the prisoner gets used to the smell of excrement and the smell of the disinfectant supplied in an effort to prevent an outbreak of disease.

Chronic overcrowding in local prisons thrusts the shocked new admission into conditions that are a disgrace to successive governments that have allowed them to develop. Whatever fatuous excuses may be offered for treating human beings so badly, the effect is to confuse, frustrate, embitter and harden. Recently, prison staff who have to work in these filthy conditions have rebelled and refused to accept more admissions once regulatory numbers are reached. As a result, cells in local prisons designed for one man now often hold only two – a big improvement over three – but still completely unacceptable by civilized standards.

Prison staff are employed to enforce the custodial element of any sentence, and they are front-line targets for any sense of grievance prisoners may feel. Sometimes those grievances are justified – and the inability or unwillingness of staff to deal with them strengthens the aligning of prisoner against prison officer. I realized that if I wished to live successfully as a free man, and not return to prison upon release, I had to try to avoid becoming a party to that alignment. I had to try to stop my feelings of injustice and resentment, whether justified or not, from colouring and controlling basic attitudes.

My experience with Karen had made me aware of feelings I had forgotten, and had allowed me to savour just how fulfilling a good relationship could be. I determined to do all I could to lead a normal life and develop lasting relationships. I tried to interest myself in projects that would fill in the idle hours. I studied Spanish and German, and passed examinations in both languages. I wrote a novel which obtained a commendation under the Koestler Award scheme.

At Gartree prison, after a period in the workshops, I was employed as a red-band in the administration block, working mainly with civilian staff. They afforded me the chance to keep in touch with ordinary people, something that my lack of friends and visitors made especially important.

Gartree prison is a relatively new establishment. Although originally intended for prisoners with medium-term sentences and of low security risk, it has become a maximum-security prison housing long-term, high-risk men. The cells were designed for short- to medium-term prisoners, and it was envisaged that the doors would be unlocked much of the time – these cells are too small to house long-term prisoners. The prison has been the scene of two serious riots, and I was there when the last one occurred. I was asked then what I thought had caused the riot, and I said that Gartree, or any similar prison, is a riot waiting to happen. I have not changed my view. If you take men and sentence them to terms of imprisonment that are impossible to come to terms with, and then place them in cells designed for prisoners with shorter sentences, you have the recipe for a riot – and you ought not to complain when you get one. At Gartree, I found that after two years the walls of the cell I occupied seemed to close in on me. It was a slow process, but inexorable, and it caused feelings of hostility which I did not understand, but which were directed at the staff. I felt under pressure, almost like the pressure that claustrophobia brings. It was not a pleasant experience, and those prisoners serving sentences much longer than mine displayed more serious reactions than I did. Because of the violence inherent in it, imprisonment can never be humane. To argue that one can inflict deprivation and pain humanely, is nonsense. Prison will always cause physical and psychological suffering, and when this is realized it becomes naive to express surprise when riots do occur – they are simply communal reaction to the imposition of suffering.

At Gartree I was given every opportunity that the system allowed to develop attitudes that would help me to lead an honest life upon release, and, as the time for my parole consideration approached, everyone at that prison tried to help me. Their recommendations were based on the efforts they could see I had made to change my attitudes – the only way my efforts could be tested was for me to be granted parole, and they recommended me for it.

My first parole application was refused – but I was granted a ten-month review. No reasons were given for the refusal and, ironically, had I been granted parole on my first application I had a job to go to. My second attempt to gain parole was successful, and I was released on my birthday, 22 March 1979. I had served four years and three months of the ten-year sentence and, during the preceding twenty-five years, had spent a total of nearly twenty years in prison. My parole licence was to run for two and a half years, and the arrangement was that I should initially fall under the supervision of the probation service in Leicester.

I am grateful to all those who did so much to help me at Gartree prison. They hoped, as I did, that I would succeed. Subsequent events show that I failed very badly – but this was not the fault of the system of parole or of those who recommended me. What I did not know, and what the ordinary prison regime provides no answer to, was that I still harboured attitudes that would prevent me seeking help when I was unable to cope with life's problems; I still carried a very strong compulsion to gamble, and I had not come to terms with the reality of my previous way of life – nor did I really believe that I was capable of living an alternative way of life. My basic attitudes towards society had developed largely in prison, and were coloured by personal experience of injustice – like most prisoners I was quite unable to accept personal responsibility for my way of life. These basic attitudes were a barrier in forming normal friendships, and my failure to make friends, in turn, led to loneliness, frustration – and to a return to gambling.

The probation service at Leicester seemed to me to be pretty disorganized when it came to finding accommodation for ex-prisoners. In my anxiety to get out of prison I would have accepted a tent to live in, and what I was offered was not much better. It was a cubicle created by subdividing a bedroom. My section had no window and provided walk-through access to the rest of the bedroom, depriving me of any privacy. It measured five feet by eight feet, leaving me space for a bed and a small table. It was not suitable accommodation, but it was approved by the probation service and therefore acceptable to the parole board. The probation service told me that they had nothing else to offer. I hoped to improve on it as soon as I obtained work, and I left prison without a job, living on supplementary benefits of twenty-five pounds each week. My board and lodging cost eighteen pounds per week, leaving me with just seven pounds to meet all my other needs.

After I had moved into the accommodation provided, I found that the owner of the house was a hard-working single parent, who took pains to ensure that I had at least one substantial meal each day – but she had a drink problem. I woke up on several nights to hear her fighting with her men friends and, on one occasion, I was woken by the sound of splintering glass as she put her fist through the front door, having forgotten her keys. My interviews with my probation officer tended to play down my problems and emphasize my hopes. I felt very insecure, and I had an ever-present fear that were I to show any inability to cope with my problems I might be recommitted to prison. So whilst I did mention my accommodation problems I tended to conceal their seriousness, and I played down my growing disillusionment as the economic climate worsened and work became more difficult to obtain.

All my job applications were unsuccessful except one. I was offered a job selling shower units door-to-door – but the boss made it clear that he expected me to continue to draw supplementary benefits whilst working for him, so that he could pay me a lower wage. I refused this offer. High-pressure selling had got me into trouble before, and I was not yet ready to break the law, and my parole conditions, and place myself at risk.

I began to make soft toys – although my landlady disapproved. She did not like me sitting in my cubicle sewing; she thought I would be better off socializing with her drinking companions. I had neither the money to do so nor the inclination, and she accused me of being 'stuck-up'. Well, perhaps I was. I worked very hard at making soft toys, taking a very small profit, and soon I was making ten to fifteen pounds each week. But then I was told that if I earned more than four pounds per week my benefits would be stopped – so I gave up making soft toys.

The seven pounds per week left over after I had paid my board and lodging did not go very far. Quite often I did not have the cash to make telephone calls to set up appointments for jobs, or the bus fare to attend them. I began to spend days walking the streets – just to get out of the house. I visited local parks and cemeteries, and the peace and quiet were very pleasant after the noise and fighting that was increasingly a feature of life at my lodgings.

Interviews arranged by the Job Centre dried up after the girls there got to know about my prison background, and I was reduced to searching local newspapers and newsagents' notice-boards as a way of finding job vacancies. I could not take part-time work without forfeiting my benefit and no full-time work was offered to me. I was prepared to accept any position. I applied for a job as a trainee lathe-operator, only to find myself in competition with skilled men who had been made redundant by Rolls-Royce. I applied to be a machine-minder for a company manufacturing screws, but I was told I was too well qualified. I sought jobs as a quality-control clerk in an engineering firm; as a work-flow controller with a textile company; as a trainee with a firm making exhaust-systems; as a storeman, a bookkeeper, a junior accountant, a sales manager. The answer was always the same. I was too old, too well qualified, or my background made me less suitable than other applicants. I began to conceal my qualifications, but when I applied for a job packing potato crisps and was turned down I began to lose hope.

After I had been free for about eight weeks I began to visit betting shops. I used the weather as an excuse at first – when it was dry I walked the streets, when it rained I went into betting shops. Very soon I was walking the streets less and going into betting shops more. Looking back it is easy to see that what was really happening was that I wanted to bet. Gambling attracted me and it fulfilled a need – but I did not recognize that at the time. The betting shops provided me with company – not to talk to, but to be near and to be part of. Once in the betting shops it was inevitable that I began to gamble; at first in ten-pence units. Usually I lost – and so I had even less money for bus fares, telephone calls or anything else.

Strangely, I was not unhappy about losing. My satisfaction seemed to come from taking part, irrespective of the outcome. I found satisfaction in studying the form of horses and all the other things that go to make up the game of deciding what to back in a race. As I became more and more disillusioned about job prospects, gambling moved in and became more and more important to me. Reading the racing news and listening to the racing commentaries became more real and more satisfying than the round of job applications and refusals. I never really expected to win, but I had found a way of making time go by, of escaping from the reality that my life was a failure.

Then I had a succession of wins which totalled over £250, and gambling took on a different role. I reasoned that even if it was not a very secure way of making a living, at least it was not illegal – and in the euphoria of winning I fantasized that I could become a professional gambler. I made careful plans to allow myself only a certain stake each day, and I worked out a system that I believed would eliminate catastrophic losses whilst maximizing winning opportunities. Of course it was a load of rubbish – but as my gambling compulsion was reawakened all my normal instincts were submerged beneath the need to satisfy my gambling urge.

I went to the Post Office to open a savings account, but was advised that I could get better withdrawal facilities with a Girobank account. I applied for one and was issued with a cheque book and a cheque-guarantee card. I was surprised that these were issued freely and without any references being asked for. I deposited £230 in the account, and later, another £120 from winnings at the three Leicester casinos I had now joined.

Gambling was now my main occupation. I gambled on horses during the day and in casinos at night. I spent less time at my lodgings, often returning in the early hours of the morning when the casinos closed. My landlady raised no objections – she thought I was having an affair, and I did nothing to change her opinion. In talks with my probation officer I mentioned my winnings, but played down the role that gambling now played in my life. Inevitably the time soon came when I had exhausted all my winnings – and I was left with a gambling compulsion I did not recognize or understand, and no money to satisfy it.

I was in a casino at the time, and I gave no thought to the consequences when I issued a cheque for which I had no funds. I issued the cheque in my own name, giving my own address. I continued to lose, and continued to issue cheques. I was unable to stop myself, caught up in a cycle I could not break. It was two days before the gambling fever seemed to leave me and I was able to sit down and look at what I had done. I could see no way of making up the amount of money I needed to meet my commitment to Girobank. The position appeared to be hopeless. Were I to tell my probation officer what I had done I would have been recommitted to prison. When the cheques were cleared an investigation would show what I had done, and I would face charges of fraud and recommittal to prison. Faced with the option of accepting the reality of my position or running away, I did what I had been doing all my life – I elected to run away.

Once that decision had been made I used all my abilities to ensure that I would not be re-arrested. I obtained a birth certificate in the name of Newsum, and I left Leicester. By doing so I made my breach of parole conditions public, and I wrote a letter to my probation officer telling her that I was leaving, but not what I had done.

Three months after my release from Gartree prison my parole licence was revoked. I had moved to London, and it was there that I hoped to begin life again – as a fugitive.

33

After my arrival in London I secured cheap lodgings – and I continued to gamble. Within a short period, I became a member of eighteen casinos throughout the country. The cheque book I had been issued with by Girobank was soon used up, and I solved my money problems by applying for two further Girobank accounts in false names. In each case, using an accommodation address, I was issued with a cheque book and a cheque-guarantee card without any request for references. My actions were clearly illegal and fraudulent, but it would be wrong not to draw attention to the fact that present-day banking procedures, and Girobank methods at that time, were and are an open invitation to criminals. In a recent case, *Regina v McGonigle*, heard in the Snaresbrook Crown Court in London, Judge Owen Stable is reported saying:

> 'The major banks' cheque-card scheme is an invitation to fraud and forgery ... Any child of ten knows how to clean the signatures and any fool can use the cards fraudulently. The system encourages bag-snatching, pick-pocketing and mugging ... If the directors of the clearing banks were personally responsible for the losses, and were unable to pass them straight on to customers in bank charges and recover them from shareholders, something would have been done about it years ago.'

What the judge said in that case was true – I found it exceedingly easy to commit the offences I did commit; and it was easy because of the lack of proper precautions taken by the banks. The banks provided me with an open-ended source of cash to feed my gambling compulsion. Gambling now completely dominated my life. It seemed to override even the need to eat and drink. Natural bodily needs become subservient to the passion that gambling arouses, and I have seen well-dressed men and women sit at the roulette table and urinate through their clothes – unable to drag themselves away from the tables, so great was their compulsion. Vincent Teresa, in his book, *My Life with the Mafia*, describes the compulsion I experienced succinctly:

> 'You don't beat the horses no matter what anybody says. But once you've been bitten by the bug, you play. You're busy stealing with one hand and losing it with the other. It's stupid and you know it, but you don't care. That's the way it is with a gambler.'

Added to my compulsion to gamble were the pressures created by the position I had placed myself in. I had breached parole, and I could expect no sympathy when apprehended. The good intentions I had when I was released had been completely discarded – one part of me knew that what I was doing was wrong, but the dominant part seemed locked into a pattern of behaviour over which I had no control. My personality changed and I became tetchy, secretive and withdrew into myself. The realization of what I had done brought with it a sense of panic, of abandon, and I cared less and less about the consequences of my actions. I embarked on an orgy of crime and gambling – and in so doing I reawakened fugitive instincts I thought I had lost.

I opened an account with one of the major clearing banks, and in due course was issued with a cheque-guarantee card. When the cheques issued to me were exhausted, I printed my own to match the cheque-guarantee card I held. My forgeries were not very good – the equipment I used cost less than one hundred pounds – but tradesmen and businesses were very happy to accept them, supported by the guarantee card I had been issued. For two years I travelled throughout England, issuing cheques fraudulently, living quite frugally, and gambling away the proceeds of my crimes. When I was arrested on 5 June 1981, I was living in a furnished room. My only possession was a suitcase full of used clothing.

I was arrested by the regional crime squad, who had targeted me, and they treated me very fairly. My first reaction was one of enormous relief that it was all over. The arresting officer remarked that I must have had a good time, and I recall telling him that I was glad it had ended, and that I would have been happier living as a worker with a home and family to return to each night.

After one night in Tottenham police station, I agreed to spend six days at Cannon Row, where Detective Inspector Paton and Detective Constable Wyatt took up the investigation. I found these two officers honest and straightforward – and I did what I could to assist them. But the cells at Cannon Row police station are a disgrace – they are not fit to put pigs in.

When I was re-admitted to prison to serve the unexpired portion of my parole period, I was held at Wormwood Scrubs, and I remained there whilst the new charges were processed. In interviews with my solicitor he expressed the view that if I did not change my way of life, I would die in prison. At that stage I did not really care if I did – the whole situation seemed such a mess that I saw no way out of it.

I was interviewed by a probation officer who proved to be the same lady who helped me telephone Karen in Tehran in 1975. She was very concerned at my attitude and interviewed me regularly, urging me not to give up. She was the first person to put it to me quite bluntly that gambling was a serious problem in my life. My feelings at that time were that my behaviour was outside my control. I wanted to give up – to plead guilty, offer no plea in mitigation, and try to survive the sentence that would follow. It was the attitude and persistence of the probation officer that began to make me change my view. What has happened to me since can be traced to the time she spent persuading me that there was an alternative to a life in prison, and I shall always owe her a very special debt of gratitude. It would have been very easy to give up – to let fate take its course. I had failed so often in the past that it could be argued I was unable to protect myself from my own destructive tendencies. I told myself that I had criminal inclinations that I could not control – that the best thing for me to do was to accept that I was a criminal and plan my future accordingly.

The probation officer rekindled the hope that had helped me survive the hardships of prison in South Africa, and as hope re-emerged the stubborn refusal to give in that had carried me through almost twenty years of imprisonment was also reawakened. I began to listen to assurances that my condition was curable, that I could change – and when an assistant governor at the prison agreed with that view and added his voice to the suggestion that I seek medical help, I decided to do so.

I approached psychiatric help with little hope and a great deal of trepidation. Despite the view that my problem was curable, the sheer quantum of the offences I had committed, and the persistence of my offending, frightened me. Long prison sentences had done nothing to change my behaviour, and I was afraid that the doctors would tell me that my problem was too deep-seated to be treated. I took the view that nothing could be worse than my present position – I had nothing to lose and a great deal to gain – but it still took a lot of self-prompting to get me to make the first approach.

I was surprised, once I had taken the first step, at the freedom I found in communicating with those who sought to help me. The medical officer who interviewed me initially suggested that I might benefit from a period at Grendon psychiatric prison, but when I was interviewed by a psychiatrist from Grendon he told me that he thought there was no hope for me.

'I know of no institution at which you could be treated,' he told me.

'What about if I paid for the treatment myself?' I asked him.

'Well, there may be one or two in the United States,' he said. 'But where would you get the money?'

I came away from my interview with him with the strong feeling that he didn't know what he was talking about – and nothing that has happened to me since has altered that view. Fortunately for me, the medical oficer who had suggested I see him was not put off by his opinion. I was placed under the care of a visiting psychotherapist – and my hope that things could be different grew.

I found my interviews with doctors sometimes confusing, sometimes depressing, but their continued interest in me made me realize that they thought we were making progress. I began to realize how much resentment I had harboured over the years, and the process of self-examination was very painful indeed. I found that as I did face up to the past my confidence grew – as I came to terms with attitudes that had led to past failures the future took on a meaning it had lacked – I began to feel that I could contribute to society and that, in doing so, I would be able to find a place in the community for myself.

As the date of my trial drew nearer, I became very conscious of the support of the prison doctors and of the probation officer. On 29 March 1982, I appeared before Judge Cox, at the Inner London Crown Court. The prosecution acknowledged the help I had given to the police during their investigation, and my counsel introduced reports from the prison doctors. In an unusual show of support the prison probation officer came to court and gave evidence for me. It was the first time that a court had been told how my criminal record had been built up, and what effect my addiction to gambling had had on my life.

In addition to the charges the police brought against me I asked the court to take into consideration 1,572 other matters I was guilty of. It was a very serious matter, and the police anticipated a sentence of ten years' imprisonment. My own view was that a sentence of seven years would be unappealable.

I was sentenced to four years' imprisonment, to run from 29 March 1982. The effect of the sentence was to add just two years to the term I still had to serve for parole violation. It was an extraordinary gesture on the part of the judge, and in passing sentence he said that he accepted that gambling might have played a role in my offending. I was conscious of the goodwill the court showed to me, and the judge encouraged me to look to the future:

'It may not be easy,' he said in sentencing me. 'But you are not too old to begin again.'

The judge's remarks, the efforts of the doctors, my probation officer and my barrister, combined to make me realize that people really did care – and this realization has helped me to learn again how to care about myself. I had been offered help, and I was determined to accept it. My barrister came to the court cells to see me before I was taken back to the prison. He had visited me more often than he had need to, and I was conscious that the outline of my life story, which had been a part of his brief, had aroused his interest and concern. I told him that I was compiling notes in order to write a book, and he encouraged me to go through with it.

'Don't give up,' he urged me. 'Whatever you do, don't give up.'

Later that evening, when I returned to the prison, I received the congratulations and good wishes of both prison staff and prisoners I had come to know.

'They've given you a chance,' one staff member told me. 'I hope you take it.'

Shortly after my trial ended I had to make a decision as to whether to continue the treatment I had been receiving or accept transfer to another prison. From the point of view of someone looking for the easiest option, transfer to another prison would have given me very much better living conditions and, with my experience of working my way through prison, far less pressure than continuing with the treatment. The doctors offered me the chance to be referred to the Hospital Annexe at Wormwood Scrubs, and I opted for that. Early in April 1982, I was interviewed by a member of the Annexe staff, and admitted to the unit.

34

The Hospital Annexe at Wormwood Scrubs prison was opened in December 1972, offering in-patient treatment to between forty and fifty prisoners with addiction and personality problems. The aim has been to create a social environment where men who have been rejected by society, and who have previously rejected society, can come to see themselves as part of the community within the unit. In this environment prisoners are encouraged, whilst dealing with their problems, to develop a sense of social responsibility. My admission to this unit came twenty-eight years after my first criminal conviction.

Between 1954 and 1982, I had built up a criminal record of some 2,600 offences, and received sentences which led to me spending more than twenty years in prison. My prison experiences had not deterred me in any way – nor had they changed my basic anti-social attitudes. The ordinary prison regime makes it very hard indeed for anyone to discard anti-social instincts. It is largely an environment without morals – where callous, irresponsible behaviour often confers status and privilege. The vast majority of prisoners are simply drawn into the prison sub-culture and are confirmed in the attitudes that brought them to prison. This is because, with a very few notable exceptions, reform and rehabilitation have been abandoned as practical aims in prison institutions. The Hospital Annexe at Wormwood Scrubs is one of the few exceptions.

Upon admission I was thrust into an environment where thirty years of allegiance to crime and gambling were challenged. I was confronted with the reality of my past behaviour and asked to accept responsibility for it – I had to choose whether I wanted to live the rest of my life as a criminal and gambler, or as a useful member of society. That choice may sound fairly simple, but I found it extremely difficult to make. It meant cutting myself free from a way of life I had grown used to and which had a very strong hold over me. I had to elect to venture out into a new social environment that would probably be quite hostile on occasion – an environment I knew very little about.

At first I resisted the efforts of staff and fellow-prisoners to make me accept that there was a constant need to examine myself – and to admit that my personality growth had been stunted in many areas. But I came to admire the dedication and care shown by the staff and I accepted the support of my fellow-prisoners – and this has made it possible for me to face the past honestly, and look to the future with hope and confidence.

Without the benefit of personal experience, I would not have believed it possible that a unit operating within the walls of a maximum-security prison could effectively dedicate itself to changing men's lives. The Annexe demonstrates that prisoners and prison officers can work together to break down the traditional attitudes of 'them and us'. The staff in the unit are drawn from prison-hospital officers and discipline staff, and are supported by visiting psychotherapists, the probation service, and a member of the educational facility within the main prison. But the day-to-day group therapy and counselling falls squarely on the shoulders of prison officers and the prisoners themselves – and its success shows that a viable alternative to the current prison regime is available, if only there were the political will to introduce it.

Since I have been in the Annexe I have been encouraged to write and I have been given the opportunity to develop my interest in penal reform. I have been surprised by the number of people both within and outside the prison who have offered me support. Very early on in my present sentence my barrister wrote to me and introduced me to a well-known author, who has encouraged me with my writing. My barrister ended his letter to me with the words:

'My very best wishes to you, and remember, I certainly have faith in you, and so have others.'

I have remembered those words whenever I felt depressed and the going got tough. The Annexe is a demanding environment, it is not an easy option in terms of prison treatment, and the efforts that others have made on my behalf, and are still making, have helped me cope with the pressures that a decision to change brought with it.

I do not expect the future to be easy – but for the first time in many years I am aware that I do have a future. I now know that I can choose the direction I take and that I am personally responsible for what happens to me. And that is a really good feeling. In the past I have rationalized that my actions were controlled by others or by circumstances I could not do anything about – that I was not responsible for them. Now I know that I am free to break away from my past, and that I can plan my own future.

The years of deprivation and waste are something I cannot undo. Anger and frustration still exist – but they have been exposed and I have learned to cope with them. The bitterness I lived with for so long has lost its edge and, now, the challenge of the future seems so much more important than the failures of the past.

My fugitive years are now over – I am quite sure that Judge Cox was right – it may not be easy, but I am not too old to start again.

PART 2
REFLECTIONS

Attitudes and Influences

Anti-social attitudes, leading to illegal activities, very often have their origin in an environment of social and economic deprivation, in turbulent home life and broken marriages: I enjoyed a caring family and financially we were quite well-to-do. Yet I did experience deprivation. My religious upbringing deprived me of normal, healthy friendships.

I believe the anti-social postures I later developed may have had their origin in the need I felt to reject and criticize the world outside the religious sect I belonged to. As a child I was constantly reminded that whilst I was *in* the world I was not *of* the world, and I came to believe this. I was conditioned to feel that I was in some ways a little different to other people, that I belonged to a chosen few, and in this way I was superior. Later, when I was rejected by the Exclusive Plymouth Brethren and by my family, I tried to become part *of* the world, and I found that the insularity of my upbringing had created defensive attitudes that made the development of normal friendships and relationships very difficult.

I had never learned the art of joining in and becoming part of a social gathering. I was uncomfortable and felt out of place where people met, and I had a fear of relationships that my religious upbringing had taught me were 'unclean'. I began to realize that I was happiest when I was alone – then it was no longer necessary to be defensive and I could relax: the anxieties that stemmed from contact with other people were quietened. Solitude became pleasant – and then it became a retreat.

It was at this stage of my life that I discovered gambling, and it answered my need for a solitary pastime with a limited social ambience.

As a gambler I could be part of a crowd – yet quite alone. It filled the lonely hours created by my failure to form stable relationships and, without realizing what was happening, I became addicted to it. At first it *filled* a need, but later it *became* a need.

I believe that my general attitude towards money made it easier for me to become involved in gambling. My father had always been contemptuous of economic planning – he conducted his affairs carelessly, professing to believe that the Lord would provide, and quoting scripture to defend his attitude. 'Consider the lilies of the field. They neither toil nor spin. Yet I tell you that Solomon in all his glory was not arrayed like one of these [Matthew 6.28–9],' he would say to me. Or, 'Do not lay up for yourselves treasures on earth where moth and rust consume, and where thieves break in and steal; but lay up treasures in heaven ... For where your treasure is there will your heart be also ... [Matthew 6.19].' These, and other scriptures were taken literally as an excuse to justify indifference to the reality of life, and they moulded the attitude towards money that influenced me in later years. The fatalism in this approach fitted in very neatly with a wish to gamble.

I have never operated a regular savings account or budgeted for future obligations. The idea of saving for a holiday never occurred to me – I took leave when I had money or put it off until a windfall occurred. This lack of planning has meant that, even without the difficulties created by my gambling, my private affairs have always been a mess. Even in the commission of crime I had no thought of accumulating wealth. I stole in order to spend and to gamble – with no thought for the future. There is, in my experience, not a great deal of difference between the attitude 'the Lord will provide' and the parallel belief that 'something will turn up' – both excuse personal responsibility.

Indifference to the future, together with my inability to handle the problems that indifference created, caused a reaction against those people who did manage their affairs well – those who did plan and save. I began to dislike them and then, because I needed to justify my own position, I began to despise them – to regard them as 'mugs'. Once I had attached the label 'mugs' to 'straight' people, I was able to rationalize my own position as being more intelligent than theirs. In my experience all criminals regard normal working people as 'mugs' – they have to in order to justify their own criminality.

My whole upbringing had been as an outsider in the community and I had grown comfortable in that role. One of the effects of this was that later, when I committed offences, I was not conscious of having offended against the community. I had never been part of the community and did not feel any responsibility towards it. Both in childhood and later, as a criminal, I operated as a loner. The sense of being apart from other people was very strong, and it made it easy for me to act without regard for communal rules – but at the same time it led to indignation and rebellion when communal rules interfered with or censured my actions – widening the gap between myself and society. I found myself more and more in the now familiar role of an outsider, and I felt strangely comfortable there, developing the ability to suppress reaction to the moral turpitude my criminal status involved. I felt more comfortable as a loner than I had done when trying to become part of the community.

Criminality brought with it not only rejection by society, but also acceptance as a member of the criminal fraternity. My escapes and illegal exploits gave me status, and as a con-man I was well up the ladder in criminal circles. The criminal fraternity made no demands on me – it provided recognition without responsibility. I had exchanged membership of a group who rejected society for membership of a group whom society rejected. Amongst the Exclusive Plymouth Brethren I had been bound by a great many rules – as a criminal I could make my own.

My early prison experiences did nothing to make me feel that society was any better than the criminal community I had joined. What actually happens under the cloak of justice often confirms anti-social beliefs. There is an inscription over the huge doorway leading into the courts at the Old Bailey. As far as I can remember it reads, 'Defend the children of the poor and punish the wrongdoer.' In my experience neither law courts nor prisons worry too much about defending the children of the poor – both in South Africa and in England my experience has been that they get pretty horribly punished along with the wrongdoer. But what is cause for concern is that present systems are geared to punish, with no real attempt being made to reform. I am quite sure that my early experience of a punitive penal system hardened my anti-social attitudes, and was a very real factor in my subsequent behaviour.

In South Africa a special situation exists because of the black-versus-white postures within the community. I believe that apartheid is morally indefensible, yet, in South Africa, it rests on legislation introduced by a church-going nation that claims greater piety than many others. The ambivalence that is a feature of white South Africans' thinking may account for the very bad conditions black prisoners are subjected to.

The farmers who hired black prisoners from their local gaols and then starved and whipped them to death were usually regular church-goers. A large number of prosecutions under South African laws prohibiting sexual intercourse between blacks and whites have involved black girls taken advantage of by white clergymen. I was aware of the hypocrisy that existed among white South Africans, and I rationalized that society's failure was in some way justification of my own.

I was never able to accept the attitude of indifference to blacks my fellow-prisoners in South Africa adopted. To me human suffering was human suffering – and it made no difference whether it was white, black or any other colour. My personal experiences at the Fort in Johannesburg, in Durban and Cape Town prisons, at Baviaanspoort and Pretoria Central Prison, led to a feeling of disgust for a society that allowed such inhuman practices to be carried out in its name, and reinforced my contempt for a system that deprived human beings of all dignity, making little or no attempt to examine or deal with what caused the conduct it punishes. These experiences confirmed my commitment to a role outside the community. I was alienated because of my own illegal actions – and I had no wish to join a society that sanctioned the injustice I witnessed. My experience at Vooruitsig prison, under the benevolent regime inaugurated by Brigadier Fourie, was a hiatus which, had it been developed, might have saved me from the consequences of the attitudes I had adopted; but even there I chafed at my impotence when faced with the treatment of young white offenders and some black prisoners.

My deportation from South Africa back to England in 1972 gave me the chance to make a fresh start in a country where no one knew about my past. But, ironically, it was the very determination not to reveal my past that made me unable to take advantage of this opportunity. My decision not to reveal my past was only partly because of the embarrassment this might have caused me – I believe a more dominant consideration was the rejection it might lead to. After spending a continuous twelve years in prison, and given my upbringing, I was ill-equipped to tackle the task of re-entering society. Like a child I sought instant gratification, immediate acceptance – I had not learned to wait, and I was surprised and hurt when I was refused rewards I had not earned. Like a child I withdrew, baffled, and soon slipped back into the solitary role I had found familiar and comfortable in South Africa. That role made it easy for me to act without regard to the law – in contempt of communal rules. My reversion to gambling was part of the process of building a life that was self-contained, where, by avoiding contacts that might have developed into lasting relationships, I avoided the hurt and embarrassment that rejection might have caused.

Gambling became an obsession and began to control my life. It provided me with instant satisfaction, the illusion of status, of membership of a group; and it suppressed any concomitant sense of responsibility. It was peculiarly suited to my needs, allowing me the pretence of freedom whilst imposing a very real hold over me until, eventually, the hold of gambling, the compulsion, became stronger than my fear of returning to prison. My history shows that long periods of abstinence proved no safeguard. Once I rekindled the urge it emerged stronger than ever. I believe that I shall always have to avoid situations where my compulsion to gamble may be reawakened.

Once I had crossed the line between lawful behaviour and unlawful action, an entirely new set of factors came into play. It is one thing to be contemptuous of society, to ignore custom and paddle a lone canoe against the stream; but it is quite another thing to be a fugitive, living by crime, pursued by the police. Fugitive instincts are very real – man's preference for freedom is innate and, when that freedom was threatened, I developed sensitivities I did not know I possessed.

My offences were mainly repetitious cheque and credit-card frauds, each one like the one before. I believe that over the years I became addicted to crime – it provided me with a challenge, an element of danger, and a sense of achievement. I would end each day with a strange satisfaction in having committed a number of crimes and having done so successfully. Looking back it is clear that just as my gambling became more rampant over the years, so did my criminal activity. Between 1955 and 1960, my offences totalled about one hundred. During my next period of freedom, between 1972 and 1974, I committed some nine hundred offences – whilst between 1979 and 1981, the figure was almost one thousand six hundred. The need to offend seemed to grow and keep pace with my need to gamble.

In a very real sense my criminal activities were a form of gambling, too. They developed into a game in which to lose would mean imprisonment, in which the tension was never eased but built up until the moment of arrest. I have no doubt that the excitement of committing a crime is addictive to some men. I have met many prisoners who have told me of the thrill they experienced as a burglar, a safe-breaker or a car thief. I can relate to their experiences – I found a thrill in doing what I was doing, in living as I lived, and I have no doubt that my addiction to crime was strengthened by the repetitiveness of my behaviour.

During the past two years, and especially in the Hospital Annexe at Wormwood Scrubs, I have examined the attitudes that made me act as I did. I don't suppose that I shall ever fully understand why I did what I did – and I believe that it is not necessary that I do. What was necessary was for me to face the past honestly, to discard the unreal expectations I had imposed on other people, and to revise my own expectations. By doing this I have been able to see myself as having a role within the community, no longer as an outsider, but as someone with a useful contribution to make. I have come to terms with the barrenness of a life of self-sufficiency, and I look forward to forming real friendships and relationships when I leave prison – and developing those I have already begun to make.

I am no longer afraid. I know myself so much better than before – I have a better understanding of my weaknesses and my failings. For the first time I shall leave prison fully aware of the danger gambling holds for me – aware of the need to avoid situations where criminal instincts might be aroused.

I no longer have anything to hide; my life has been made public. I have regrets, but I am not ashamed – I have admitted my failures to myself, and I can look back and see the terrible price I have paid for those failures. I have paid my debt many times over, and there is nothing now to prevent me taking my place in society at whatever level circumstances determine. I am free to begin again, to build a new life based on real values. Whenever that opportunity is allowed me I shall leave prison without the bitterness and fear that made me an outsider, and having rejected the criminal way of life I had grown used to; I am busy, even now, developing interests and prospects that will enable me to lead a full and satisfying life as a law-abiding member of the community.

I have not achieved this on my own, nor do I believe I would have been able to do so. I shall always be indebted to staff and fellow-prisoners in the Hospital Annexe, I shall always remember the way many other people offered me encouragement and guidance when I was struggling to come to terms with my past. I have made friends with members of Gamblers Anonymous, and I believe their support has been a big factor in developing the confidence I now feel. But what I have achieved is possible for anyone. I asked for help and I accepted it even when it seemed more hurtful than staying the way I was. I believe that the key to change lies in a genuine commitment to face reality and accept the obligations and responsibilities that freedom imposes. There is no magic formula, no sweet-tasting medicine – change comes from a combination of constructive objectives and hard work.

Institutions and Criminal-Justice Procedures

I am often asked what I think about the police, prisons, the legal system and other institutions I have had experience of. The notes that follow set out what my experience has taught me is true. They only touch on the very real problem of finding an intelligent and effective response to crime, but they do highlight aspects which are often ignored or pigeon-holed as being embarrassing. I have levelled criticism where I believe it is necessary to do so, and I have tried to make that criticism constructive by suggesting alternatives to present procedures. I hope that what I say may be a useful contribution to the debate on these matters.

Institutions concerned with the prevention, detection and treatment of crime are often criticized, seldom praised. In general they are the poor relations in socio-economic planning and the butt of uninformed abuse. I accept the difficulties financial constraints and political emphasis place on these institutions; but this does not relieve us of a duty to say something is wrong when we are confronted with ongoing malpractice and inhuman, senseless policy decisions.

One of the matters that causes me concern is that people best qualified to contribute to the debate are prevented from doing so by the iniquitous Official Secrets Act. When prison officers and prison governors, and a host of civil servants, are gagged by legislation, they become frustrated and, eventually, resigned to the continuance of practices they know to be contrary to the public interest. The laws that effectively muzzle the people best qualified to speak about bureaucratic incompetence and political opportunism are designed to protect incompetents and opportunists from the embarrassment of public accountability. These laws serve no public interest and should be scrapped.

Nothing in these notes excuses my past behaviour – but that behaviour in no way invalidates the comments and suggestions I have made. Indeed, my personal experience of the matters I deal with may lend some weight to what I have written.

POLICE CUSTODY AND INTERROGATION METHODS

During the years I have spent in prison I have seen a great many injustices, and many of these arose from the improper use of criminal-justice procedures. There is little to be gained by repeating what is already known about the interrogation methods used by BOSS, South Africa's Bureau of State Security. The deaths of prisoners in their care, whether those deaths be suicide or murder, are eloquent testimony to the cruelty and inhumanity of their methods. We have all read reports of how prisoners in Ulster have similarly been subjected to physical ill-treatment. But what is not always realized is that many of the methods used in South Africa and Ulster are simply an extension of standard police procedures, and it is a matter of concern that these standard police procedures are judged acceptable by many who have knowledge of them.

It has long been realized by interrogators that psychological stress is a far more potent weapon than physical abuse – although some authorities combine both. My experience of British police methods is that physical abuse is seldom used, whilst psychological stress is a standard weapon used to obtain advantage at every stage of the procedure. The unfair use of psychological stress and misuse of custodial powers are daily occurrences, and they occur because the police want to bypass safeguards supposedly ensured by so-called Judges' Rules.

On the occasions I have been interviewed and detained by police in England I have been denied access to a solicitor for up to two days after arrest. I have been locked up without washing facilities or access to clean clothing for long periods. I have been refused contact with friends, denied cigarettes and normal refreshments. I have been refused bail, and told that only my co-operation would cause police objections to bail to be withdrawn. The conditions in police cells I have been held in are disgusting. The size of the cell, the lack of furnishing, deprivation of even basic comforts, and the tendency to allow them to become stinking, combine to attack the standards normal people expect. It is naive to claim that anyone subjected to arrest, police custody and interrogation is treated fairly. The system is designed to be unfair – to give advantage to the police.

The part that British police play in prosecution procedures is open to abuse, and is daily abused. Prosecution procedures ought properly to be the province of a completely separate authority. My experience in England is that police witnesses regularly sit in court listening to the evidence, enabling them to tailor their own evidence and advise prosecution witnesses of what is expected of them. A separation of duties would take the police out of the courtroom except when testifying, dramatically reducing the opportunities to manipulate evidence – something I personally experienced. Successful prosecutions ought not to be a factor influencing police promotions, as I believe they are at present, and a by-product of relieving the police of prosecuting duties would be to release large numbers for their more necessary detective and prevention roles.

A grievance that is very common indeed in prison is that the police 'verballed' a prisoner. It is far too common to be dismissed as the product of embittered criminal minds. 'Verballing' occurs when the police alter what a prisoner actually said in a way that unfairly incriminates him, or where they invent statements having the same effect. The police tend to operate in pairs, and the word of a single accused person as to what was actually said is seldom accepted in court against the word of two policemen.

It is quite common for an accused person to be advised by his solicitor not to pursue an allegation that the police evidence is not a true record of what was said.

'You will antagonize the judge,' the solicitor will say – and unfortunately this is true. Judges are invariably antagonistic to attacks on the veracity of police witnesses. The accused then has to decide whether to go against the advice of his solicitor, and risk the wrath of the judge, or accept the introduction of police evidence he knows is false.

As an additional disincentive, any questioning of police evidence is regarded as an attack on the character of the police witness, and leaves the prosecution free to expose any previous convictions the accused person may have. This is an iniquitous rule that provides unlimited cover for police witnesses who do lie, and its effect is to condone and facilitate misinformation. It ought to be abolished. There is no reason for it to exist other than to protect dishonest police witnesses. No accused is free from challenge as to the veracity of what he is saying when testifying, and that challenge is regarded as wholly fair. Why then should police witnesses be protected from similar challenges? The present rule smacks of double standards – protection for police witnesses and exposure for the accused.

Occasionally 'verballing' occurs inadvertently, and without any malice. Policemen do make mistakes, and the unintentional alteration of just one word can have dire consequences for an accused. I am quite sure that because of the seriousness of the consequences of wrongly recorded statements, there can be no excuse for not reforming present procedures governing recording what prisoners say to the police. Basically there are three types of statement, and each presents its own problems.

Voluntary statements and confessions

When an accused expresses the wish to make a voluntary statement it is reduced to writing by the police. This procedure is open to abuse and malicious challenge. It needs reforming to protect both the police and the accused.

In South Africa, when an accused wished to make such a statement, he was taken to a magistrate where he was interviewed in a room from which the police and prosecution were excluded. There the magistrate inquired whether the accused had been put under any pressure to make a statement, or whether he had been made any promises. He would then warn the accused that anything he said would be recorded and would be made a part of the trial record. After the statement had been recorded it was read over, and the accused was asked to sign it and swear to the truth of it. Whether it was exculpatory or incriminating it then formed part of the trial record.

I believe that system is as safe and fair as it is possible to get. It may be suggested that such a procedure should make use of tape recordings, and this would certainly reduce the margin for error, but in my experience magistrates very seldom have any axe to grind – and I believe that they are eminently suitable to perform this duty. I would like to see the British system changed to follow the South African procedure.

Statements of question and answer

The present interrogation method in England is for the police to interview a suspect and record the questions they put to him, and his answers to those questions, contemporaneously. This type of one-sided interrogation, where the questions determine the parameters of what is said and left unsaid, is designed to give advantage to the interrogator – it is undesirable. It is open to the use of omission and manipulation in the creation of a false impression. A skilled interrogator has little difficulty in wording questions to include allegations which, although unsupported, then become part of the record – and colour the thinking of all but the most observant reader. The system also offers no real opportunity to counter false allegations.

A suspect may ask for a solicitor to be present at such an interview, but my experience is that the police always bring pressure to bear to have the interview without the solicitor present. Of course the police have a legal right to ask questions, and no investigation could proceed were this not so. What seems to me to be very wrong is that the police do on many occasions press those questions, without a solicitor being present, when the suspect has asked to be allowed to exercise his legal right to have a solicitor present. The police have powerful weapons which are freely used to achieve their objective. They can and do refuse contact with solicitors and friends. They can and do withhold bail or oppose it. They can and do play on the prisoner's fears for his family and friends. Petty physical deprivations can be and are used to gain a psychological advantage. These abuses are commonplace. They are third-degree methods that are a blot on the system, and they can be eliminated quite simply.

All interviews between the police and a prisoner ought to be in the presence of the prisoner's legal adviser, and ought to be recorded both aurally and visually. A carbon copy of any writings made by the police at such an interview should be handed to the prisoner or his legal adviser at the conclusion of the interview.

The main reason the police prefer interviews without a solicitor present is because, working in pairs, they can bring unfair pressure to bear on the prisoner and, in some cases, make the record show what they want without regard to what was said. The suggestion that the presence of a solicitor would interfere with police processes is a slur on the legal profession, who have a rather better malpractice record than the police do.

The case-load that each police officer carries is a source of unending pressure, and this pressure can create a tendency to overstep the proper limits of behaviour in order to clear cases and so avoid censure from superiors. My suggestion would relieve the police of the very real pressures that arise when they, and they alone, are the arbiters of what was or was not said. The prisoner needs protecting from unscrupulous policemen, whom we know do exist, and the police need protecting from the false and malicious allegations that are often made by prisoners in their care. My suggestion answers both needs.

Ex tempore *remarks*

Statements made *ex tempore* give rise to the majority of complaints of 'verballing', and they present the most difficult control problem. By its very nature this type of statement may be taken out of context, be the subject of an honest mistake, be misunderstood, misinterpreted or wrongly recorded from memory. It can also be manufactured.

In real life it is difficult to remember a conversation verbatim, even for a short period. Any two parties to a conversation will later record it a little differently. Despite the myths that we are brought up to believe, policemen have the same strengths and weaknesses as anybody else – and this is true in respect of memory. In general we tend to forget what we don't want to hear, and remember what we want to hear. I am always amazed when reading police statements at how two policemen can produce records of a conversation identical down to the last comma and full stop. What amazes me is not that the accounts tally so exactly, but that anyone can be fooled for an instant into believing that they are not cooked in some way. My private belief is that the police use lots of carbon paper in producing these identical statements or, alternatively, that they reconstruct the conversation together afterwards – no other explanation makes sense. If this is true then the dangers of error and manipulation are multiplied many times over.

Despite the problems, there are measures that could and should be taken to control *ex tempore* statements. To leave matters as they are is to leave a festering wound on the fabric of suspect–police relations that can only lead to unending dispute and confrontation. I believe the following suggestions would do much to eliminate irregularities that at present occur.

a) *Notification to the defence*

Where it is the intention to introduce evidence of *ex tempore* statements made by the accused, a copy of them should be furnished to the accused or his legal representative at the earliest opportunity, but not later than seventy-two hours after the alleged statements have been made. The accused should have the right to place on record his reaction to such police evidence. This would prevent the police from 'remembering' things weeks after they were allegedly said, concealing them from the defence, and springing them as a surprise much later.

b) *Opportunity to question the police*

Police evidence of *ex tempore* statements should be put to the accused as part of the first formal interview after they were made, in the presence of his legal adviser. At such an interview, the accused or his legal representative should have the right to question the police and challenge the veracity of the police record of such statements. The written record of this part of any interview should be kept quite separate from any other writings.

c) Where *ex tempore* statements are contested, and there is no evidence other than police evidence to corroborate them, the trial judge should caution the jury and advise them of the dangers inherent in such evidence. The danger of honest mistake makes this essential, and where a conviction rests solely upon such a contested statement, it should not be allowed to stand.

Whatever measures are taken to tighten control of this part of police work, there will be misgivings by one party or the other. But this is no excuse for not reforming a procedure that gives rise to more complaints against the police than any other, and is so vital to the administration of justice. The present system is open to abuse, and to false allegations of abuse – the suggestions made would go a long way towards eliminating both possibilities.

My misgivings at present police procedures are shared by others. Recently Lord Salmon, whose career spanned terms as a High Court judge, a Lord Justice of Appeal and a Lord of Appeal in Ordinary, spoke of cases he had dealt with where the police had lied and said: 'Justice is calling loudly for tape recording to be used *now*; and there is no real excuse for this to be refused . . . it is essential . . . to allow the interrogation process to be tape recorded.' The Home Office have taken tentative steps towards the introduction of tape recordings. At a recent press conference, Mr Patrick Mayhew, Minister of State at the Home Office, said that tape recording police interviews would allow a more 'even-handed' approach – an acknowledgement that the present system needs to be changed. But my own view is that whilst tape recording interviews is essential, it may well lead to interrogation techniques that give a false impression of all the facts in a matter, and the only way to prevent this is to make the attendance of a legal representative at all police interviews where the suspect is in custody a requirement of the procedure.

It may be said that I don't trust the police, and this colours my thinking. I can only say that my experience is that not many policemen are careful of a prisoner's rights, and some set out to manipulate evidence in order to ensure a conviction. My experience is no different to that of a great many men who have passed through police stations up and down the country, and is largely supported by the attitude of all solicitors I have met, who say unequivocally, 'never tell the police anything – they may misuse it'.

BAIL

The effect of refusing bail

The effect of refusing bail is to sentence an accused person to imprisonment without trial. It is a fact that a very large proportion of people refused bail under present procedures are later acquitted or receive non-custodial sentences at their trial. The effect of the present system, therefore, is to gaol men and women without trial who may well not be guilty, and who may not warrant imprisonment at all.

Deciding whether or not to grant bail

There is a legal presumption of innocence at all times until a guilty verdict has been reached by a properly constituted court. In my experience this presumption is largely ignored in bail considerations. The basis on which bail appears to be decided is the seriousness of the allegations made against an accused person. These accusations are invariably made by the police without any supporting evidence at all, and my experience is that the police invariably exaggerate matters in order to keep an accused person in custody – especially if he has not made a statement saying he is guilty. They have a vested interest in doing so – under present procedures the refusal of bail is a weapon used daily by the police to bring pressure to bear on accused persons. The present basis for deciding bail leaves a great deal to be desired and, in my view, there is only one answer to this shabby treatment of suspects – bail as a right.

BAIL AS A RIGHT

Bail ought to be a right except in a murder investigation, where it should be at the discretion of a superior court to grant it. Of course, there will always be cases where the police justifiably feel that bail ought not to be granted and, in those cases, evidence supporting those feelings should be submitted and tested in court. Unsupported police evidence should never be a good and sufficient ground for refusing bail. Where the police claim that they need time to produce evidence, as they usually do, a police officer of not less than Superintendent rank should testify in court to this effect and, even in such cases, bail should be reviewed every seventy-two hours by the court. Failure to produce evidence within ten days should require bail to be granted.

Bail ought never to be fixed beyond the means of the accused, as to do so is in effect to refuse bail.

These procedures would eliminate one evil from the present criminal-justice process – the use of bail as a lever by the police to obtain statements and confessions that would not otherwise have been made. They would also make corruption in respect of bail a non-starter and would help to alleviate overcrowding in local prisons – freeing hundreds of men and women who are currently held for months without trial and then acquitted or given non-custodial sentences at their trial.

PROCEDURES IN COURT

I have already spoken of the need to ensure that the police are taken out of the courtroom except as witnesses. The opportunities for malpractice at present have to be cut back. It is an affront to the whole concept of a fair judicial process to see a policeman in court giving a thumbs-up sign to one of his witnesses as he or she leaves the witness box. The criminal-justice process ought not to be a gladiatorial spectacle – much as that may appeal to the more theatrical members of the legal profession. It is about people and people's lives – it is not a game.

Prosecuting counsel's address to the jury

At present the prosecuting counsel open their case by a so-called outline of the evidence, in order to give the jury the background to what witnesses may say. It is undoubtedly desirable that the jury be given such an outline of the case so that they can follow the evidence more easily – but that outline must be confined to a précis of evidence to be presented and not, as at present, develop into rhetoric aimed at furthering the prosecution case. Prosecutors regularly exaggerate matters in an attempt to sensationalize the charges, the better to impress the jury and, in my experience, occasionally in order to get press coverage for the matter. There is no excuse for allowing this procedure to be continued. The jury ought to be in a position to listen to and adjudicate the evidence with an open mind. It is impossible for them to do this when they have been subjected to a lengthy oration designed to create sympathy for the prosecutor's case.

As a safeguard against the jury being unfairly influenced by allegations that, in my experience, are not always substantiated by the evidence, I believe the judge should inform the jury that they have been listening to one side of the matter, part or all of which may be contested by the defence. The defence should also be invited to reply to such harangues.

Pleas in Mitigation

When determining what sentence to impose it is essential that the court be in possession of all the facts. In my experience many judges cut short carefully prepared pleas in mitigation, showing an impatience and prejudgement of the matter that does not inspire confidence. No court should presume to know enough about an accused person without the benefit of a probation and home-circumstance report. In my experience, the need that some judges feel to dispose of sentencing matters quickly is indicative of judicial ignorance as to the effect of the sentences they impose in general.

SENTENCING POLICY

Mr Ian Dunbar, Governor of Wormwood Scrubs prison, describing prison conditions as appalling, went on to say: 'If the objective is to reduce the amount of crime in society, and to minimize its effect on innocent people, the present sentencing policy does not appear to be working, and may be counter-productive.' That statement expresses exactly my own views.

In Britain, sentencing is in the hands of magistrates and the judiciary, subject to statutory provisions. There does not appear to be any rule which determines an appropriate sentence for any category of offence. Disparity in sentencing seems to be the rule rather than the exception. It is fairly uniformly the case that where an accused elects to exercise his legal right to plead not guilty and contest a matter, he receives a longer sentence than he would have had had he pleaded guilty. The effect of this is that quite often an accused person will be advised to plead guilty to an offence even when he is innocent – especially a first-time offender who can expect to be given a suspended sentence if he takes this course. The reasoning is that, given the danger of a capricious guilty verdict, it is better not to take a chance on judicial displeasure at the court's time being wasted. Whatever the expediency that gives rise to this trend, it is clearly inimical to the accused's unfettered right to plead not guilty. The present position is that an accused has to elect whether to plead guilty and receive a light sentence or contest the matter, gamble on getting an acquittal, and expect a heavy sentence if he loses. Sentences ought not to rest on a gamble.

It is said that public opinion determines sentences to some degree. It is certainly true that the disparity between sentences passed in rural areas and those passed in urban areas reflect the conservatism of the former – but is that justice? As a criterion for assessing sentences, public opinion must rank as the least predictable and least suitable it is possible to imagine. It is sobering to think that it was public opinion that burned witches at the stake, clamoured for public executions and hanged children for petty thefts. Public opinion is notoriously ill-informed, and it is dangerous to be guided by uninformed reaction. The use of public opinion as a factor influencing sentencing is shown as even more dangerous in the light of recent surveys that throw into sharp relief the fact that judges are out of touch with ordinary people.

Disparity in sentences imposed is the most important factor in the lack of confidence in present policy. It is undoubtedly true that the prospects of a light sentence increase in direct relation to the accused's social standing. Recently a man was given a suspended sentence for two armed robberies in which he used considerable violence, clubbing a bank cashier about the head with a sawn-off shotgun. Another man, at the same time, was sentenced to sixteen years' imprisonment for one armed robbery where care had been taken not to injure anyone. The man who received the suspended sentence was an ex-guardsman who belonged to the same regiment as that the sentencing judge had served in. The man who received a sixteen-year sentence was from a poor family in the East End of London. It is impossible to reconcile differences like this.

Recently a judge was widely reported as telling an accused that he was fortunate to appear before him on that particular day, as he was in a good mood – the accused received a suspended sentence. It may be relevant to ask what sentence would have been imposed had the judge been in a bad mood. Sentences ought not to be determined by the mood of the judicial officer.

Statistics show conclusively that when Parliament introduced remission, and later parole, the judiciary discounted legislative intention by increasing sentences in direct proportion to the remission and parole allowed. In doing so I believe that the courts acted unconstitutionally with the intention of negating legitimate legislation. When interpreting law, the judiciary have a constitutional duty to follow the spirit and the intention of the legislature – and this constitutional duty supersedes any imagined obligation to appease public opinion. Were this not so we would be faced by judges subservient to public opinion in open defiance of properly enacted legislation. I believe that there is an element of conservative defiance in the way the courts have ignored repeated reminders of Parliament's wishes, and continue to impose sentences in excess of what public opinion has indicated society would accept. Sentences for robbery in which no one is injured frequently exceed sentences imposed on killers. Property offences frequently attract more severe sentences than those where persons are physically harmed.

Imprisonment is one of society's reactions to crime. It is a violent reaction and the use of force to impose it is common – and is always implied. Just as society's disapproval leads to this violent reaction so, too, imprisonment itself creates violence. It would be naive to suppose that someone can be deprived of their freedom without reacting – men and women sentenced to imprisonment do react; sometimes with violence.

A mixture of disbelief, shock and a small amount of grim satisfaction, greeted the imposition of the barbaric sentences in the Great Train Robbery; and it is my belief that the upsurge in violent crime since then is not a coincidence. These sentences were so violent that they caused a violent reaction. Whatever the intention may have been, the sentences in that case introduced an entirely new factor into the pattern of criminal thinking and, in consequence, criminal behaviour. Would-be robbers were faced with the prospect of sentences it was impossible to relate to, and the reaction of many men serving long sentences I have met since then is almost uniformly the same as the one I once harboured – next time they will leave no witnesses; next time they will kill. The difference between eighteen years for robbery and life for murder is not a deterrent at all – the mind cannot relate to either of them. It may be argued that long sentences do deter others from offending, but that is not the picture that emerges from studies of countries where long sentences are used even more freely than in Britain. One thing is clear, and that is that long sentences seem to have a perverse effect – they result in imitative offences, they tend to glamorize violence in the eyes of those most likely to offend, making 'heroes' out of those sentenced to them. Young offenders seem to find a perverse satisfaction in being the recipient of a sentence longer than that their fellow prisoners are serving. Why this is I do not know – but it is a fact that in prison a long-term man, a robber or a killer, is usually more respected by up-and-coming criminals than a man with a lesser sentence. I believe that this 'image' of big-time gangsters leads many young offenders to progress to more serious crimes. All the evidence I have seen shows that long sentences are counter-productive.

I believe that the whole scale of sentencing needs to be reviewed. Judges appear to have been goaded into losing their sense of proportion by an upsurge in serious crime which their own sentencing policy may have been partly responsible for.

The sheer cost of housing increasing numbers of long-term prisoners is economically and socially unacceptable. Prison is now recognized as the least effective and most expensive response to crime there has ever been. Public opinion has changed, and a recent National Opinion Poll carried out on behalf of the Prison Reform Trust shows that there is wide support for change in the way courts deal with offenders. Despite the rhetoric of some politicians seeking publicity and the exaggerated language of some newsmen, there is a growing realization that prison is not a sensible way of dealing with a wide range of anti-social acts. There is public concern at the disparate treatment offenders receive and, too, at judicial indifference to the fact that present sentencing and bail policies have created totally unacceptable conditions in overcrowded prisons. Dr Stephen Shaw, a director of the Prison Reform Trust, is reported as saying: 'On prisons and penal policy the majority ... are more sympathetic to reform than anyone has previously believed. People are concerned about crime, but they also realize that using prison to detain petty and non-violent offenders actually diminishes rather than strengthens the public's defences against crime.'

There is a limit to how much prison space is available, but the courts consistently ignore this when considering sentence. Judicial independence is all very well but, when it becomes divorced from reality, problems arise. The use of scarce prison space to imprison petty and non-violent offenders is the major cause of overcrowding in prisons today. It is also an expensive and ineffective way of dealing with this type of offender. The growing trend in the United States is to concentrate on detecting and imprisoning professional criminals and persistent offenders. Non-custodial measures are used to deal with less serious matters. There has to be concern when the cost of keeping people in prison reaches present proportions. It is reported that at a new juvenile centre in West Yorkshire it will cost £600 per week for each inmate. To house a top-security prisoner costs £370 per week; a young offender at borstal costs £180 each week; medium security and remand prisoners cost more than £170 per week. It is estimated that petty non-violent offenders account for 15,000 of the daily prison population – well over £100,000,000 per year is spent on imprisoning people who ought properly to be treated in the community.

Despite these facts, certain sections of the press, and a few politicians, have taken the present increase in crime figures as justification for a campaign to toughen prison sentences. This campaign is based on the theory that inhuman and frightening sentences deter criminals. That theory is fallacious and unsound. Three examples of countries with very harsh penal sanctions are the USSR, South Africa and the United States of America. It is believed that the USSR has the highest prison population of any country in the world – South Africa comes second only to the USSR as the country with the highest percentage of its population in prison, whilst the USA comes third in the world with over 400,000 persons actually in prison, or one for each 600 members of the population. In Britain approximately one person in each 1200 of the population is in prison.

The USSR, South Africa and, particularly, the USA, where political offences do not distort statistics, are well-documented, long-term examples of the fact that harsh penalties do not bring down the crime rate and therefore cannot be said to deter. If they did, then the USA, with its range of indeterminate sentences, would have the lowest crime rate in the western world. Horrific sentences of life, meaning natural life, sixty to eighty years, meaning a minimum of sixty years, fifty years' minimum for two-time robbers in Texas, and many more examples ought, if the deterrent theory is right, to terrify would-be offenders, and so prevent crime happening. In fact the USA has not only the longest sentences in the western world, it also has the highest serious-crime rate in the western world. The message is very clear – long sentences do not deter, they appear to provoke a violent reaction.

One of the effects of increasingly severe sentences is to polarize two sections of the community – the law-abiding section and the section that does not respect the law. Whether society likes it or not, criminals are a part of society – a dissenting part maybe, but still a part. I believe that crime is a symptom of conflict within society, and I cannot see how that conflict will ever be resolved by the parties to it taking up entrenched positions and making little effort to resolve whatever gives rise to the conflict. The effect of long sentences is to express a hardening of social attitudes and at the same time to drive the offender into a position where shock and a sense of injustice only confirm the attitudes that made him offend in the first place. It is an exacerbating and self-perpetuating policy – and the current position in the U S A is conclusive evidence that this is so.

There is an urgent need to review the effect and the purpose of sentences the courts impose. My own view is that there is no justification for sentences exceeding four years for property offences. Confiscatory and compensatory orders would enable the sentencing authority to ensure that crime does not pay. I do not believe that a sentence of twelve years has any greater deterrent effect than one of four years. People committing crimes do not expect to get caught and, if they do consider prison at all, do not sit down and work out how long they are likely to have to serve. A four-year sentence is just as likely to deter someone on the borderline between lawful and unlawful conduct. Put another way, if a four-year sentence does not deter a would-be offender, then the prospect of a twelve-year sentence is unlikely to.

There are some offenders, and there always will be, from whom the public have to be protected. They are relatively few in number, certainly less than one thousand out of a prison population exceeding 44,000. They require special consideration and do not fall within my general proposition that sentences need to be drastically reduced, and in many cases replaced by non-custodial measures.

My experience over the years has led me to the inescapable conclusion that the courtroom is the least suitable place to assess a sentence. My experience is that despite the myth that judges are well informed and good assessors of how long a sentence should be, the majority are guided by a misconception of what public opinion is. They operate in what is often a theatrical and emotion-charged forum, and they continually ignore Parliament's guidelines and wishes, causing chaos within the prison system. The record shows just how badly many judges carry out sentencing duties. There have been, and there are, judges who display extraordinary ability in dispensing justice, but in my experience they are, sadly, in the minority.

I believe that the courtroom ought to be used only to determine guilt or innocence. Thereafter the judicial function should be to release a prisoner on bail if a short-term sentence is envisaged, or to remand the prisoner in custody if a long-term sentence is envisaged. Sentencing ought then to be determined by a tribunal made up of members of the legal profession, medical officers, social workers and probation officers, a representative of the prison service and members of the local community. Such a tribunal would be able to take into account the reality of options open to it – and being conscious of the scarcity of some options would more seriously consider suitable alternatives. Appeals under such a system could follow the present course.

PRISONS

My experience of British prisons has been confined to Brixton, Pentonville, Wandsworth and Wormwood Scrubs in London, and Gartree in Leicestershire.

The London prisons would be a disgrace in any civilized society and ought to be demolished. I do not believe that any amount of renovation will make them suitable for the role they have to play. Staff are at present forced to work in conditions that are often utterly depressing and degrading. Prisoners are subjected to overcrowding and a resultant deprivation of facilities that would have caused an outcry in Victorian times.

Crowded conditions result in close contact with other offenders, and the interchange of information and development of new contacts make London's prisons the most fertile breeding-ground for crime I have ever seen. Any properly directed inquiry would show that a great many serious offences were planned as a direct result of contacts made in these and other prisons. Under present conditions, there is nothing the staff can do to change this. Public outrage at crime would be more meaningful if it were directed in part at the conditions that breed the crime complained of.

Staff attitudes are influenced by the conditions they work in, by the reality of what can be achieved under those conditions. Decades of indifference to human needs have resulted in a prison regime that has given up any pretence of reform or rehabilitation – it is as much as overcrowded and understaffed establishments can do to ensure containment. Prison officers know that it is futile to spend time working on a prisoner's attitudes, and then be forced to lock him up in a cell with one or two other prisoners who are dedicated to crime. Prison staff are faced with the reality that they have no say in how long a prisoner is in their care – they watch men attain a degree of commitment to change and then slip back, drawn into the ordinary prison environment. There is nothing prison staff can do about it – and so they learn to live with it.

Successive Home Secretaries have made eloquent speeches dealing with the need to do something about prison conditions, but none of them has done anything worthwhile. New building programmes and renovations simply perpetuate and add to a system that has been seen to fail. What is needed is a serious rethink about the role prison should play in society – what is its purpose. If its purpose is to combat the crime rate then it is conspicuously ineffective. Men and women are daily sentenced to imprisonment in conditions that breach the European Convention on Minimum Rules for the Treatment of Prisoners, to which Great Britain is a signatory, yet few citizens appear interested in asking what it is hoped to achieve by embittering and hardening these men and women. If prison is seriously considered as providing an answer to crime, then surely one of its objectives must be to reform the offender.

Ideally, one would hope for a regime where prison staff and prisoners mix freely and there is an ongoing dialogue; where initiative and self-respect are encouraged and conflict is resolved by consensus, with words rather than violence; where ex-prisoners feel able to maintain links with the staff and fellow prisoners after release. I believe that the Hospital Annexe is just such a regime. It is the only unit I have seen where the aim is to reverse the process of hardening and embitterment, seeking to restore self-respect and a sense of social responsibility. I believe it is an example of how to use custodial sanctions constructively – to help men come to terms with reality and develop the ability to cope with the problems that brought them to prison. I am not alone in thinking as I do. Sir James Hennessy, KBE, CMG, HM Chief Inspector of Prisons, recently spoke of overcrowded, old-fashioned buildings, and of how under present conditions a long-term prisoner might be led to despair and bitterness – but, he went on: 'Amidst all this, any visit to the Annexe stands out like a beacon. Walking around and talking to the occupants and the staff, one could not fail to be impressed by the positive and relaxed atmosphere, by the air of purpose, and sense of hope that for all a new beginning was indeed possible. It was clear to me that this owed much to the hard work and commitment to this unique venture by prisoners and staff alike.'

John McCarthy, ex-governor of Wormwood Scrubs prison, has described the Annexe as 'a model of how ... most prisons should be run'. What is clear is that prison can be used far more constructively than at present. But, before any reform can take place, sentencing policy, which sends four hundred men to a prison designed to hold only two hundred, will have to be reviewed. At present, prison staff work in shocking conditions, and a large number of prisoners have to live in them. Unless there is a radical change in the way prisons are used, in the numbers sent to them and the treatment they can offer, they will continue to spew out jail-shocked men and women, and the good intentions many prison staff harbour will continue to be frustrated.

No discussion of prisons would be complete without reference to some of the petty and unnecessary hardships a large number of prisoners are subjected to.

TOBACCO: A shortage of smoking requisites causes more problems in British prisons than any other single issue. Prisoners are paid a small 'wage' – in 1983 it was between two and three pounds per week at Wormwood Scrubs. From this they have to buy tobacco, privilege letters, and anything else they do not have private cash to pay for. The tax on tobacco makes up more than two-thirds of its price, and the effect is for the revenue account to claw back prisoners' earnings at rates in excess of super-tax. The answer is to increase earnings or to remit the excise duty on prisoners' tobacco. There is evidence to show that an adequate tobacco issue decimates prison misconduct.

EARNINGS: The present very low earnings of prisoners are not justified on any grounds at all. Under such restrictive financial constraints, every penny becomes extremely important. The recent riot at Albany prison on the Isle of Wight, which led to more than £1,000,000 worth of damage, is said to have stemmed from some prisoners having between sixty and seventy-five pence deducted from their earnings. That proved to be an expensive deduction, but it highlights the fact that such low earnings leave no room for disciplinary action. The effect of stopping a prisoner's earnings is to take away his ability to write and receive letters from his family, and to take away his tobacco. It is not really surprising that, given the fact that other conditions are not very good, prisoners often react violently to loss of earnings.

CONTACTS WITH FAMILY AND FRIENDS: Very little attention is given to the social consequence of imprisonment. Few marriages survive a medium- or long-term sentence – many break up quite quickly. My experience is that a prisoner receives a lot of support during the early days of his sentence, but this falls away as the months become years. Much greater efforts must be made to enable prisoners to maintain contact with friends and relations.

LETTERS: There is no excuse for any restriction on letter-writing. Letters pose hardly any security problem – no one has ever escaped in an envelope. Spot censorship would meet any security requirement in respect of easily identifiable risks. The knowledge that one's letters have been read by someone else is demeaning and is not conducive to the re-establishment of the self-respect prison regulations require the regime to aim for.

VISITS: At present visits are curtailed because of the numbers of men held in local prisons. Facilities should be quadrupled to meet the social need to support and encourage contacts with families and friends.

TELEPHONES: There is no excuse for not installing telephones in every prison unit. They pose no security risk and offer contact quickly, cheaply and conveniently.

Present regulations which regard contact between the prisoner and his family and friends as a privilege are wrong. Communication must be a right. To deny it is to ignore the need of human beings for support and encouragement from those they love. Present regulations are archaic and should be scrapped. Prison officers who find censoring duties distasteful should be relieved of this duty, and the few who enjoy reading other people's letters ought not to be allowed to indulge themselves.

PAROLE: The present practice is to grant or withhold parole without disclosing the reasons. This system is cruel and uncaring of the family and friends of the prisoner concerned. I know of several instances where the wife of a prisoner has been quite unable to accept that the decision to withhold parole had nothing to do with her husband's behaviour in prison – and the resulting conflict has led to a marriage breaking up. Frequently prisoners with good prison records are refused parole whilst others with blemished records are granted it. I believe that complaints about the secretive way decisions are reached are justified. Prisoners are given no chance to correct misinformation or to improve conduct in an area causing concern. No one is told the truth when parole is withheld for reasons quite outside circumstances over which the prisoner has control. I believe to play fast and loose with prisoners' freedom in this way is most undesirable. The present practice smacks of dishonesty – parole is offered as a carrot to encourage good behaviour and is then withheld – despite good behaviour.

To eliminate the undesirable features of present procedures I believe that parole should be granted as a right in the same way as good-conduct remission – subject to good behaviour. Where parole is not granted then the reasons should be stated and notification given simultaneously to reduce the cruel effects of refusal on innocent parties.

RIGHTS AND RESPONSIBILITY

In my introduction to this book I have said that it would never have been written without the support and encouragement of a large number of people. Those people include members of the prison staff. Many prison officers and governors are aware of the need for change within the prison system. Jonathan Uzzel, a governor at Wormwood Scrubs, writing in the *Prison Service Journal*, expresses concern that the emphasis in decision-making has shifted from what it is right to do to what is administratively convenient. He writes: 'The regime within any prison, if it is to have an ethical content, must have a concern for rights and responsibilities. Indeed it may be argued that a denial of rights, the lack of acceptance of responsibility together with absence of a *demand* that prisoners, as well as staff, accept personal responsibility for their behaviour is at the root of a great deal of the conflict that abounds.' At present the prison regime lacks a concern for the rights and responsibilities of both prisoners and staff. The administration of justice takes second place to a requirement that the Home Secretary should not be embarrassed. Prison staff are prevented from voicing legitimate complaints publicly, and until they are free to do so there is little prospect of prisoners being allowed to say collectively what their grievances are.

I hope that this book may add something to the debate about prison conditions as they affect both staff and prisoners. I believe that governor Uzzel is right when he says: 'It is surely important that an organization within the judicial system should itself be concerned for true justice.'

MORE ABOUT PENGUINS, PELICANS, PEREGRINES AND PUFFINS

For further information about books available from Penguins please write to Dept EP, Penguin Books Ltd, Harmondsworth, Middlesex UB7 0DA.

In the U.S.A.: For a complete list of books available from Penguins in the United States write to Dept DG, Penguin Books, 299 Murray Hill Parkway, East Rutherford, New Jersey 07073.

In Canada: For a complete list of books available from Penguins in Canada write to Penguin Books Canada Ltd, 2801 John Street, Markham, Ontario L3R 1B4.

In Australia: For a complete list of books available from Penguins in Australia write to the Marketing Department, Penguin Books Australia Ltd, P.O. Box 257, Ringwood, Victoria 3134.

In New Zealand: For a complete list of books available from Penguins in New Zealand write to the Marketing Department, Penguin Books (N.Z.) Ltd, Private Bag, Takapuna, Auckland 9.

In India: For a complete list of books available from Penguins in India write to Penguin Overseas Ltd, 706 Eros Apartments, 56 Nehru Place, New Delhi 11019.

A CHOICE OF PELICANS AND PEREGRINES

☐ ***The Knight, the Lady and the Priest***
Georges Duby £6.95

The acclaimed study of the making of modern marriage in medieval France. 'He has traced this story – sometimes amusing, often horrifying, always startling – in a series of brilliant vignettes' – *Observer*

☐ ***The Limits of Soviet Power*** **Jonathan Steele** £3.95

The Kremlin's foreign policy – Brezhnev to Chernenko, is discussed in this informed, informative 'wholly invaluable and extraordinarily timely study' – *Guardian*

☐ ***Understanding Organizations*** **Charles B. Handy** £4.95

Third Edition. Designed as a practical source-book for managers, this Pelican looks at the concepts, key issues and current fashions in tackling organizational problems.

☐ ***The Pelican Freud Library: Volume 12*** £5.95

Containing the major essays: *Civilization, Society and Religion, Group Psychology* and *Civilization and Its Discontents*, plus other works.

☐ ***Windows on the Mind*** **Erich Harth** £4.95

Is there a physical explanation for the various phenomena that we call 'mind'? Professor Harth takes in age-old philosophers as well as the latest neuroscientific theories in his masterly study of memory, perception, free will, selfhood, sensation and other richly controversial fields.

☐ ***The Pelican History of the World***
J. M. Roberts £5.95

'A stupendous achievement . . . This is the unrivalled World History for our day' – A. J. P. Taylor

A CHOICE OF PELICANS AND PEREGRINES

☐ ***A Question of Economics*** **Peter Donaldson** £4.95

Twenty key issues – from the City and big business to trades unions – clarified and discussed by Peter Donaldson, author of *10 × Economics* and one of our greatest popularizers of economics.

☐ ***Inside the Inner City*** **Paul Harrison** £4.95

A report on urban poverty and conflict by the author of *Inside the Third World*. 'A major piece of evidence' – *Sunday Times*. 'A classic: it tells us what it is really like to be poor, and why' – *Time Out*

☐ ***What Philosophy Is*** **Anthony O'Hear** £4.95

What are human beings? How should people act? How do our thoughts and words relate to reality? Contemporary attitudes to these age-old questions are discussed in this new study, an eloquent and brilliant introduction to philosophy today.

☐ ***The Arabs*** **Peter Mansfield** £4.95

New Edition. 'Should be studied by anyone who wants to know about the Arab world and how the Arabs have become what they are today' – *Sunday Times*

☐ ***Religion and the Rise of Capitalism***
R. H. Tawney £3.95

The classic study of religious thought of social and economic issues from the later middle ages to the early eighteenth century.

☐ ***The Mathematical Experience***
Philip J. Davis and Reuben Hersh £7.95

Not since *Gödel, Escher, Bach* has such an entertaining book been written on the relationship of mathematics to the arts and sciences. 'It deserves to be read by everyone . . . an instant classic' – *New Scientist*